Labor and Punishment

Labor and Punishment

WORK IN AND OUT OF PRISON

Edited by Erin Hatton

UNIVERSITY OF CALIFORNIA PRESS

University of California Press
Oakland, California

© 2021 by The Regents of the University of California

Library of Congress Cataloging-in-Publication Data

Names: Hatton, Erin Elizabeth, 1974– editor.
Title: Labor and punishment : work in and out of prison / edited by Erin
    Hatton.
Description: Oakland, California : University of California Press, [2021]
    | Includes bibliographical references and index.
Identifiers: LCCN 2020051368 (print) | LCCN 2020051369 (ebook)
    | ISBN 9780520305335 (cloth) | ISBN 9780520305342 (paperback)
    | ISBN 9780520973374 (epub)
Subjects: LCSH: Prisoners—Employment—United States. |
    Ex-convicts—Employment—United States. | Precarious employment—
    United States.
Classification: LCC HV8925 .L335 2021 (print) | LCC HV8925 (ebook)
    | DDC 331.1086/927—dc23
LC record available at https://lccn.loc.gov/2020051368
LC ebook record available at https://lccn.loc.gov/2020051369

30 29 28 27 26 25 24 23 22 21
10 9 8 7 6 5 4 3 2 1

Contents

Introduction

Erin Hatton

Mass incarceration and economic inequality and insecurity are among America's most pressing social problems. Each has been the subject of extensive research, and together they provide the scholarly scaffolding for this book.

Contemporary America has been dubbed "The Age of Mass Incarceration."[1] More than two million people in the United States are incarcerated in prisons and jails, and another four and a half million people are under criminal justice supervision via probation or parole, and therefore are surveilled, regulated, and one misstep away from incarceration.[2] These numbers are shocking, and thus, despite being widely reported, they must be dwelled upon—again and again—rather than glossed over as a mere backdrop.

Yet, as astonishing as such incarceration rates are, they do not tell the full story of mass incarceration in the United States. For incarceration rates have not been evenly distributed across the American population. Black men have been the primary target of America's incarceration project: the consequence of the 1970s cultural and political turn toward "getting tough" on crime, drugs, and welfare that was directed at poor Black (and Brown) populations.[3] As a result, while African Americans represent just 12 percent of the US population, they constitute 33 percent of its prison population (and that number was even higher just a few years ago).[4] Even more to the point: while Black *men* represent just 6 percent of Americans, they make up 32 percent of America's prisoners.[5] Indeed, the criminalization of Black men has been so pervasive that, as sociologists Bruce Western and Becky Pettit have shown, fully one-third of young Black men are likely to be incarcerated at some point in their life and, for those without high school diplomas, the cumulative risk of imprisonment is 68 percent.[6] This is worth repeating: *more than two-thirds* of young Black men who have not finished high school are likely to be incarcerated over the course of their lives. Thus, if incarceration rates (and criminal justice entanglement more broadly) have soared in the United States since the 1970s, Black male incarceration has rocketed to space.

Despite their dramatic and disturbing overrepresentation in the criminal justice system, however, Black men represent less than a third of America's sprawling prison population.[7] Meanwhile, women—particularly women of color—are currently the fastest-growing population behind bars.[8] Still, white men and women constitute 30 percent of the US prison population (though, with 64 percent of the adult population, they are significantly underrepresented).[9] Thus, while mass incarceration has reached most deeply and destructively into Black lives, families, and communities, it has also harmed those of many other Americans. In fact, recent reports suggest that nearly half of all adults in the United States have had at least one of their immediate family members put behind bars.[10] Again: *almost half of all adults* have experienced firsthand the painful, deep, and lasting consequences of incarceration.[11] In short, as legal scholar John Pfaff writes, "Mass incarceration . . . is one of the biggest social problems the United States faces today," one that imposes "staggering economic, social, political, and racial costs."[12]

At the same time, Americans have faced escalating economic inequality and insecurity. Since the 1970s, various human-driven socioeconomic forces—including global competition, changing corporate ownership, and neoliberalization as enacted through de- and reregulation, changing tax policy, stagnating wages, de-unionization, and retrenchment of labor and welfare protections—have produced a sharply divided economy.[13] From 1979 to 2015, the top 1 percent of US earners more than doubled their share of national income (and the top 0.01 percent nearly octupled theirs), while other Americans' incomes increased only minimally, stagnated, or even declined.[14] Yet wealth inequality has grown even more and, because measures of wealth account for household assets and debts (in addition to income), such data more accurately reflect families' lived experiences of security and insecurity and, thus, inequality. Since 1983, the average household wealth of the top 0.1 percent has increased 230 percent, reaching almost $101 million per household; meanwhile, the wealth of the bottom 40 percent of American households dropped by 130 percent, falling from an average of nearly $7,000 in assets to $9,000 in debt.[15] In short, the very rich have become *much* richer, while the poor and working classes have become *much* poorer, losing their modest savings and going into debt.

Much like mass incarceration, moreover, economic insecurity is not evenly distributed. While the median white family's wealth has increased by one-third since 1983, that of Black families has decreased by half.[16] As a result, today, middle-of-the-road white families have *forty-one times* more wealth than comparable Black families and *twenty-two times* more wealth than Latinx families, and both Black and Latinx families are more than twice as likely to have no wealth at all or negative net worth.[17] Meanwhile, gender inequality has remained a remarkably stalwart feature of the contemporary economy; women of color, in particular, earn less, have greater debt and fewer assets, and experience higher rates of poverty than white men and women.[18] Thus, although not all women and ethno-racial minorities have suffered in this era of economic inequality and insecurity—and, to be sure, not all men and whites have benefitted—growing class divides have exacerbated already stark race, ethnic, and gender divides, as both a product of past inequalities and a producer of future ones.

Employment precarity has helped propel this era of economic insecurity for many Americans. Since the 1970s, all jobs—but particularly those of the poor, working, and middle classes, including disproportionate numbers of ethno-racial minorities—have become worse on nearly every measure of job quality.[19] Wages have stagnated, benefits have shrunk, job stability and security have declined, and long-term unemployment and underemployment have grown; as a result, workers have increasingly sought to make ends meet through short-term "gigs" and other forms of casualized labor.[20] In short, work has become more precarious—more uncertain, more unstable, and more insecure—for a growing number of people.

The socioeconomic consequences of such precarity exacerbate the race and gender inequalities already in place, though it is also true that this era is characterized by an unusual "democratization" of precarity: white men—similar to and sometimes even more than other groups—have faced significant levels job instability and insecurity.[21] (This stands in stark contrast to the postwar era, a historically anomalous time in which white men, but not other groups, experienced high levels of employment stability and security in the United States.) Ultimately, then, even though pronouncements of America's new "gig economy" are often overstated, these trends underscore very real changes in normative expectations and experiences of work. The result is a culture of insecurity that, as Pierre Bourdieu and Judith Butler have argued, is itself a form of labor governance and social control.[22]

Though economic insecurity and mass incarceration have not typically been studied side by side, a growing number of scholars have examined their concurrent rise. In fact, scholars such as Katherine Beckett, Bruce Western, Julilly Kohler-Hausmann, and Loïc Wacquant have argued that these social forces have become deeply intertwined: that expanding the carceral state and contracting the welfare state constituted America's two-pronged approach to governing social marginality in the late twentieth century.[23]

As scholars have shown, it is an approach that stemmed from the 1960s. At that time, the problem of poverty—particularly Black urban poverty—gained new visibility in the United States.[24] In 1964, President Johnson declared an "unconditional war" on poverty, and for a short time, welfare programs expanded.[25] Meanwhile, African American women began organizing around issues of poverty and welfare, which included class action lawsuits against the pervasive racial discrimination that had blocked their access to public assistance programs.[26] As a result, by the end of the 1960s, African American women and their families gained unprecedented access to expanding social welfare programs that, combined with their activism in the welfare rights movement, increased Black (female) vis-ibility in the welfare system.[27] This intensified the stigmatization of both welfare and (feminized) Blackness in American culture—stigmatization that was cemented in American culture by Ronald Reagan's persistent use of the "welfare queen" trope in the 1970s and '80s, which equated welfare receipt with unfounded claims of Black women's fraudulence and indo-lence.[28] Thus, poverty was criminalized, and welfare recipients were seen as a population to be disciplined, not helped.[29]

Meanwhile, the "race riots" of the late 1960s, in combination with the Black Power movement, increased the visibility—and fear—of (male) Black-ness in the white American imagination.[30] Because this fear was fixated on Black violence and crime, it was intensified by rising crime rates in the 1960s and '70s.[31] This laid the foundation for the racially targeted "War on Drugs" in the 1970s and '80s, which became one of several forces driv-ing America's incarceration project.[32] As prisons and jails were filled with more and more people (and as more and more prisons were constructed and filled again)—particularly with disproportionate numbers of young Black men—the cultural rhetoric of prisoner rehabilitation was replaced with the rhetoric of punishment and segregation, and US prisons were increasingly seen—and sometimes used—as semi-permanent warehouses for socially marginalized groups.[33]

Thus, previous scholarship has highlighted a driving force behind the concomitant expansion of the criminal justice system and contraction of the welfare system in late twentieth-century America: the subjugation of already marginalized groups. The consequence of this double-edged dynamic, scholars have shown, is a self-reinforcing system in which such groups are kept disproportionately incarcerated and poor. Criminal con-victions often leave a long-lasting "mark" that impairs former prisoners' employment prospects, particularly among African Americans.[34] In numer-ous ways, moreover, incarceration negatively affects prisoners' long-term health, as well as that of their families.[35] Indeed, children whose parents have been behind bars—particularly racial minorities—suffer a wide range of negative consequences, including increased antisocial behav-ior, criminal involvement, and drug use, as well as decreased educational achievement.[36] All of these dynamics impede the economic security and stability of former prisoners and their families: perpetuating poverty and increasing the risks of re-incarceration, while transferring such risks across generations.

Labor and Punishment: Work in and out of Prison builds on this already rich literature by exploring the intersections between work and prison. In doing so, it identifies two new crucially important mechanisms that drive the looping effects between mass incarceration and economic insecurity. The first is that incarceration not only acts as an external stigmatizing "mark" that former prisoners bear, much like Hester Prynne's scarlet *A*, but it also produces internal change in prisoners' expectations and experiences of work. Through compulsory and coercive labor in prisons, jails, and immigrant detention centers, as well as in the pervasive job "preparation" and "counseling" programs to which prisoners, parolees, and probationers are subjected, carceral subjects come to expect—and sometimes embrace—low-wage precarious work outside of prison.[37] Thus, just as Karl Marx and other theorists argued that labor produces *worker subjectivities* in addition to goods and services, the authors in this volume show that labor and job training within the criminal justice system produce *carceral subjectivities* centered on labor compliance and acceptance of degraded and precarious work.[38]

Carcerally mandated precarity is the second key mechanism identified in this book, a mechanism that sustains the iterative relationship between incarceration and economic insecurity. For, regardless of whether carceral subjects internally embrace precarious work, their docility and compliance are actively *enforced* by the criminal justice system. This is because, in fact, many Americans entangled in the criminal justice system are compelled to work under the threat of incarceration. People on probation and parole, as well as those with court-ordered debt and in court-mandated addiction treatment programs, are often required to maintain employment as a condition of their freedom from incarceration. This requirement effectively compels them to accept and keep any job—no matter how degraded—thereby intensifying their exploitability and socioeconomic marginality. In short, the criminal justice system mandates labor compliance among the carcerally entwined precariat, fueling the insidious feedback loop between mass incarceration and economic insecurity.

The essays in this book thus show that labor precarity is not simply a product of shrinking government and declining employment standards.

Nor is it simply one of two distinct prongs of the state's approach to governing social marginality. Precarity is also actively produced by government investment in carcerality, an investment that has not only strengthened the carceral state but has also stretched it beyond its traditional confines and into the labor market. The result is that America's expansive carceral state is a regime of labor discipline: one that molds and enforces worker compliance, vulnerability, and insecurity, thereby compounding already-marginalized groups' stigmatization and disadvantage.

. . . . .

In chapter 1, "Working Behind Bars: Prison Labor in America," I argue that prisons are a key site of labor and labor making in America today. First, drawing on secondary literature, I outline the history of prison labor in the United States. Then, by analyzing a range of incomplete and disaggregated data, I delineate the contours of US prison labor today, for this category of work has been understudied and overlooked, in no small part because aggregate data are not available. Finally, drawing on in-depth interviews with forty-one formerly incarcerated workers, I analyze prisoners' own experiences and interpretations of their labor. In describing their labor as prison janitors, groundskeepers, food servers, legal assistants, welders, forklift operators, and more, these formerly incarcerated workers characterize prison labor as everything from highly valuable to intensely abusive, exploitative, and dangerous. Indeed, such descriptions are not mutually exclusive. Rather than being valuable *or* exploitative, a source of dignity *or* a site of coercion, prison labor is often all of the above. But even when prisoners gain value and meaning from their labor, I argue that prison labor—at least as currently constructed in the United States—is deeply exploitative and coercive and, as a result, is often a site of abuse and endangerment. Because work produces worker subjectivities, moreover, and because such subjectivities do not remain behind bars when prisoners are released, prison labor primes workers for degraded work in the mainstream economy.

In chapter 2, "From Extraction to Repression: Prison Labor, Prison Finance, and the Prisoners' Rights Movement in North Carolina," historian Amanda Bell Hughett traces the recent history of prison labor and labor

activism in North Carolina. In particular, Hughett examines a key moment
in North Carolina's prison labor history: the gap between the abolition of
the chain gang in 1971 and its reinstatement—and expansion—in 1975.
Why, Hughett asks, was prison labor brought back in force just four years
after its idealistic abolition? She finds the answer at the intersection of
prisons' changing finances, the growing number of prisoners, and heightened prisoner activism. Even though prison labor had become less profitable, Hughett argues that state prison officials embraced it anew in order
to undermine prisoners' solidarity and labor activism. In this, Hughett
finds, they were largely successful, and their efforts laid the groundwork
for today's prison labor regime predicated on suppressing and controlling
(rather than rehabilitating) prisoners.

In chapter 3, legal scholar Jacqueline Stevens shifts our attention to
another form of incarcerated labor: that of immigrants in ICE detention
centers. In this chapter, "The Political Economy of Work in ICE Custody:
Theorizing Mass Incarceration and For-Profit Prisons," Stevens outlines
immigrant detention in the United States today—a corner of the carceral
landscape that has rapidly changed in recent years. For although the number of people incarcerated under criminal law has recently declined in
some states, the number of people detained under immigration law has
increased dramatically. Unlike most conventional prisoners, moreover,
the vast majority of immigrant detainees are held in for-profit prisons,
and their labor in such facilities is central to the prisons' profitability.
Through analysis of recent litigation challenging the legality of these
detainee work programs, Stevens seeks to develop a causal theory of mass
incarceration, one that points to "kleptocracy"—rather than racism, nativism, or neoliberalism—as a key driver of America's incarceration project.

In chapter 4, "The Carceral Labor Continuum: Beyond the Prison
Labor/Free Labor Divide," legal scholar Noah Zatz expands our analytical
lens to recast prison labor as part of a broader continuum of labor in the
criminal justice system, which includes the court-ordered work requirements imposed on probationers, parolees, and debtors (e.g., those with
child support obligations or criminal legal debts). Even though such labor
does not take place behind bars, Zatz argues, it is governed by the threat
of incarceration and is therefore part of the carceral state. He develops the
concept of "carceral labor" to accommodate this sprawling yet unexamined

landscape of court-ordered labor, revealing how the criminal justice system has reached deep into the conventional economy. Zatz's analysis thus disrupts conventional understandings of punishment and economy as separate spheres—understandings that have not only hidden these practices from view, but have also led critics of mass incarceration to embrace these forms of carceral labor as viable "alternatives to incarceration" and valuable opportunities for "reentry." Yet this spread of carceral labor into the mainstream economy, Zatz shows, is destructively reshaping the low-wage labor market and the precariat who work there.

In chapter 5, anthropologist Caroline Parker identifies another realm of Zatz's "carceral labor": the unpaid labor that serves as a centerpiece of many residential therapeutic communities for addiction in Puerto Rico. In this chapter, "Held in Abeyance: Labor Therapy and Surrogate Livelihoods in Puerto Rican Therapeutic Communities," Parker argues that, in order to understand why such therapeutic communities and labor therapies continue to thrive as a treatment for addiction, we must recognize the work they perform as "abeyance mechanisms": institutions that provide alternative kinds of work opportunities and housing to populations who would otherwise be excluded from formal labor markets and family homes. However questionable the success of these therapies as treatments for addiction, Parker argues that their proliferation reflects their capacity to provide people who are struggling with addiction surrogate jobs, a sense of purpose, and civic recognition in a context of unemployment, isolation, and stigmatization.

In chapter 6, "'You Put Up with Anything': On the Vulnerability and Exploitability of Formerly Incarcerated Workers," sociologist Gretchen Purser examines the everyday workplace experiences of formerly incarcerated men. Though such men's paltry job prospects have been widely studied, surprisingly little is known about their day-to-day experiences when they do find employment. Drawing on in-depth interviews with sixty formerly incarcerated men in Syracuse, New York, Purser examines the overlapping challenges they face at work: status degradation ceremonies, pervasive presumptions of criminality, and the coercive pressures of parole supervision. In so doing, Purser shows how the criminal justice system exacerbates formerly incarcerated workers' vulnerability to exploitative labor practices and degraded working conditions in the lower rungs of the labor market.

In chapter 7, geographer Anne Bonds examines another key site of post-prison work: the care work that formerly incarcerated women must perform in order to resume—indeed, reclaim—their roles as mothers and caregivers. In this chapter, "Working Reentry: Gender, Carceral Precarity, and Post-incarceration Geographies in Milwaukee, Wisconsin," Bonds draws from her research with formerly incarcerated women in Milwaukee to show how women returning home from prison must not only comply with the coercive pressures of parole, which entail securing employment and housing while bearing the "mark" of a criminal record, but must also *labor* to regain custody of their children and rebuild disrupted family relationships. This reentry care work is both implicitly and explicitly mandated by the carceral state and, as Bonds shows, is a deeply racialized and gendered form of labor. The chapter thus reveals yet another way in which carcerality and capitalism rely on and reinforce gender and race hierarchies.

In the conclusion, criminologist Philip Goodman underscores the importance of this volume, particularly in the context of the COVID-19 pandemic. "People are living (and dying) as prisoners, detainees, and people subject to surveillance in the community," Goodman writes. "They are also suffering as people pressed or coerced to work under what are likely to be worsening labor conditions." Yet this volume will be crucial reading long after this public health crisis, Goodman maintains. Because it explores the (often complex) intersections between people's experiences of carceral labor and the broader structures of exploitation and inequality, Goodman argues that *Labor and Punishment* provides much-needed insight into the depth and breadth of the systemic reform that is required to build a "more just and less brutal society."

· · · · ·

Taken together, these chapters depict carceral labor in high relief, providing a panoramic view of this little-known landscape as well as detailed portraits of some of the people and institutions within it. In doing so, these chapters reveal the connections between labor in prisons, detention centers, and addiction treatment programs; between work *instead of* prison, work *in* prison, and work *after* prison; and between the gendered care work of formerly incarcerated mothers and the routine degradation of formerly incarcerated men in their jobs. They highlight how the past shapes the present, while also pointing to ways in which the present will shape the future. They expose harsh social inequalities, while also showing how people experience such inequalities in their everyday lives.

This volume is thus of crucial importance, for American society is profoundly structured by both mass incarceration and socioeconomic insecurity. Previous research has connected these two social forces, documenting their historical co-emergence and some of their contemporary intersections. *Labor and Punishment* pushes this literature in new directions by showing how the criminal justice system penetrates the mainstream labor market, facilitating and enforcing labor precarity, particularly among those who are already socioeconomically marginalized. Together, the chapters in this volume demonstrate that mass incarceration—this punitive racialized system of social governance and labor control—does not have neat or narrow psychological, legal, and social boundaries. Indeed, its disciplinary tentacles have pervaded the lower rungs of the labor market. Thus mass incarceration has not only entailed the *upward* growth of the criminal justice system (in terms of numbers of prisoners), but also the *outward* growth of the criminal justice system (in its institutional reach well beyond prison walls). The result is the amplification of the detrimental cycle between criminal justice entanglement and socioeconomic disadvantage, and a redoubling of the brutal social inequalities of race, class, and gender that characterize American society.

NOTES

1. See, for example, the October 2015 issue of *The Atlantic*, https://www.the atlantic.com/projects/mass-incarceration/ (accessed January 21, 2020).

2. Even these high numbers of incarceration and criminal justice supervision represent a significant drop from their respective peaks in 2008 and 2007. For these and other data, see, US Department of Justice, *Correctional Populations in the United States, 2016* (Washington, DC: US Department of Justice, 2018), file:///C:/ Users/USER/Documents/Working%20But%20Not%20Employed/1-Prison%20 Workers/BJS%20data%202016.pdf (accessed February 11, 2019). For more on probation and parole, see, Michelle Phelps, "Mass Probation and Inequality: Race, Class, and Gender Disparities in Supervision and Revocation," in *Handbook on*

Punishment Decisions: Locations of Disparity, ed. Jeffery Ulner and Mindy S. Bradley (Abingdon, UK: Routledge, 2018), 43–67; also see Columbia University Justice Lab, *Too Big to Succeed: The Impact of the Growth of Community Corrections and What Should Be Done about It*, https://justicelab.columbia.edu/sites/default/files/content/Too_Big_to_Succeed_Report_FINAL.pdf (accessed February 27, 2019).

3. Julilly Kohler-Hausmann, *Getting Tough: Welfare and Imprisonment in 1970s America* (Princeton, NJ: Princeton University Press, 2017); also see, Michelle Alexander, *The New Jim Crow: Mass Incarceration in the Age of Colorblindness* (New York: New Press, 2012); Elizabeth Hinton, *From the War on Poverty to the War on Crime* (Cambridge, MA: Harvard University Press, 2016); John Pfaff, *Locked In: The True Causes of Mass Incarceration and How to Achieve Real Reform* (New York: Basic Books, 2017).

4. Latinx Americans have also been disproportionately incarcerated, but not to the same degree as African Americans. For these and other descriptive statistics of the prison population, see Bureau of Justice Statistics (BJS), "Correctional Statistical Analysis Tool (CSAT)—Prisoners," https://www.bjs.gov/index.cfm?ty=nps (accessed February 11, 2019).

5. In fact, this number represents a significant drop in recent years (BJS, "Correctional Statistical Analysis Tool"; also see, John Gramlich, "The Gap between the Number of Blacks and Whites in Prison Is Shrinking," Pew Research Center, January 12, 2018, http://www.pewresearch.org/fact-tank/2018/01/12/shrinking-gap-between-number-of-blacks-and-whites-in-prison/ (accessed February 11, 2019).

6. Bruce Western and Becky Pettit, "Incarceration and Social Inequality," *Daedalus* (Summer 2010): 8–19; also see Bruce Western, *Punishment and Inequality in America* (New York: Russell Sage Foundation, 2006); Phelps, "Mass Probation and Inequality."

7. BJS, "Correctional Statistical Analysis Tool.

8. Vera Institute of Justice, *Overlooked: Women and Jails in an Era of Reform* (New York: Vera Institute of Justice, 2016); Aleks Kajstura, "Women's Mass Incarceration: The Whole Pie 2018," *Prison Policy Initiative*, November 13, 2018, https://www.prisonpolicy.org/reports/pie2017women.html (accessed March 12, 2019).

9. Gramlich, "The Gap between the Number of Blacks and Whites in Prison Is Shrinking."

10. FWD.us, *Every Second: The Impact of the Incarceration Crisis on America's Families* (Ithaca, NY: Cornell University and FWD.us, 2018), https://everysecond.fwd.us/downloads/EverySecond.fwd.us.pdf (accessed February 27, 2019). Because such numbers only count those with family members who have spent time in jail or prison, they do not include all of the roughly 3.6 million Americans on probation. For more on probation, see, US Department of Justice, *Correctional Populations in the United States, 2016.*

11. FWD.us, *Every Second*; Eric Martin, "Hidden Consequences: The Impact of Incarceration on Dependent Children," *National Institute of Justice Journal 278* (2017), https://nij.gov/journals/278/pages/impact-of-incarceration-on-dependent -children.aspx (accessed March 12, 2019); Michael Massoglia and William Alex Pridemore, "Incarceration and Health," *Annual Review of Sociology* 41 (2015): 291–310.

12. Pfaff, *Locked In*, 18.

13. Arne Kalleberg, *Good Jobs, Bad Jobs: The Rise of Polarized and Precarious Employment Systems in the United States, 1970s–2000s* (New York: Russell Sage Foundation, 2011); Paul Osterman, *Securing Prosperity: The American Labor Market: How It Has Changed and What to Do about It* (Princeton, NJ: Princeton University Press, 1999).

14. Emmanuel Saez, "Striking It Richer: The Evolution of Top Incomes in the United States," University of California–Berkeley, 2016), https://eml.berkeley.edu /~saez/saez-UStopincomes-2015.pdf (accessed March 12, 2019); Economic Policy Institute, "Strong Across-the-Board Wage Growth in 2015 for Both Bottom 90 Percent and Top 1.0 Percent," EPI.org, https://www.epi.org/blog/strong-across-the -board-wage-growth-in-2015-for-both-bottom-90-percent-and-top-1-0-percent/ (accessed March 12, 2019); Congressional Research Service, *Real Wage Trends, 1979 to 2017* (Washington, DC: Congressional Research Service, 2018), https:// www.everycrsreport.com/files/20180315_R45090_9ca7ba485312c5f8fc00ff7e9c 11561322f6cb1b.pdf (accessed March 12, 2019).

15. Edward Wolff, "Household Wealth Trends in the United States, 1962 to 2016: Has Middle Class Wealth Recovered?" NBER Working Paper No. 24085, November 2017, https://www.nber.org/papers/w24085 (accessed March 12, 2019).

16. Chuck Collins, Dedrick Asante-Muhammed, Josh Hoxie, and Sabrina Terry, *Dreams Deferred: How Enriching the 1% Widens the Racial Wealth Divide* (Washington, DC: Institute for Policy Studies, 2019), https://inequality.org/wp-content /uploads/2019/01/IPS_RWD-Report_FINAL-1.15.19.pdf (accessed March 12, 2019); Wolff, "Household Wealth Trends."

17. While about 16 percent of white families have zero/negative net worth, 37 percent of Back families and 33 percent of Latinx families have none (Collins et al., *Dreams Deferred*).

18. AAUW, "Women's Student Deb Crisis in the United States," AAUW.org, May 2018, https://www.aauw.org/research/deeper-in-debt/ (accessed March 12, 2019); Paula England, "The Gender Revolution: Uneven and Stalled," *Gender & Society* 24, no. 2 (2010): 149–66; National Women's Law Center, *National Snapshot: Poverty among Women and Families, 2016* (Washington, DC: National Women's Law Center, 2017), https://nwlc-ciw49tixgw5lbab.stackpathdns.com /wp-content/uploads/2017/09/Poverty-Snapshot-Factsheet-2017.pdf (accessed March 12, 2019).

19. Kalleberg, *Good Jobs, Bad Jobs*.

20. Kalleberg, *Good Jobs, Bad Jobs*; also see, Erin Hatton, *The Temp Economy: From Kelly Girls to Permatemps in Postwar America* (Philadelphia: Temple University Press, 2011); Arne Kalleberg and Steven Vallas, "Precarious Work: Theory, Research, and Politics," *Research in the Sociology of Work* 31 (2017): 1–30; Lawrence Katz and Alan Krueger, "The Rise of Alternative Work Arrangements in the United States, 1995–2015," NBER Working Paper No. 22667, September 2016, https://www.nber.org/papers/w22667 (accessed March 12, 2019); Economic Policy Institute, "State of Working America: Jobs," http://stateofworkingamerica.org/subjects/jobs/ (accessed March 12, 2019).

21. Kalleberg and Vallas, "Precarious Work," 17.

22. Pierre Bourdieu, *Acts of Resistance: Against the Tyranny of the Market*, translated by Richard Nice (New York: The New Press, 1999); Judith Butler, foreword, in *State of Insecurity: Government of the Precarious*, Isabell Lorey, ed. (London, UK: Verso, 2015); also see, Kalleberg and Vallas, "Precarious Work."

23. Katherine Beckett and Bruce Western, "Governing Social Marginality: Welfare, Incarceration, and the Transformation of State Policy," *Punishment & Society* 3, no. 1 (2001): 44; Kohler-Hausmann, *Getting Tough*; Julilly Kohler-Hausmann, "Guns and Butter: The Welfare State, the Carceral State, and the Politics of Exclusion in the Postwar United States," *Journal of American History* 102, no. 1 (2015): 87–99; Jamie Peck, "Zombie Neoliberalism and the Ambidextrous State," *Theoretical Criminology* 14, no. 1 (2010): 104–10; Loïc Wacquant, *Punishing the Poor* (Durham, NC: Duke University Press, 2009); Bruce Western and Katherine Beckett, "How Unregulated Is the U.S. Labor Market? The Penal System as a Labor Market Institution," *American Journal of Sociology* 104, no. 4 (1999): 1030–60; also see, David Garland, *The Culture of Control: Crime and Social Order in Contemporary America* (Chicago: University of Chicago Press, 2001).

24. This was largely due to Michael Harrington's 1962 book, *The Other America: Poverty in the Unites* States (repr., New York: Simon & Schuster, 1997), which sought to bring attention and sympathy to the problem of poverty even as it also espoused problematic and inaccurate tenets of the "culture of poverty" ideology.

25. Kohler-Hausmann, *Getting Tough*; Julilly Kohler-Hausmann, "'The Crime of Survival': Fraud Prosecutions, Community Surveillance and the Original 'Welfare Queen,'" *Journal of Social History* 41, no. 2 (2007): 329–54; Robert Moffitt, "The Deserving Poor, the Family, and the U.S. Welfare System," *Demography* 52, no. 3 (2015): 729–49.

26. Kaaryn Gustafson, *Cheating Welfare: Public Assistance and the Criminalization of Poverty* (New York: New York University Press, 2012); Kohler-Hausmann, "'The Crime of Survival'"; Felicia Kornbluh, *The Battle for Welfare Rights: Politics and Poverty in Modern America* (Philadelphia: University of Pennsylvania Press, 2007); Premilla Nadasen, *The Welfare Rights Movement in*

the United States (New York: Routledge, 2005); Kenneth Neubeck and Noel Cazenave, *Welfare Racism: Playing the Race Card against America's Poor* (New York:
Routledge, 2001); Joe Soss, Richard Fording, and Sanford Schram, *Disciplining
the Poor: Neoliberal Paternalism and the Persistent Power of Race* (Chicago: University of Chicago Press, 2011).

27. For more on the welfare rights movements, see, Kornbluh, *The Battle for
Welfare Rights*; Nadasen, *The Welfare Rights Movement*.

28. Gustafson, *Cheating Welfare*; Kohler-Hausmann, "'Crime of Survival'";
Neubeck and Cazenave, *Welfare Racism*; Rickie Solinger, *Beggars and Choosers:
How the Politics of Choice Shapes Adoption, Abortion, and Welfare in the United
States* (New York: Hill and Wang, 2002).

29. Gustafson, *Cheating Welfare*; Neubeck and Cazenave, *Welfare Racism*;
Soss, Fording, and Schram, *Disciplining the Poor*.

30. For example, Steve Chapman, "Black Demands and White Fears," *Chicago
Tribune*, July 13, 2016, http://www.chicagotribune.com/snews/opinion/chapman
/ct-dallas-race-war-blacks-white-anxiety-perspec-20160713-column.html
(accessed August 10, 2018); Alice George, "The 1968 Kerner Commission Got It
Right, But Nobody Listened, *Smithsonian Magazine*, March 1, 2018, https://www
.smithsonianmag.com/smithsonian-institution/1968-kerner-commission-got
-it-right-nobody-listened-180968318/ (accessed August 10, 2018); Mark Hare,
"Riots Still Haunt Rochester," *Rochester City Newspaper*, July 16, 2014, https://
www.rochestercitynewspaper.com/rochester/riots-still-haunt-rochester/Content
?oid=2408308 (accessed August 10, 2018). Also see, Jane Rhodes, *Framing the
Black Panthers: The Spectacular Rise of a Black Power Icon* (New York: New Press,
2007); Sabrina Sérac, "Between Fact and Fiction: The Use of Fear in the Construct and Dissemination of the Black Panther Party Image," *Review de Recherche
en Civilisation Américaine*, http://journals.openedition.org/rrca/273 (accessed
August 10, 2018).

31. For more on crime rates and fears of crime, see, Garland, *Culture of Control*;
Kohler-Hausmann, *Getting Tough*.

32. Alexander, *The New Jim Crow*; Kohler-Hausmann, *Getting Tough*; Doris
Marie Provine, *Unequal Under Law: Race and the War on Drugs* (Chicago: University of Chicago Press, 2007).

33. Garland, *Culture of Control*; Wacquant, *Punishing the Poor*; but see,
Michelle Phelps, "Rehabilitation in the Punitive Era: The Gap between Rhetoric
and Reality in U.S. Prison Programs," *Law & Society Review* 45, no. 1 (2011):
33–68.

34. Devah Pager, "The Mark of a Criminal Record," *American Journal of Sociology* 108, no. 5 (2003): 937–75; Devah Pager, *Marked: Race, Crime, and Finding Work in an Era of Mass Incarceration* (Chicago: University of Chicago Press,
2007).

35. Massoglia and Pridemore, "Incarceration and Health."

36. Massoglia and Pridemore, "Incarceration and Health"; Martin, "Hidden Consequences."

37. Also see Erin Hatton, *Coerced: Work under Threat of Punishment* (Oakland: University of California Press, 2020).

38. On worker subjectivities, see for example, Michel Foucault, *Discipline and Punish: The Birth of the Prison* (New York: Random House, 1977); Karl Marx, *Capital: A Critique of Political Economy, Vol. I* (New York: Penguin, [1906] 1992); Max Weber, *The Protestant Work Ethic and the Spirit of Capitalism* (New York: Charles Scribner's Sons, 1958); Kathi Weeks, *The Problem with Work: Feminism, Marxism, Antiwork Politics, and Postwork Imaginaries* (Durham, NC: Duke University Press, 2011).

1 Working Behind Bars

PRISON LABOR IN AMERICA

Erin Hatton

Work is a centerpiece of American culture. Both the idea and the doing of work are—and have long been—essential to American notions of morality, sovereignty, and citizenship.[1] Most often, as political theorist Judith Shklar observed, its cultural importance is framed in the negative: a deep and abiding abhorrence of idleness.[2] Stemming from the Protestant work ethic, idleness (whether real or perceived) is construed as an individual moral failing and therefore any consequences of such idleness are perceived to be warranted, as illustrated by contemporary interpretations of St. Paul's dictum, "If a man will not work, he shall not eat."[3] Accordingly, there is said to be "dignity" in all kinds of work, even the very worst of jobs, an ideological tenet that Americans broadly embrace, as they seek and find dignity in labor, even the "dirtiest" of jobs.[4] Meanwhile, those who are unemployed and underemployed struggle to maintain a basic standard of material well-being, since so many economic and social rights are tied to employment in the United States, while also struggling to maintain a sense of dignity and belonging.[5] Indeed, for the vast majority of Americans, family-supporting rights-bearing work is the only entrée to full citizenship, as T. H. Marshall conceptualized it, for only through such work can most Americans gain "a modicum of economic welfare and security."[6]

Yet not everyone has—or has had—access to such work. As a wide range of scholars have shown, the very definition of what rights-bearing work is and who can get it are predicated on logics of race, gender, and nationality.[7] (Two of many such examples are the gendered exclusion of unpaid domestic labor from cultural and legal definitions of "real" work and the raced and gendered exclusion of paid domestic labor from legal definitions of employment.) Logics of race, gender, and nationality have also infused allegations of idleness and indolence.[8] (For example, after emancipation, the formerly enslaved people who sought to work for themselves as independent farmers rather than for their former masters were widely accused of laziness, and such accusations were used to justify debt peonage and other strategies deployed to compel and control their labor.)[9] Thus, work is not only a centerpiece of American culture, it is a centerpiece of American inequality: a splitting wedge used to marginalize, exploit, and exclude some groups of workers while advantaging others.

Given the centrality of work to American culture and inequality, it is perhaps not surprising that it is also a centerpiece of American punishment. Prisoners are the sole exception to the Constitution's prohibition of slavery, and their compulsory labor has long been an integral component of US prisons.[10] Indeed, prison labor was not only vital to the development of the modern prison system, it was also essential to America's emergence as a modern, industrial, capitalist economy.[11] As historians have shown, in the nineteenth and early twentieth centuries, prisoners in the American North were compelled to work in newly modernized corporate factories.[12] In the South, they were leased to private companies and forced to build railroads, mine coal, pave roads, and pick cotton.[13] In both cases, their labor was central to American modernization and industrialization, yet they labored in horrendous conditions: "worse than slavery," as historian David Oshinsky said of Mississippi's notorious (and deadly) Parchman State Penitentiary.[14] For such prisoners, there was no "dignity" in their work, only punishment.

In the South, moreover, prison labor was not solely an economic project to rebuild and modernize the region—though it was that.[15] It was also a racial project. Through the late nineteenth and early twentieth centuries, hundreds of thousands of African Americans (including children) were incarcerated in the American South, often on trumped-up charges of "vagrancy" (levied against those who could not prove employment at any given moment) as well as through outright kidnapping.[16] This overtly racialized criminalization and incarceration of African Americans was a broad-based effort to maintain the South's racial hierarchy and recapture former enslaved people's labor after emancipation. "For whites no longer able to mete out arbitrary punishment to their former black chattel," historian Alex Lichtenstein writes, "the criminal justice system served as a prime means of racial control and labor exploitation."[17] The result, historian Douglas Blackmon observes, was "slavery by another name."[18]

Prison labor remained largely unregulated until the 1930s. Then, in the aftermath of the Great Depression's mass unemployment, an increasingly vocal coalition of critics—led by business leaders and supported by unions—successfully pressured the federal government to restrict corporate use of incarcerated labor.[19] Yet such restrictions did not actually curb prison labor, only its use by private-sector companies. Even more, as historian Heather Ann Thompson has argued, this same legislation "formalized and legitimated" the institution of prison labor itself by legalizing it in the public sector with the formation of the Federal Prison Industries (FPI), a government program for using prison labor to produce goods and services for government agencies.[20] As a result, even as corporate use of prison labor was curbed, public use of it flourished and prisoners were put to work in factories behind bars, making a wide array of products for state and federal governments, including clothes, furniture, mattresses, metal castings, and more.[21] In such factories, Thompson shows, prisoners' exploitation and abuse remained widespread. As a result, through the postwar era, incarcerated workers became increasingly organized and militant in challenging their low wages, long hours, harsh treatment, and dangerous working conditions: they went on strike, they refused to eat, they organized sit-ins, and they formed labor unions.[22]

In the 1970s, however, prisoners' labor activism was dealt two significant blows. First, the 1977 court case *Jones v. North Carolina Prisoners' Labor Union* restricted prisoners' First Amendment rights to free speech and assembly, which circumscribed their ability to organize unions.[23] Second, in 1979, in order to exert more control over prisoners and their labor—particularly their labor activism—prison officials and neoliberal politicians pushed through legislation known as the PIE program (or the Prison Industry Enhancement certification program), which lifted restrictions on the private-sector use of prison labor, while also allowing prisons themselves to be privatized so that they could be operated as for-profit entities.[24] Meanwhile, incarceration rates had begun to soar. Though US incarceration rates had remained steady for much of the twentieth century (hovering around 0.1 percent of the population), beginning in 1972, they increased dramatically each year.[25] This rapidly growing population of prisoners pushed state officials to rethink prisons and prison labor—and, importantly, find new ways to control them.[26] The private-sector use of prisoners' labor was one of many strategies they used to do so.

Incarceration rates continued to increase through the 1990s, peaking at 1 percent of the adult population in 2008, amounting to more than two million people behind bars.[27] The United States had unequivocally become the world's leader in incarceration. And because most prisoners who are deemed able-bodied are required to work, this era of mass incarceration recalls elements of the post-emancipation South.[28] For the current entrenchment and expansion of the US criminal justice system is not only a raced and gendered penal institution, it also as a raced and gendered labor market institution. Though concrete numbers of incarcerated workers are not available, estimates suggest that well over half of prisoners have jobs at any given time, and most prisoners work for some substantial portion of their sentence.[29] This is not an insignificant population of workers. The combined prison and jail population in the United States equals the number of employees that Walmart, the world's largest employer, employs across the globe, and the prison population alone (minus jail inmates) is equivalent to Walmart's US employee base.[30] But unlike Walmart's workers, who themselves are not always adequately protected by US employment laws, incarcerated workers do not have access to even the most basic employment rights: the minimum wage, overtime, unemployment benefits, workers' compensation, social security, and more.[31] Thus America's disproportionately Black and Brown prison population is also a disproportionately Black and Brown population of unprotected workers.

CATEGORIES OF CONTEMPORARY PRISON LABOR

Incarcerated workers are usually assigned to one of four types of jobs: (1) facility maintenance jobs, also known as "regular" or "non-industry" jobs, in which they do much of prisons' upkeep and operations work, (2) "industry" jobs in the government-run prison factories launched in the 1930s, also known as the "correctional industries," (3) jobs with private-sector companies that have contracted with prisons for their labor, as restarted in 1979 with the PIE program, and (4) jobs outside of prisons and jails through various inmate labor programs. While evidence suggests that there is significant variation across these types of work in terms of their prevalence, wages, and opportunity for skill development, documenting such variation is an impossible task. There are remarkably little aggregate data available about prison labor in general and any given type in particular. In the remainder of this section, I synthesize a range of primary and secondary research in order to outline—insofar as possible—the contours of these categories of incarcerated labor.

The first category, basic facility maintenance, is the largest. Though concrete data are not available, estimates suggest that the vast majority of prisoners who work perform this type of labor.[32] They cook and serve food in prison mess halls; they clean prison dorms, bathrooms, school-houses, hospitals, and recreation yards; they cut lawns and shovel snow on prison grounds; they fix prisons' electrical and plumbing systems; they paint prison walls and wash prison windows. In short, they do the work required to keep the institution running, and because their wages for this work are invariably minimal, they save prison operators significant sums of money by supplanting free-world, full-wage workers.[33] In Alabama, Arkansas, Florida, Georgia, Mississippi, South Carolina, and Texas, in fact, state prisoners do not earn anything for these prison upkeep jobs. Meanwhile, in West Virginia they earn $0.04–$0.58 an hour, in Utah they earn a flat rate of $0.40 an hour, and in Wyoming they earn $0.35–$1.00 per hour. Prisoners' wages top out at $2.00 an hour in Minnesota and New Jersey for this type of work, though their pay scales start at $0.25 and $0.26, respectively.[34]

Yet prisoners' already minimal wages are routinely reduced—by 50 percent or more—through wage deductions for restitution fines, family support payments, court fees, and discharge money.[35] From such reduced wages, in addition to any money sent to them from family members, prisoners must cover the not-insignificant costs of living behind bars. Most often, studies show, they spend their wages on food, toiletries, and over-the-counter medicines from the prison commissary.[36] These items—ramen noodles, peanut butter, hot sauce, candy bars, deodorant, tampons, antacids, and toilet paper—are deemed essential by prisoners because US prisons consistently provide insufficient servings of unappetizing food and inadequate supplies of only the most basic (and low-quality) toiletries.[37] Though the cost of such items is often—though not always—less than in the free world, it nonetheless amounts to a significant portion of incarcerated workers' wages. According to the Prison Policy Initiative, for example, Massachusetts state prisoners earning $0.14 an hour must work more than thirteen hours to pay for a month's supply of dental floss.[38] Similarly, by my own calculation, New York State prisoners who earn $0.10 an hour must work eighteen hours for a month's supply of dental floss and twenty-two hours for a jar of peanut butter.[39] In addition to paying for these basic amenities, moreover, prisoners are often required to pay (sometimes very high) fees for phone use, room and board, email use, mandatory DNA testing, medical treatment, and more.[40] Living in prison is not cheap.

Though all prisoners' wages are subject to such deductions and fees, those working in the three other types of prison jobs—industry jobs, private-sector jobs, and outside jobs—tend to earn higher wages than those in facility maintenance. Such jobs may also offer more satisfying work and skills training (though not always, as we will see below), and are therefore often sought-after by prisoners. In truth, however, such jobs are rare. Still, it is important to examine them in order to understand the full landscape of prison labor: what incarcerated workers experience firsthand as well as what they know is possible, what types of jobs they may be working toward as well as those they may be trying to avoid, and all of the ways in which these types of labor intersect with free-world work.

Industry jobs, the second category of prison labor, account for nearly 5 percent of state and federal prisoner employment.[41] These are the government-run prison factory jobs that were formalized in the 1930s with the establishment of the Federal Prison Industries, and today nearly every state prison system (in addition to the federal prison system) has its own division of correctional industries.[42] Prisoners who labor in such factories produce a wide range of goods and services for sale to government agencies. They build office furniture and filing cabinets for government offices, schools, libraries, and other public institutions; they make uniforms, linens, and mattresses for prisons and hospitals; they make body armor for the military and police; they fabricate metal grills and wooden benches for public parks; they manufacture road signs and license plates; they do data entry and answer phones in call centers; they work in print shops and binderies.[43] In Texas, Georgia, and Arkansas, state prisoners do not earn any wages for such labor but, on average, state and federal prisoners earn $0.33–$1.41 an hour for this work (as compared to an average of $0.14–$0.63 an hour for the facility maintenance jobs described above).[44] At the high end of the pay scale, state prisoners in Nevada can earn as much as $5.15 an hour for this industry work, though their pay starts at $0.25 an hour.[45]

Working for private-sector companies through the PIE program is the third category of prison labor. Such jobs are even less common than industry jobs, employing just 0.3 percent of the prison population in the United States.[46] These are the highest-paid prison jobs by far, because private-sector companies are legally obligated to pay prisoners "prevailing wages" in order to avoid undercutting non-prison labor.[47] However, reports suggest that prisoners are typically paid the minimum wage, not the prevailing wage, and legal loopholes allow some companies to pay even less.[48] Moreover, prisoners' wages are subject to the many deductions described above, which are capped at a whopping 80 percent of their gross earnings.[49] Moreover, some states have mandatory savings programs that take away another chunk of their wages.[50] Thus, for many incarcerated workers, even free-world wages in private-sector jobs are reduced so much that they begin to resemble prison-world wages.

Consider, for example, private-sector prison jobs in South Carolina. In the third quarter of 2018, South Carolina had the largest PIE program in the United States, with 744 prisoners working for private companies, representing about 14 percent of prisons' private-sector workforce across the country.[51] These 744 prisoners labored for companies in the hardwood flooring, electronics, commercial signage, and garment industries, earning nearly $2 million in gross wages over the three-month period.[52] Fifty-four percent of their wages was deducted for various reasons: 20 percent for victim compensation and restitution funds, 19 percent for room and board, 4 percent for family support, and 10 percent for taxes; in addition, another 10 percent of their wages was deducted and deposited in mandatory savings accounts.[53] Thus, South Carolina prisoners received 36 percent of their gross wages, or an average of $963 per worker for three months' work.[54] (Compare this to US prisoners' average three-month earnings for facility maintenance work: $55–$245 *before* deductions. Though, in fact, prisoners in South Carolina are not paid at all for facility maintenance work.) Thus, the very few prisoners who labor in these private-sector jobs are paid handsomely by prison-world standards but deplorably by free-world standards, and critics widely condemn what they see as the corporate exploitation of prison labor at the expense of free-world workers.[55]

Finally, prisoners work outside of the prison itself through various labor arrangements—work-release programs, outside work crews, and work camps—in which they perform a wide range of labor for public works, nonprofit agencies, and private companies.[56] Reports suggest that such jobs are more common than both public and private industry jobs behind bars, but not as common as facility maintenance work.[57] Reliable data, however, are not available, as this is a particularly under-researched category of work in an already under-researched labor relation. It is also a highly heterogeneous one, as the various work programs differ dramatically from each other. In work-release programs, for example, prisoners typically maintain free-world jobs—at free-world wages, though subject to prison-world deductions—but must otherwise remain in the correctional facility.[58] In prison work crews, groups of prisoners or jail inmates are sent outside of the facility during work hours to perform public works, or "community service" jobs, such as cleaning highways, park grounds, and abandoned lots.[59] Their work clearing homeless encampments has been particularly well publicized. In California, for example, a sheriff's office reportedly boasted that the jail's work crew "cleaned up more than 1,300 pounds of trash from a homeless encampment . . . that was packed with hypodermic needles."[60] Wages for such labor vary significantly: in some states, prisoners on work crews earn the same as they would in prison maintenance jobs (including nothing in no-wage states); in other states, depending on the job, they may earn closer to correctional industry wages.[61]

Prisoner work camps are similar to work crews, except that they do not return to the prison at the end of the work day. Because they work in longer-term labor projects, prisoners in work camps are housed in facilities near the site of their labor and, although such facilities are still prison-like, prisoners often see them as better than full-scale prisons.[62]

California's "fire camps" are the best-known example of such work camps. Approximately 3,700 prisoners labor in these camps—about 3 percent of the state's prison population—where they fight wildfires, clear brush and fallen trees, build sandbag barriers, and perform other disaster prevention and remediation work.[63] For this labor they earn $2 per day, plus another $1 an hour while fighting active fires.[64] Their low-cost labor has been so valuable to the State of California, in fact, that—in order to preserve it—prison officials have actively resisted Supreme Court mandates to reduce the state's prison population. In 2011, the US Supreme Court ruled that overcrowding in California state prisons violated prisoners' right to be free from cruel and unusual punishment; as a remedy, the Court ordered California prison officials to grant early parole to all minimum-security prisoners.[65] Three years later, however, the California prison system was once again on trial, this time for not adhering to the Court's mandate. As the centerpiece of their defense, prison officials argued that because California depended on prisoners' cheap labor in the fire camps, prisons needed to reserve early parole exclusively for those who "volunteered" to work in them. Otherwise, state officials argued, prisoners "would choose to participate in [other programs] rather than endure strenuous physical activities and risk injury in fire camps" and "fire camp beds [would be] even more difficult to fill."[66] In short, state officials were willing to forgo prisoners' Eighth Amendment rights in order to compel them to take on the difficult and dangerous work of fighting fires—even though, for some prisoners at least, it could also be deeply rewarding work.[67]

PRISONERS' EXPERIENCES WORKING BEHIND BARS

In general, popular and scholarly accounts of prison labor portray it as one of two extremes: as the outright and unjust exploitation of prisoners *or* as a valuable and sought-after opportunity for skills training, dignity, and purpose behind bars.[68] However, as Philip Goodman's study of prisoners in California's fire camps suggests, this is a simplistic binary, as prisoners themselves often understand their labor as *simultaneously* exploitative and valuable.[69] In my own interviews with New York State prisoners, some incarcerated workers also understood their labor as simultaneously exploitative and valuable, though their views varied—not only across workers but also within individuals, for how they understood their labor behind bars depended on the particular job and, even more, how they were treated at work.[70]

Yet prison labor is not unique in this regard. *All* labor relations embody this duality—this tension between economic exploitation and personal worth—at least to some degree. Because the workplace is a converging point of power, it is a site of worker exploitation and domination *as well as* one of worker power and dignity. It is a site in which power is enacted upon workers through the extraction of surplus value from their labor (exploitation) and the exertion of control over their activities and bodies (domination).[71] Yet it is also a site in which workers themselves obtain and embody power by resisting such domination and exploitation, while also occupying the socioeconomic status that (at least some) work yields.[72]

Prison labor is an acute manifestation of these dual dynamics. It is indeed a site of intensive exploitation. As described above, prisoners can be legally forced to work, they are paid significantly (and often exorbitantly) less than the value of their labor, and they cannot make legal claims as workers. Moreover, as I have examined elsewhere, prisons are sites of intensive labor coercion.[73] Corrections officers (COs), who are also often labor supervisors, have expansive punitive power over their subordinate workers: prisoners. If prisoners do not comply with their demands—whatever they are—officers can impose a range of punishments: they can withdraw the basic entitlements that become "privileges" behind bars (e.g., phone use, family visits, exercise, and commissary purchases); they can put prisoners in solitary confinement (also known as "the box," which entails the loss of all privileges as well as human interaction); and they can keep prisoners behind bars longer (through disciplinary charges that block parole for "good behavior" as well as through additional criminal charges). In short, COs have far-reaching power over incarcerated workers' bodies, activities, and futures, rendering prison labor profoundly coercive.

At the same time, however, at least some prison jobs are crucial sources of meaning and dignity in a place where such things are severely lacking. In fact, some prisons might be best described as dignity black holes: sites that actively seek to extract and extinguish prisoners' sense of dignity and self-worth.[74] Within this context, those jobs that allow prisoners to understand themselves as productive and valuable workers—as productive and valuable *people*—are profoundly important.[75] Such jobs give prisoners access to the dignity of work that is pervasively promised in American culture, but is not usually available behind bars.[76] In many states, work also increases prisoners' access to material well-being by allowing them to buy the food and amenities they deem essential for living behind bars.

Of course, not all prisoners view any given job in the same way. Those jobs that some incarcerated workers see as exploitative "modern-day slavery" others view as valuable opportunities—to gain skills, perhaps, or simply to fulfill the moral obligation to work and avoid the idleness that is so deeply abhorred in American culture (and experienced as mind numbing behind bars). Meanwhile, others view their labor as simultaneously exploitative and valuable: economically extractive but also personally advantageous. Thus, like any subset of Americans, prisoners are not a homogeneous group. They have diverse experiences and interpretations of their labor.

In order to explore such experiences and interpretations, I now turn to prisoners themselves. As part of a broader study of coerced labor, I interviewed forty-one people recently released from New York State prisons. Eighty-three percent of them identified as non-Hispanic Black, 7 percent as Hispanic or Black and Hispanic, and 4 percent as non-Hispanic white. Five were women and thirty-six were men; their ages ranged from nineteen to sixty years old, with a median age of twenty-seven. All of them had worked in prison, usually in multiple jobs over the course of their sentences, which ranged from six months to nearly forty years (with an average sentence of seven years). They had worked three to six hours a day, five or six days a week. All of them had labored in some kind of facility maintenance job, though some had also worked on outside work crews or in factories for Corcraft, New York State's correctional industries company.[77]

Here I present a cross-section of these former prisoners' work lives across different types of jobs and experiences: the good, the bad, and the middling. As much as possible, I present their experiences in their own words, because their own interpretations of their labor—the ways that they make sense of their work—are just as important to this analysis as the work itself.

Among my informants, the one with the most unambiguously positive work experience was Miguel Fine.[78] While in prison, this Hispanic twenty-seven-year-old man worked on the Inmate Grievance Committee, first as an elected representative and then as chairperson. These committees were started in New York State prisons in the aftermath of the 1971 Attica prison uprising in order to give prisoners a formal mechanism for filing complaints. Most of the ex-prisoners I interviewed said that they had filed a grievance, and some had filed many. But they also said that their grievances were not usually successful, as there are strict regulations governing grievances' content and procedures.[79] While working on the grievance committee, Miguel's primary job was to mediate between the prisoners who had filed a grievance and the target of their grievance. His first task of every day, Miguel said, was to resolve such complaints informally. He would approach the prisoner and officer to discuss the situation, perhaps convincing the officer to allow the prisoner to change jobs, for example, or, more often, explaining to the prisoner that his complaint was not "grievable" because of prison policy. As Miguel said,

> I was the face of the grievance committee, so anytime we had a grievance, my job was go try to informally resolve it. . . . And I had good success with that, because I had a good relationship with both the inmates and the staff. It was kind of a unique position because, as an inmate, you're wearing their same colors, you know. You wear green [like the other prisoners]. . . . But I kind of had to educate people as to the process. I let them know, "Listen, I'm not on anyone's side here. I'm siding with the facts. And if you have a legitimate issue, then I can help you. . . . But, if you don't have a legitimate issue," and, [as Miguel said to me,] this is when I'll try to pull out something in black and white and let them know this is why you really don't have a good issue, because the rules prohibit you from having blue sneakers or something.

If he could not resolve the grievance informally in this way, Miguel said that he would see it through a multistage process with a formal hearing, findings, and possibly appeals. "It's almost like a courtroom," he said of the hearing, "and I was the neutral party, just making sure everybody stayed in line and let them know what the rules were." Thus, in his job, Miguel had to navigate the often tense divide between officers and prisoners, working closely with each side to clarify, question, and enforce prison rules.

For Miguel, it was valuable work. It was a "prestigious job" behind bars, he explained, giving him social standing and privileges that other prisoners did not have, including (relative) autonomy, freedom of movement, and perks such as access to newspapers and coffee. He also learned a great deal from it, he said, "about process, about policy and procedures and how to interpret those things." But, above all, for Miguel the work was valuable because of how his boss treated him. "Despite me being an inmate," Miguel said, "he always looked at me as—just a person." They read the newspaper together every morning and discussed news and politics. Their relationship was deeply meaningful for Miguel. As a result, Miguel said that he was not bothered by earning just $0.25 an hour for this work. "I never really looked at it as 'us versus them' or 'slavery' or, you know, the pay," he explained. "I learned to accept it as a condition of my actions. So, it took me a little while to kind of adjust my mind, to wrap my mind around that way of thinking. But I just knew that, in order to get through . . . I had to keep an open mind. . . . I knew that I just had to get through this process, this temporary condition, make the best out of it."

Jack Johnson also found value in his job as a facilitator in the prison's anger management class. He had first been a participant in the class, this sixty-year-old Black man explained, "because I was a very angry person." He learned a lot from the class, he said, and so when a facilitator job opened up, he applied for it, thinking to himself, "I'm doing some time, so why not take advantage of it?" "After a while," Jack said, "it became part of me, because I said, 'Wow, I could be of help with this.' So, you know, I looked past how much they were paying me. I was giving the knowledge to help somebody else. You know, we take so much from our community, why not give something back?" Of course, "there were times," Jack recalled, "private times, we talked about, 'Man, they're just dogging us for thirty-seven cent, blah, blah, blah.'" As he explained to me, "I talk [like that], because I'm human and I'm locked up, I got greens just like you do,[80] so let's talk about how they're just working us to death." But in general, Jack said, echoing Miguel above, that he focused more on the value of the work than its meager wages.

Yet there were important preconditions for Jack's ability to find value in his work, just as there were for Miguel. First, Jack was getting financial support from his church and his family, so he did not need to rely on his prison wages. "I was getting a lot of support from the ministry," he said. "I was getting a lot of support from my family. So, I didn't look at it [like] that." Second, Jack said that his boss treated him with respect. "[My supervisor] was really good," he said. "I said to myself, '*I* can do that.' And we made their jobs easier for them. . . . There were some times we could talk to inmates better than the officers could. They will go, 'Hey man, could you please talk to this guy?'" He would then counsel his fellow prisoners, Jack recalled, perhaps helping them avoid further punishment. He took pride in his ability to do so, as well as in his ability to make his bosses' "jobs easier for them." Thus, like Miguel, Jack was able to find value, respect, and dignity in his work behind bars, but only because his supervisors treated him with respect. Once this condition was met, both Jack and Miguel could find self-worth in their labor by deliberately overlooking their low rate of pay.

Yet such conditions are relatively unusual behind bars because, as "total institutions," prisons are predicated on prisoners' domination and subjugation.[81] Therefore, unlike Jack and Miguel, most of the incarcerated workers I interviewed—some 80 percent—did not feel like respected "workers" on the job. At best, they simply felt like "prisoners," subject to the routine (and sometimes extreme) forms of subjugation that pervaded their lives and labor behind bars. At worst, they felt like "slaves" or "animals." "Let me put it like this," nineteen-year-old Mike Russ said. "You know how if you had a dog and you abuse it? Like, they will treat you like you're an animal, an animal that they don't care about."

Fifty-two-year-old James D. described the everyday subjugation that permeated prison life and prison labor. In addition to many rudimentary jobs, James—like Jack and Miguel—worked in several ostensibly rewarding jobs behind bars, including in the prison law library, where he helped other prisoners pursue legal remedies. Like Jack and Miguel, James felt that he gained important skills and knowledge from this work. "There are a lot of things that I learned," this African American man explained, particularly the art of writing legal briefs, which he has continued to use in his work outside of prison. Unlike Jack and Miguel, however, James did not find dignity and self-worth in his labor. "Honestly, I don't think you could feel like a real working man in there," he said. "It ain't just because of the pay. It's because usually you're so subjugated no matter what you're doing. The staff people weren't all nasty and bad but, you know, there is always that sense of—not like working for [my current boss] where you, you know, you have a boss who respects you. Even though he *is* the boss of you. You know, the atmosphere is just *totally* different. It's a *prison.* You're never not a prisoner. *Never.* And you're reminded [of that] by everything that's said and done around you—even on those valued jobs." Thus, regardless of the job, for James, one's subjugated status as prisoner is overt and ever present behind bars. "You're never not a prisoner," he said. No matter how valuable the work, his interrelated sense of sovereignty and masculinity was diminished: one could never feel "like a real working man" behind bars.

Echoing James, prisoners repeatedly described their sense of domination and subjugation on the job. John D., for example, recounted a typical incident of incarcerated workers' subjugation. One of his jobs in prison was dorm porter, cleaning the dormitory where he and his fellow prisoners lived. He worked six hours a day, five days a week, earning about $6 every two weeks. "Sometimes," this twenty-year-old African American man said, "Like, say if I got off on Wednesday, [and the officer] asked me to do something. Like, they will never actually do it presentably. Like, they kick your bed [and bark,] 'Ain't you a porter?' 'I'm off today.' 'No, not today while I'm working, nobody's off.' And it go like that. They'd make us do it. You got to look at it like: If I don't, they'll probably going to put hands on me or I'll end up in the box." In other words, as John said, if he did not comply with the officer's order to work on his day off, he believed that he would be physically beaten, or put in solitary confinement. In fact, as described by the workers I interviewed, these two consequences usually went together.[82] So he complied, John said, even though he would not be paid for that work and he would lose his day off.

John D. also worked in lawn and grounds, "just cleaning up basically the whole jail, picking up cigarette butts, and all the cutting grass." He did not like this job. "None of that was something I wanted to do," John said. "Especially waking up eight in the morning and [you] got to walk around the jail, you just pick up cigarettes. You know, everybody smokes cigarettes, they just throw them on the ground. There's a million cigarettes." He and his coworkers had to pick up the cigarettes and other trash with their bare hands, he explained, unless they could afford to buy gloves from the commissary. "You got to have your own gloves, because nine times out of the ten, they're going to say, 'Oh, we don't got any.'" Intensifying his sense of injustice about this, John believed that the prison actually had "a locker full" of gloves that remained unused while the workers labored barehanded. Moreover, John continued, they often had to labor in extreme weather conditions: on 90° days and in blizzards alike, he said, but with only push mowers and snow shovels (rather than electric lawnmowers and snow blowers). As a result, John believed that prison labor was subjugating by design: it was meant to be a "pain" for prisoners. "I always look at it as like they're trying to teach you a lesson, like, *this is not a place you want to be or get comfortable.* But at the same, I don't think they taught that. . . . They just going off straight ignorance. Like, they're just doing it to make this a pain for us." Thus, in John's view, prison labor was subjugating without any redeeming lesson behind it, and so he saw it as a "waste of time . . . just garbage, something I didn't want to do."

Unlike John D., twenty-four-year-old Ron did not usually mind working behind bars, though he was not particularly fond of it either. While in prison, Ron worked the breakfast shift in the mess hall, earning $0.22 an hour. "I liked to work," this African American man said, "just to get the time to go by." Beyond that, however, he did not see much "good" about prison labor. "You wasn't getting paid nothing," he explained, "and they want you to work *hard.* They want you to slave and," he repeated, "you're not getting paid nothing." In addition to their lack of decent pay, Ron said, was the problem of bad bosses. "Some of them was alright," he allowed. "But then you got the ones that are just, I don't know, assholes." Of course, this is true of all jobs but, in prison, the consequences for workers are significantly more severe. Once, Ron recalled, his supervisor threw out all of the food just as the African American kitchen workers were about to eat (and eating this self-prepared food is the primary benefit of working in the mess hall). "The rule is, you're supposed to finish your job and then eat," Ron explained. That day, however, Ron said that the "white guys" who worked in the kitchen had already eaten their meal but, "when the real Black crowd started to come, [the supervisor] just picked up both trays and put it in the garbage.[83] Ron was upset, and only more so when the supervisor asked him to clean the bathroom, a task that was not normally his job. He refused. "I said, 'I'm not cleaning the bathroom. Why should

I clean the bathroom? You're not even letting us eat. The rule is to do our job and then we could eat.' He said, 'You guys can't eat. Why you guys can't eat back at your dorm?'" Ultimately, Ron said, he called his boss "a racist bastard" and this insubordination—in addition to his refusal to clean the bathroom—landed him in solitary confinement. "I went to the box for thirty days," he said. "And I never ever go worked back in the mess hall again."

For many of the former prisoners I interviewed, however, such overt insubordination was not a prerequisite for being sent to the "box." As I have written elsewhere, any form of noncompliance, including work refusals, can land prisoners in solitary confinement—an enclosed and segregated cell for twenty-two to twenty-four hours a day without human interaction—and so going "to the box" is a relatively common occurrence behind bars.[84] Estimates suggest that nearly ninety thousand people in the United States (forty-five hundred in New York State prisons) are in some type of isolation at any given time, and often for long periods: prisoners are kept in solitary confinement for an average of five months in New York and eighteen months in Colorado, though such sentences can be indefinite.[85] There is no legal limit. The mental and physiological consequences of such prolonged isolation are both severe and long lasting, including PTSD, anxiety, depression, suicide, paranoia, insomnia, hallucinations, psychosis, dizziness, headaches, lethargy, heart palpitations, and more.[86] Thus at least one bioethicist has called solitary confinement "the worst kind of psychological torture."[87]

While the pervasive threat of solitary confinement led most of the incarcerated workers I interviewed to comply with officers' work orders most of the time, some—like Ron above—recounted incidents of refusal and resistance. Twenty-three-year-old Bruce described two such incidents, both while he was working as a porter. "They had wanted me to clean the bathrooms," this African American man recalled. "I feel, like, we all men, we all know hygiene, how to keep ourselves clean. But it was at the point where people are using the bathroom in the shower. I mean we're just talking about *feces*. I'm not going to clean no feces. I don't care what gloves you give me." He refused to do the job and, as a result, he was put in solitary confinement for thirty days. "The other incident I didn't want to clean," Bruce continued, was in "a robo-station that oversees the unit.

The CO [who worked there] was nasty. He used to chew snuff and he spit on the floor and he expects people to clean it. I wasn't cleaning that stuff." Once again, Bruce said, he "went to the box" for a month.

For John Smith, however, solitary confinement was not the primary punishment he faced for work refusal and on-the-job missteps. He, along with three other former prisoners I interviewed, had a different work and punishment experience because he was incarcerated in one of New York State's "shock" facilities, also known as "boot camp" prisons, in which younger nonviolent offenders serve shorter sentences in exchange for intensive military-style physical training, labor, and discipline.[88] According to the National Institute of Justice, prisoners in these facilities typically spend one-third of their time doing "hard labor on facility and community projects," 26 percent of their time in physical training, 28 percent in addiction treatment, and 13 percent in educational programs.[89] Thus labor—or "work therapy" as the New York State Department of Corrections and Community Supervision describes it—is even more central to these boot camp prisons than it is to regular state prisons.[90] "They work you like crazy," John Smith said. "They work you to the bone." And if officers, called "DIs" or "drill instructors," perceive prisoners to step out of line in any way, this white twenty-four-year-old man explained, those prisoners would face intensive physical discipline, as well as risk losing their spot in the shock program and their curtailed prison sentence. "Like, we were cleaning the basement," John recalled, by way of example, "and I was cleaning the one window. And the DI comes up and he thought I was peeking into the window, when in reality I'm cleaning it." The officer asked if he had been "peeking in there," John said, and he answered, "Sir, no sir!" For, as John explained to me, that was the only response he was allowed to give. But the officer did not believe him, and so John said that he was "worked out for an hour and a half": required to do "pushups, flutter kicks, jumping jacks" on the basement floor.

But even worse than such physical discipline, John Smith said, was the officers' disrespect. "It's outrageous at that place," he recalled. "Just how all the DIs talk to you. They talk to you like you're the scum of the earth. . . . Some of them call you names like, you know, 'You little shithead, hurry up.'" Then, after recounting several incidents of extreme prisoner abuse, he explained, "You get pissed off, but you can't jeopardize your program."

In John's view, no matter what happened, he needed to submit to every demand and form of discipline, however unjust, in order to stay in the program and get out of prison on time. He ultimately succeeded, unlike some 37 percent of New York State's shock prisoners, who are removed from those facilities and returned to regular state prisons where they must serve longer sentences.[91] "I had to do what I had to do just to get home," John said.

Jarome Wilks was also incarcerated in a shock prison, where he worked on the outside work crew. "The worst day," this African American twenty-year-old man recalled, was the day his crew labored in one of the natural gorges that dot Central New York's landscape. These gorges are popular tourist attractions, with hiking trails winding up hundreds of feet along steep cliffs, rivers, and waterfalls. Jarome's work crew was tasked with bringing in large pieces of slate to rebuild the steps that line the gorge, each of which was "probably like 150 pounds," Jarome recalled. "Those things are heavy," he said again and again. "It could have taken two of us to carry them, and it would *still* be heavy—like, crazy heavy. Like, we couldn't even put them on a dolly, no nothing. And it was raining and slippery out there." (Indeed, I have been to the specific gorge where Jarome worked and the trail is remarkably slippery, even without carrying heavy pieces of slate in the rain.) The work crew, Jarome recalled, had to carry the slate from the top of the gorge to the bottom, descending several hundred feet on narrow moss-covered steps, and then "run all the way back" to the top to do it again. "We had to go up there like twenty times in that one day," he said. "I've never sweat like that. I mean, it was a workout for me within itself, but at the end of the day my back was hurting. And I still be having back problems." After describing this grueling job, Jarome said—almost offhandedly—that he did not understand why they had not simply unloaded the slate at the bottom of the gorge. "We could have drove," he said, "I don't know why the drill instructor chose for us to carry it like this. . . . I guess that was the task for the day," he said resignedly. According to New York State guidelines, such arduous (and seemingly unnecessary) labor was likely deemed his "work therapy."

Finally, Mary, Qwon, and A.T. were three of the five former prisoners I interviewed who had worked in industrial jobs in Corcraft factories.[92] These factories can be found in thirteen New York State prisons, and include the metal shop in Attica, the eyeglasses shop at Wallkill, the printing shop in Elmira, and the DMV call center at Bedford Hills.[93] While she was in prison, Mary worked as a welder in one of these factories and generally enjoyed the work, though she said it was "very hot." "You know, it's a dirty job. I mean, just very hot, because you're welding." But the work was not too difficult or dangerous, this fifty-two-year-old white woman said, and she felt that she got training that may "benefit [her] somewhere down the road." She worked her way up to $0.35 an hour, so that, with bonuses, she could earn as much as $35 every two weeks. "I was grateful to make at least some money to get me by," she said, "because you don't really get a lot of money in prison." But for Mary, like Miguel and Jack above, even more important than the pay was the fact that her boss was "really good." He was "highly intelligent" and "funny," Mary recalled. "He had a humorous side to him, but a serious side. You got to keep the girls working, you know, so it was good. I liked it." (By contrast, she did not like working as a porter in prison—not because of the work, she explained, but because her supervisor was "nasty" and took "an instant dislike" to her. "I must have needed to have that guy in my life for whatever reason," she speculated.)

For the most part, Qwon also valued the experience he gained working as a forklift operator in a Corcraft factory, which this thirty-one-year-old African American man described as a "legit" workplace. "You got the proper equipment, the hard hats, the proper labor. They teach you," he said. "They play the courses on a video tape, so you can understand. You sign your papers and everything. So it goes legit. But it's just the pay. Like, everything they do is going to be a working atmosphere. It's going to be a legitimate atmosphere. . . . It's just the pay is, instead of bringing home X amount [i.e., a normal free-world wage], you're getting X amount [i.e., a prison wage]." For Qwon, that wage was $22 every two weeks. "That's the crappy thing," he said, "because you sweatin'." "You *work*," he emphasized again and again. "You're going to work. Them industries, oh, you're going to work. By all means, you're going to be hot, sweaty, everything." But, because of that experience, Qwon said that he was able to get a temporary job once he got out of prison, which became permanent after three weeks, though he was laid off just two months later. "The experience is priceless," he said, "[that's] the only thing you can go for in [such] hard labor. Other than that, you're going to be sweaty. You get dirty. Everything.

People get their fingers cut off in there. . . . It's just *crazy*. It's a crazy working atmosphere. It's not worth it, but . . ." His voice drifted off. He seemed torn between the value of the work experience and its difficulty, danger, and low wages.

Qwon's description of the work environment in his Corcraft factory recalled A.T.'s account of the Attica metal shop in the early 1970s, before it was rebranded a Corcraft factory in the 1980s. A.T. had worked in many prison jobs since that time, as he had been incarcerated for nearly forty years, but he remembered the early-1970s metal shop vividly, even though he had worked there for only nine days. As this sixty-four-year-old Black man explained, "The Attica metal shop was one of the most egregious examples of lack of safety, concern, pay. It's the closest thing to slave labor that I've experienced, *ever*. . . . I had worked at Bethlehem Steel before I got arrested. Bethlehem Steel didn't scare me like this place. . . . It was not unheard of for people to lose fingers." A.T. said that he quit the metal shop when "they came and gave me a pay slip . . . for fifty-four cents." Imagine, he said to me, "six cents a day to work in those conditions," while "a mirror costs seventy cents" in the prison commissary.[94] Because he refused to continue working in the shop, A.T. said that he was written up in a disciplinary report and was put on "keep lock" for seven days, which meant that he was confined to his cell but not in solitary confinement. ("Back then," he told me, "they never gave you more than thirty days in the box. Now, they'll send you to the box for years. I mean *years*."[95])

"Over the years," A.T. continued, "I worked in the school, hospital, tailor shop—various jobs from prison to prison. And the one thing that all these jobs have in common is just, like, no matter how menial the labor is, it's forced. It's forced. . . . Even if the work is light, when someone is standing over you all the time, you know, looking for something wrong or you're not working fast enough, you know, that gets very tiresome." Thus, even though there were a few jobs that he liked (particularly working in the prison gym where he "learned a *lot* about physical fitness"), A.T. argued that all prison labor is fundamentally "coercive." "You're in prison," he said, "you're going to have a [job] assignment." And if prisoners refused to comply with that assignment, he explained, they would lose their recreation time, their ability to purchase commissary goods, and other important "privileges." "They use prison assignments—good jobs, bad jobs, plum jobs—to control people, to get what they want," he said of prison officials. Though, he allowed, "in prison, everyone's truth is different. Every single person who goes to prison has a different experience."

·　·　·　·　·

My research confirms A.T.'s perspective on both counts: prisoners, like all people, have dramatically different "truths." They experience and interpret their labor—and their lives—behind bars in different ways. Yet at the same time, as A.T. argued and as I have argued elsewhere, their labor is profoundly coercive.[96] Officers, as supervisors of their labor, have expansive punitive power over their lives in ways that most other labor supervisors do not. Through solitary confinement, keeplock, and disciplinary reports, officers can impede prisoners' relationships with their families and friends by limiting their phone use, visitation, and interaction with fellow prisoners; they can restrict prisoners' recreation and freedom of movement; they can block prisoners from buying food and other consumer items in the commissary; and they can refuse prisoners' parole, that is, freedom from prison.

But, while prison labor is extreme, it is not unique. Prison labor is part of the landscape of work in America, despite being persistently differentiated from "regular" work—legally, culturally, and spatially.[97] Economically, there is unavoidable overlap between free-world and prison-world labor. Even though there are no official estimates, perhaps by design, some *not insignificant* portion of incarcerated workers directly replaces free-world workers. As California's reliance on incarcerated firefighters suggests, county and state governments across the United States economically rely on prisoners' low-wage or no-wage labor. Yet the intersections between these two realms of work are not only economic. As described above, the power dynamics that shape prison labor are similar to those that govern all labor relations. *All* workers contend with coercion, subjugation, and exploitation on the job, at least to some degree, and all workers struggle for dignity and respect at work. Because such dynamics emerge in high relief behind bars, incarcerated labor is a valuable lens to understand them more broadly.

For, at the most basic level, incarcerated workers are not that different from "normal" workers. In fact, they are the same people. Incarcerated workers leave prison to work in "regular" jobs, and "regular" workers are incarcerated and put to work behind bars. In both directions, moreover, their labor shapes their subjectivities. As Karl Marx and, more recently, Kathi Weeks have argued, "Work produces not just economic goods and services but also social and political subjects."[98] Prison labor, like any labor relation, shapes incarcerated workers' subjectivities: how they experience and interpret their labor and even themselves.

My previous research has uncovered one of the ways that this labor relation shapes workers' subjectivities: by priming incarcerated workers to embrace low-wage precarious work outside of prison.[99] For instance, as Qwon told me, the "bare minimum, nothing" he earned in prison made him willing to accept low wages outside of prison. "How can I come out here and *not* appreciate a job in society, in the real world, where it matters, when I was just working for thirty-eight or fourteen or twelve cents?" he asked rhetorically. "How can I *not* come out here and appreciate it, even if it had to be a minimum wage or, you know, a stepping stone [to a better job]?" Thus, even if prison labor did not extend beyond prison walls through its economic effects and the other forms of carceral labor examined in this volume, it nonetheless reaches far beyond those walls because it produces *workers*: "disciplined individuals, governable subjects."[100]

Therefore, I argue that studies of work and employment need to better account for incarcerated labor. Rather than reifying the material and symbolic boundaries that divide this sector from "regular" work, scholars should problematize such boundaries by studying them: not as separate and idiosyncratic labor relations, but as key elements of the broader landscape of labor.[101] Doing so will deepen—and perhaps even transform—our understanding of work and labor in America today.[102]

ACKNOWLEDGMENTS

I have many people to thank for this research, but above all are the workers who shared their experiences with me. Thank you. You taught me so much. For this research I received financial support from several gems at the University at Buffalo: Errol Meidinger and the Baldy Center for Law & Social Policy, Erik Seeman and the Humanities Institute,

Kari Winter and the Gender Institute, and Laura Mangan and UB Civic Engagement and Public Policy. Thank you. This research would not have been possible without your support. Finally, a million thanks to my home team: David, Nicky, and Felix.

NOTES

1. Evelyn Nakano Glenn, *Unequal Freedom: How Race and Gender Shaped American Citizenship and Labor* (Cambridge, MA: Harvard University Press, 2002); Linda Kerber, *No Constitutional Right to Be Ladies: Women and the Obligations of Citizenship* (New York: Hill and Wang, 1998); Judith Shklar, *American Citizenship: The Quest for Inclusion* (Cambridge, MA: Harvard University Press, 1991); Kathi Weeks, *The Problem with Work: Feminism, Marxism, Antiwork Politics, and Postwork Imaginaries* (Durham, NC: Duke University Press, 2011).

2. Shklar, *American Citizenship*; also see Glenn, *Unequal Freedom*.

3. Max Weber, *The Protestant Work Ethic and the Spirit of Capitalism* (New York: Charles Scribner's Sons, 1958), 159; also see Weeks, *The Problem with Work*.

4. Randy Hodson, *Dignity at Work* (New York: Cambridge University Press, 2001).

5. Ofer Sharone, *Flawed System/Flawed Self: Job Searching and Unemployment Experiences* (Chicago: University of Chicago Press, 2013).

6. T. H. Marshall, *Class, Citizenship and Social Development* (New York: Doubleday, 1964 [1949].

7. For example, Jeanne Boydston, *Home and Work: Housework, Wages, and the Ideology of Labor in the Early Republic* (New York: Oxford University Press, 1994); Nancy Fraser and Linda Gordon, "A Genealogy of Dependency: Tracing a Keyword of the U.S. Welfare State," *Signs* 19, no. 2 (1994): 309–36; Glenn, *Unequal Freedom*; Kerber, *No Constitutional Right*; Alice Kessler-Harris, *Out to Work: A History of Wage-Earning Women in the United States* (New York: Oxford University Press, 1982); Mae Ngai, *Impossible Subjects: Illegal Aliens and the Making of Modern America* (Princeton, NJ: Princeton University Press, 2004); David Roediger, *The Wages of Whiteness: Race and the Making of the American Working Class* (New York: Verso, 1991); Weeks, *The Problem with Work*; also see Erin Hatton, "Mechanisms of Invisibility: Rethinking the Concept of Invisible Work," *Work, Employment and Society* 31, no. 2 (2017): 336–51.

8. Eric Foner and Olivia Mahoney, *America's Reconstruction: People and Politics after the Civil War* (New York: HarperCollins, 1995); Fraser and Gordon, "A Genealogy of Dependency"; Kenneth Neubeck and Noel Cazenave, *Welfare Racism: Playing the Race Card against America's Poor* (New York: Routledge, 2001); Weeks, *The Problem with Work*.

9. Foner and Mahoney, *America's Reconstruction*, 58.

10. As the Thirteenth Amendment states, "Neither slavery nor involuntary servitude, except as a punishment for crime . . . shall exist within the United States ("Primary Documents in American History," https://www.loc.gov/rr/program/bib/ourdocs/13thamendment.html [accessed October 27, 2017]). For the history of prison labor, see Douglas Blackmon, *Slavery by Another Name: The Re-enslavement of Black Americans from the Civil War to World War II* (New York: Doubleday, 2008); Alex Lichtenstein, *Twice the Work of Free Labor: The Political Economy of Convict Labor in the New South* (New York: Verso, 1996); Rebecca McLennan, *The Crisis of Imprisonment: Protest, Politics, and the Making of the American Penal State, 1776–1941* (Cambridge: Cambridge University Press, 2008); David Oshinsky, *Worse Than Slavery: Parchman Farm and the Ordeal of Jim Crow Justice* (New York: Free Press, 1997); Heather Ann Thompson, "Rethinking Working-Class Struggle through the Lens of the Carceral State: Toward a Labor History of Inmates and Guards," *Labor: Studies in Working-Class History of the Americas* 8, no. 3 (2011): 15–45.

11. Lichtenstein, *Twice the Work of Free Labor*; McLennan, *The Crisis of Imprisonment*.

12. McLennan, *The Crisis of Imprisonment*.

13. Lichtenstein, *Twice the Work of Free Labor*.

14. Oshinsky, *Worse Than Slavery*; also see Blackmon, *Slavery by Another Name*; McLennan, *The Crisis of Imprisonment*.

15. Lichtenstein, *Twice the Work of Free Labor*.

16. Blackmon, *Slavery by Another Name*.

17. Lichtenstein, *Twice the Work of Free Labor*, 17–18

18. Blackmon, *Slavery by Another Name*.

19. Matthew Pehl, "Between the Market and the State: The Problem of Prison Labor in the New Deal," *Labor: Studies in Working-Class History of the Americas* 16, no. 2 (2019): 77–97; Thompson, "Rethinking Working-Class Struggle."

20. Thompson, "Rethinking Working-Class Struggle," 718.

21. Thompson, "Rethinking Working-Class Struggle"; also see Unicor, *Factories with Fences: 85 Years Building Brighter Futures* (Washington, DC: Federal Prison Industries, Inc., Federal Bureau of Prisons, US Department of Justice, 2018), https://www.unicor.gov/publications/corporate/FactoriesWithFences_FY19.pdf (accessed February 11, 2019).

22. Thompson, "Rethinking Working-Class Struggle."

23. Amanda Bell Hughett, "A 'Safe Outlet' for Prisoner Discontent: How Prison Grievance Procedures Helped Stymie Prison Organizing During the 1970s," *Law & Social Inquiry* 44, no. 4 (2019): 893–921; also see Thompson, "Rethinking Working-Class Struggle"; Jones v. North Carolina Prisoners' Labor Union, Inc., 433 US 119 (1977).

24. Thompson, "Rethinking Working-Class Struggle"; National Correctional Industries Association (NCIA), "Prison Industry Enhancement Certification Program (PIECP)," https://nationalcia.org/piecp-2 (accessed February 11, 2019); Barbara Auerbach, *The Prison Industries Enhancement Certification Program: A Program History* (Baltimore: National Correctional Industries Association, 2012), https://nationalcia.org/wp-content/uploads//PIECP-a-Program-History.pdf (accessed February 12, 2019).

25. US Department of Justice, *Correctional Populations in the United States, 2016* (Washington, DC: US Department of Justice, 2018), https://www.bjs.gov/content/pub/pdf/cpus16.pdf (accessed February 11, 2019).

26. See Amanda Belle Hughett's chapter in this volume, "From Extraction to Repression: Prison Labor, Prison Finance, and the Prisoners' Rights Movement in North Carolina."

27. Such numbers include people incarcerated in jails as well as prisons. This population peaked at 2.3 million in 2008, and dropped to 2.1 million in 2016, with the prison portion of that population at 1.5 million (US Department of Justice, *Correctional Populations in the United States, 2016*).

28. Though there is likely significant variation across states and institutions. For more, see Title XXIX: Prisons, Crime Control Act of 1990, S.3266, 101st Congress (1990), https://www.congress.gov/bill/101st-congress/senate-bill/3266 (accessed February 11, 2019); "Inmate Participation and Status in Prison Work Programs," Montana Code Annotated 2017, https://leg.mt.gov/bills/mca/title_0530/chapter_0300/part_0010/section_0320/0530-0300-0010-0320.html (accessed February 11, 2019); US GAO, *Prisoner Labor: Perspectives on Paying the Federal Minimum Wage* (Washington, DC: US General Accounting Office, 1993).

29. Estimates from the Bureau of Justice Statistics suggest that, in 2005, half of state and federal prisoners (not including jail inmates) had work assignments, amounting to about eight hundred thousand people. See Bureau of Justice Statistics (BJS), *Census of State and Federal Correctional Facilities, 2005* (Washington, DC: US Department of Justice, 2008); also see National Center for Educational Statistics, *Highlights from the US PIAAC Survey of Incarcerated Adults: Their Skills, Work Experience, Education, and Training* (Washington, DC: US Department of Education, 2016).

30. Walmart officials report that the company employs about 2.2 million workers across globe and 1.5 million workers in the United States. See Walmart, "Company Facts," https://corporate.walmart.com/newsroom/company-facts (accessed January 21, 2019).

31. Excluding those prisoners working for private companies on work release or in private industrial jobs behind bars. For more on employment law and incarcerated labor, see Noah Zatz, "Working at the Boundaries of Markets," *Vanderbilt Law Review* 61, no. 3 (2008): 857–958; Noah Zatz, "Prison Labor and the Paradox

of Paid Nonmarket Work," in Nina Bandelj, ed., *Research in the Sociology of Work, Vol. 18* (Bingley, UK: Emerald Publishing Group, 2009), 369–98.

32. In 2005 the Bureau of Justice Statistics estimated that 88 percent of prisons and jails had facility maintenance labor programs (BJS, *Census of State and Federal Correctional Facilities*).

33. US GAO, *Prisoner Labor*; also see Robbie Brown and Kim Severson, "Enlisting Prison Labor to Close Budget Gaps," *New York Times*, February 24, 2011, https://www.nytimes.com/2011/02/25/us/25inmates.html (accessed February 11, 2019); Daniel Moritz-Rabson, "'Prison Slavery': Inmates Are Paid Cents While Manufacturing Products Sold to Government," *Newsweek*, August 28, 2018, https://www.newsweek.com/prison-slavery-who-benefits-cheap-inmate-labor-1093729 (accessed February 11, 2019); Beth Schwartzapfel, "Taking Freedom: Modern-Day Slavery in America's Prison Workforce," *Pacific Standard*, April 12, 2018, https://psmag.com/social-justice/taking-freedom-modern-day-slavery (accessed February 11, 2019).

34. These wage data, along with those of other state prisons' non-industry and industry jobs, are available at: Prison Policy Initiative, "State and Federal Prison Wage Policies and Sourcing Information," PrisonPolicy.org, https://www.prisonpolicy.org/reports/wage_policies.html (accessed January 21, 2019). For a summary of these data, see Prison Policy Initiative, "How Much Do Incarcerated People Earn in Each State?" PrisonPolicy.org, https://www.prisonpolicy.org/blog/2017/04/10/wages/ (accessed February 11, 2019).

35. Prison Policy Initiative, "How Much Do Incarcerated People Earn in Each State?"; also see Prisoners' Legal Services of Massachusetts, "Fees Charged to Prisoners," PLSMA.org, http://www.plsma.org/prisoner-self-help/pro-se-materials/property-and-fees/fees-charged-to-prisoners/ (accessed February 11, 2019); Chandra Bozelko, "Give Working Prisoners Dignity—and Decent Wages," *National Review*, January 11, 2017, https://www.nationalreview.com/2017/01/prison-labor-laws-wages/ (accessed February 11, 2019).

36. Prison Policy Initiative, "The Company Store: A Deeper Look at Prison Commissaries," May 2018, https://www.prisonpolicy.org/reports/commissary.html (accessed February 11, 2019).

37. Prison Policy Initiative, "The Company Store"; Alysia Santo and Lisa Iaboni, "What's in a Prison Meal," The Marshall Project, July 7, 2015, https://www.themarshallproject.org/2015/07/07/what-s-in-a-prison-meal (accessed February 11, 2019); David Reutter, Gary Hunter, and Brandon Sample, "Appalling Prison and Jail Food Leaves Prisoners Hungry for Justice," *Prison Legal News*, April 15, 2010, https://www.prisonlegalnews.org/news/2010/apr/15/appalling-prison-and-jail-food-leaves-prisoners-hungry-for-justice/ (accessed February 11, 2019); "Short-Term Deprivation of Toilet Paper Does Not Violate Detainee's Rights," *Prison Legal News*, February 2014, https://www.prisonlegalnews.org/news/2014/feb/15/short-term-deprivation-of-toilet-paper-does-not-violate-detainees

-rights/ (accessed February 11, 2019). For reporting on the issue of tampons and other menstrual products in particular, see Erin Polka, "The Monthly Shaming of Women in State Prisons," Public Health Post, September 4, 2018, https://www .publichealthpost.org/news/sanitary-products-women-state-prisons/ (accessed February 11, 2019); Zoe Greenberg, "In Jail, Pads and Tampons as Bargaining Chips," *New York Times*, April 20, 2017, https://www.nytimes.com/2017/04/20/nyregion /pads-tampons-new-york-womens-prisons.html; Michael Alison Chandler, "Federal Prisons Must Provide Free Tampons and Pads to Incarcerated Women," *Washington Post*, August 24, 2017, https://www.washingtonpost.com/local/social-issues /federal-prisons-must-provide-free-tampons-and-pads-to-incarcerated-women /2017/08/23/a9e0e928-8694-11e7-961d-2f373b3977ee_story.html?noredirect= on&utm_term=.d9e398035c56 (accessed February 11, 2019).

38. Prison Policy Initiative, "The Company Store."

39. According to the Attica Correctional Facility Commissary Buy Sheet, which I obtained in my own fieldwork, a bag of thirty flossers costs $1.80 and a jar of peanut butter costs $2.17.

40. For an overview of fees charged to prisoners, see Lauren-Brooke Eisen, "Paying for Your Time: How Charging Inmates Fees Behind Bars May Violate the Excessive Fines Clause," Brennan Center for Justice, July 31, 2014, https:// www.brennancenter.org/analysis/paying-your-time-how-charging-inmates-fees -behind-bars-may-violate-excessive-fines-clause (accessed February 11, 2019); Prisoners' Legal Services of Massachusetts, "Fees Charged to Prisoners," PLSMA .org, http://www.plsma.org/prisoner-self-help/pro-se-materials/property-and -fees/fees-charged-to-prisoners/ (accessed February 11, 2019).

41. This is based on my own analysis of state and federal correctional industries data. Older reports give a slightly higher estimate of 6 percent (e.g., see State of Minnesota, Office of the Legislative Auditor, "Evaluation Report: Minncor Industries," February 2009, appendix A, https://www.auditor.leg.state.mn.us /ped/pedrep/minncor.pdf (accessed February 11, 2019)).

42. Alaska is the sole exception.

43. For example, Unicor, "Products and Services," https://www.unicor.gov /Category.aspx?iStore=UNI (accessed February 11, 2019); Corcraft, https:// www.corcraft.org/webapp/wcs/stores/servlet/TopCategoriesDisplay?langId=-1 &storeId=10001&catalogId=10051 (accessed February 11, 2019); Washington State Correctional Industries, "Products & Services," https://www.washingtonci .com/products-services.html (accessed February 11, 2019); Colorado Correctional Industries, https://www.coloradoci.com/ (accessed February 11, 2019).

44. Prison Policy Initiative, "How Much Do Incarcerated People Earn in Each State?"

45. Prison Policy Initiative, "How Much Do Incarcerated People Earn in Each State?"

46. At the end of 2018, according to PIE reports, 5,207 prison and jail inmates were employed in PIE programs across U.S. prisons. See NCIA, Prison Industry Enhancement Certification Program, "Certification & Cost Accounting Center Listing," Statistics for the Quarter Ending September 30, 2018, https:// nationalcia.org/wp-content/uploads/2018/12/Third-Quarter-2018-Certification -Listing-Report.pdf (accessed February 12, 2019). PIE program quarterly statistical reports are available at: NCIA, "PIECP Quarterly Statistical Reports," https:// nationalcia.org/piecp-2/quarterly-statistical-reports (accessed February 12, 2019).

47. PIECP Final Guideline, 64 Fed. Reg. 66, 17000-17014 (April 7, 1999), https:// nationalcia.org/piecp-2/piecp-final-guideline (accessed February 12, 2019).

48. PIECP Final Guideline, 64 Fed. Reg. 66; NCIA, Correctional Industries: FAQs, https://nationalcia.org/wp-content/uploads/2018/12/CI-FAQ-Brochure -12-5-2018.pdf (accessed February 12, 2019); Schwartzapfel, "Taking Freedom.

49. NCIA, "Prison Industry Enhancement Certification Program," https:// nationalcia.org/piecp (accessed February 12, 2019). Across the United States, wage deductions averaged 58 percent of incarcerated workers' gross wages. See NCIA, Prison Industry Enhancement Certification Program, "Quarterly Report," Statistics for the Quarter Ending September 30, 2018, https://nationalcia.org /wp-content/uploads/2018/12/Second-Quarter-2018-Statistical-Report.pdf (accessed February 12, 2019).

50. NCIA, "Quarterly Report."

51. NCIA, "Certification & Cost Accounting Center Listing."

52. NCIA, "Quarterly Report."

53. NCIA, "Quarterly Report."

54. NCIA, "Quarterly Report."

55. For example, Michelle Chen, "Prison Labor on the 'Kill Line,'" *The Nation*, August 23, 2018, https://www.thenation.com/article/prison-labor-on-the-kill -line/ (accessed February 12, 2019); Mark Maxey, "Corporations and Governments Collude in Prison Slavery Racket," *People's World*, February 7, 2018, https:// www.peoplesworld.org/article/corporations-and-governments-collude-in-prison -slavery-racket/ (accessed February 12, 2019); Joanna Zambas, "10 Companies That Use Prison Labour to Rake in Profits," *Career Addict*, October 11, 2017, https://www.careeraddict.com/prison-labour-companies (accessed February 12, 2019).

56. For an overview of work release programs, see Jillian Berk, "Does Work Release Work?" November 14, 2007, https://www.colgate.edu/portaldata/image gallerywww/2050/imagegallery/berk_wr_jobmarket.pdf (accessed February 12, 2019). For examples of such programs, see Mississippi Department of Corrections, "Community Work Centers," https://www.mdoc.ms.gov/Community-Corrections /Pages/Community-Work-Centers.aspx (accessed February 12, 2019); Oregon DOC Operations Division: Prison, "Inmate Work Crew Information," https://www

.oregon.gov/doc/ops/prison/pages/crci_workcrew.aspx (accessed February 12, 2019).

57. Though current and concrete data are not available, a 2005 report from the Bureau of Justice Statistics states that 28 percent of prisons had some type of work release program, while 44 percent had some type of public works program; to my knowledge, no data are available about such programs in jails (BJS, *Census of State and Federal Correctional Facilities*).

58. For example, North Carolina Department of Public Safety, "Work Release," https://www.ncdps.gov/adult-corrections/prisons/transition-services/work-release (accessed February 12, 2019); Spokane County Detention Services, "Work Release," https://www.spokanecounty.org/401/Work-Release (accessed February 12, 2019).

59. For example, National Crime Prevention Council, "Strategy: Requiring Inmates to Perform Community Service," https://www.ncpc.org/resources/home-neighborhood-safety/strategies/strategy-requiring-inmates-to-perform-community-service/ (accessed February 12, 2019); North Carolina Department of Corrections, "Community Work Service Jobs for State Prisoners," https://www.doc.state.nc.us/dop/CWPJOBS/tipsheets/com-work.feb.pdf (accessed February 12, 2019); 2016 Arizona Revised Statutes, Title 31: Prisons and Prisoners, § 31-142 Use of Prisoners on Public Works (AZ Rev Stat § 31-142 (2016).

60. "California Uses Prison Labor for Dirty Jobs 'Nobody Else Wants to Do,'" *Sputniknews.com*, March 31, 2018, https://sputniknews.com/us/201803311063088948-CA-Prison-Labor-Dirty-Jobs/ (accessed February 12, 2019); Thacher Schmid, "'Straight Up Bullshit': Inmates Paid $1 to Clear Homeless Camps They Once Lived In," *The Guardian*, August 9, 2017, https://www.theguardian.com/us-news/2017/aug/09/portland-homelessless-camps-inmate-clean-up (accessed February 12, 2019); Elizabeth Trovall, "City of Houston Crews Clean Up Homeless Encampment at Wheeler Avenue," Houston Public Media, November 5, 2018, https://www.houstonpublicmedia.org/articles/news/2018/11/02/310468/city-of-houston-crews-clean-up-homeless-encampment-at-wheeler-avenue/ (accessed February 12, 2019).

61. Some descriptions for these programs are included in non-industry job listings at: Prison Policy Initiative, "State and Federal Prison Wage Policies and Sourcing Information."

62. For example, Illinois Department of Corrections, "Southwestern Illinois Work Camp," https://www2.illinois.gov/idoc/facilities/Pages/southwesternworkcamp.aspx (accessed February 12, 2019); Escambia County, Florida, "Road Prison," https://myescambia.com/our-services/corrections/community-detention/road-prison (accessed February 12, 2019); also see April McCullum, "Why Vermont Could Close St. Johnsbury Prison Work Camp," *Burlington Free Press*, March 13, 2016, https://www.burlingtonfreepress.com/story/news/politics/2016/03/13

/why-vermont-could-close-st-johnsbury-prison-work-camp/81453576/ (accessed February 12, 2019).

63. California Department of Corrections and Rehabilitation, "Conservation (Fire) Camps," https://www.cdcr.ca.gov/Conservation_Camps/ (accessed February 12, 2019); also see Jaime Lowe, "The Incarcerated Women Who Fight California's Wildfires," *New York Times Magazine*, August 31, 2017, https://www.nytimes.com/2017/08/31/magazine/the-incarcerated-women-who-fight-californias-wildfires.html?module=inline (accessed February 12, 2019).

64. California Department of Corrections and Rehabilitation, "CDCR's Conservation Camp Program Frequently Asked Questions," https://www.cdcr.ca.gov/Conservation_Camps/docs/FAQ-Fire-Camps.pdf (accessed February 12, 2019).

65. Brown v. Plata, 563 U.S. 493 (2011).

66. "Defendants' Opposition to Plaintiffs' Motion to Enforce," Case No. C01-1351-THE, United States District Court, Eastern District of California and the Northern District of California (2014), 4.

67. Philip Goodman, "Hero *and* Inmate: Work, Prisons, and Punishment in California's Fire Camps," *Working USA: The Journal of Labor & Society* 15 (2012): 353–76; also see Annika Neklason, "California Is Running Out of Inmates to Fight Its Fires," *Atlantic*, December 7, 2017, https://www.theatlantic.com/politics/archive/2017/12/how-much-longer-will-inmates-fight-californias-wildfires/547628/?utm_source=twb (accessed December 20, 2017); Lowe, "The Incarcerated Women Who Fight California's Wildfires."

68. Goodman, "Hero *and* Inmate."

69. Goodman, "Hero *and* Inmate"; also see Lynne Haney, "Working through Mass Incarceration: Gender and the Politics of Prison Labor from East to West," *Signs* 36, no. 1 (2010): 73–97.

70. Erin Hatton, *Coerced Labor: Work and Punishment in Contemporary America* (Oakland: University of California Press, forthcoming); also see Erin Hatton, "When Work Is Punishment: Penal Subjectivities in Punitive Labor Regimes," *Punishment & Society* 20, no. 2 (2017): 174–91.

71. Erik Olin Wright, *Understanding Class* (London, UK: Verso Books, 2015).

72. Hodson, *Dignity at Work*; Steven Vallas, "Working Class Heroes or Working Stiffs? Domination and Resistance in Business Organizations," *Research in the Sociology of Work* 28 (2016): 101–26.

73. Hatton, *Coerced Labor*.

74. Erving Goffman, *Asylums: Essays on the Social Situation of Mental Patients and Other Inmates* (New York: Doubleday, 1961); Craig Haney, *The Psychological Impact of Incarceration: Implications for Post-Prison Adjustment* (Washington, DC: Assistant Secretary for Planning and Evaluation, US Department of Health & Human Services, 2001).

75. Goodman, "Hero *and* Inmate"; Haney, "Working through Mass Incarceration."

76. Hatton, "When Work Is Punishment."

77. Corcraft, "About Corcraft," Corcraft.org, http://www.corcraft.org/webapp/wcs/stores/servlet/WhoWeAreView?langId=-1&storeId=10001&catalogId=10051 (accessed February 11, 2019).

78. All informant names are self-chosen pseudonyms and their demographic data are self-reported.

79. New York State Corrections and Community Supervision, "Inmate Grievance Program," Directive #4040, January 20, 2016; New York State Corrections and Community Supervision, *Inmate Grievance Program, Annual Report 2013* (Albany, NY: Department of Corrections and Community Supervision); also see Kitty Calavita and Valerie Jenness, "Inside the Pyramid of Disputes: Naming Problems and Filing Grievances in California Prisons," *Social Problems* 60, no. 1 (2013): 50–80.

80. Jack's mention of "greens" (like Miguel's above) refers to New York State prisoners' green uniforms. This was commonly used among my informants to refer to prisoners' shared status and identity as prisoners.

81. Goffman, *Asylums.*

82. Hatton, *Coerced Labor.*

83. This likely stemmed from the prison's pervasive racial segregation. See, for example, Philip Goodman, "'It's Just Black, White, or Hispanic': An Observational Study of Racializing Moves in California's Segregated Prison Reception Centers," *Law & Society Review* 42, no. 4 (2008): 735–70; Julie Taylor, "Racial Segregation in California Prisons," *Loyola of Los Angeles Law Review* 37 (2003): 139–52.

84. Hatton, *Coerced Labor.*

85. Solitary Watch, "FAQ," *Solitary Watch*, http://solitarywatch.com/facts/faq/ (accessed January 14, 2018); NYCLU, *Boxed In: The True Cost of Extreme Isolation in New York's Prisons* (New York: New York Civil Liberties Union, 2012); NYSBA, *Solitary Confinement in New York State* (Albany: New York State Bar Association, 2013); Anna Flagg, Alex Tatusian, and Christie Thompson, "Who's in Solitary Confinement?" The Marshall Project, November 20, 2016, https://www.themarshallproject.org/2016/11/30/a-new-report-gives-the-most-detailed-breakdown-yet-of-how-isolation-is-used-in-u-s-prisons (accessed June 6, 2018).

86. Bruce Arrigo and Jennifer Leslie Bullock, "The Psychological Effects of Solitary Confinement on Prisoners in Supermax Units," *International Journal of Offender Therapy and Comparative Criminology* 52 (2008): 622–40; Mary Murphy Corcoran, "Effects of Solitary Confinement on the Well Being of Prison Inmates," *Applied Psychology OPUS* (2015), https://steinhardt.nyu.edu/appsych/opus/issues/2015/spring/corcoran (accessed June 5, 2018); Craig Haney, "Restricting the Use of Solitary Confinement," *Annual Review of Criminology* 1 (2018): 285–310; Terry Allen Kupers, *Solitary* (Oakland: University of California Press, 2017); Nathaniel Penn, "Buried Alive: Stories from Inside

Solitary Confinement," *GQ* (March 2, 2017), http://www.gq.com/story/buried
-alive-solitary-confinement (accessed January 14, 2018); NYSBA, *Solitary Confinement in New York State*; Andrew Urevig, "The Confined Mind," *Lateral Magazine* (December 18, 2018), http://www.lateralmag.com/articles/issue-30/the
-confined-mind (accessed December 25, 2018).

87. George Dvorsky, "Why Solitary Confinement Is the Worst Kind of Psychological Torture," *Gizmodo*, http://io9.gizmodo.com/why-solitary-confinement-is
-the-worst-kind-of-psycholog-1598543595?utm_campaign=socialflow_gizmodo
_facebook&utm_source=gizmodo_facebook&utm_medium=socialflow (accessed
January 14, 2018).

88. New York State Corrections and Community Supervision, Directive #0086,
September 13, 2017, http://www.doccs.ny.gov/Directives/0086.pdf (accessed February 12, 2019); also see National Institute of Justice (NIJ), *Shock Incarceration
in New York: Focus on Treatment* (Washington, DC: US Department of Justice,
1994), https://www.ncjrs.gov/pdffiles/shockny.pdf (accessed February 12, 2019).

89. NIJ, *Shock Incarceration in New York*, 5.

90. New York State Corrections and Community Supervision, Directive #0086.

91. NIJ, *Shock Incarceration in New York*, 7,

92. Corcraft is the brand name of New York State's correctional industries
company.

93. For a full listing, see: Corcraft, "About Corcraft."

94. In fact, A.T. said that the metal shop's low pay was one of the causes of the
Attica uprising in 1971, and his claim is confirmed in Heather Ann Thompson's
encyclopedic account of that event: *Blood in the Water: The Attica Prison Uprising
of 1971 and Its Legacy* (New York: Pantheon, 2016).

95. A.T.'s assertion is borne out by evidence. A 2016 survey of state and federal
prisons reported that 11 percent of the prisoners in solitary confinement had been
there for three years or more, and 5.4 percent had been in isolation for six years
or more (Association of State Correctional Administrators and the Arthur Liman
Public Interest Program at Yale Law School, *Aiming to Reduce Time-In-Cell* (New
Haven, CT: Yale Law School, 2016), https://law.yale.edu/system/files/area/center
/liman/document/aimingtoreducetic.pdf (accessed February 12, 2019); also see
Penn, "Buried Alive"; Solitary Watch, "FAQ").

96. Hatton, *Coerced Labor*.

97. Zatz, "Working at the Boundaries of Markets"; Zatz, "Prison Labor and the
Paradox of Paid Nonmarket Work."

98. Weeks, *The Problem with Work*, 8; also see Michel Foucault, *Discipline &
Punish: The Birth of the Prison* (New York: Random House, 1977); Karl Marx,
Capital: A Critique of Political Economy, Vol. I (New York: Penguin, [1906] 1992);
Weber, *The Protestant Work Ethic*.

99. Hatton, *Coerced Labor*.

100. Weeks, *The Problem with Work*, 8.

101. For example, Erin Hatton, "Work beyond the Bounds: A Boundary Analysis of the Fragmentation of Work," *Work, Employment and Society* 29, no. 6 (2015): 1007–18.

102. Heather Ann Thompson has made a similar argument about the history of prisoners' labor activism and labor history (Thompson, "Rethinking Working-Class Struggle").

2 From Extraction to Repression

PRISON LABOR, PRISON FINANCE,
AND THE PRISONERS' RIGHTS
MOVEMENT IN NORTH CAROLINA

Amanda Bell Hughett

In July 1971, North Carolina legislators passed a bill phasing out the state's nearly one-hundred-year-old practice of forcing imprisoned people to labor without pay on the state's roadways. Prison Superintendent Vernon Lee Bounds celebrated the move, proclaiming that North Carolina had finally "achieved its rightful place as a model of modern correctional practices."[1] Since he took office in 1965, Bounds had pushed for the chain gang's abolition. In its place, he envisioned a new model of prison labor, one that taught imprisoned men how to be effective "breadwinners" and leaders of their households. Influenced by midcentury social scientific thinking that linked criminality to "family disorganization," Bounds hoped to create prison work programs that taught men vocational skills and disciplined work habits, enabled them to work in their communities while serving their sentences, and paid minimum wages they could use to support their families and off-set the cost of their room and board.[2] Yet soon after the North Carolina General Assembly took its first step toward implementing Bounds's vision, it reversed course. In 1975, legislators not only reinstituted the chain gang but also expanded state agencies' access to forced prison labor.

This chapter uses this turn of events to illuminate how government officials reshaped prison labor to better control imprisoned people during the last third of the twentieth century. Between 1971 and 1975, North Carolina experienced a prison labor crisis. Since the 1930s, the prison system's funding had depended in part on forced prison labor on the state's roadways and in a small number of prison industries. During the early 1970s, three interrelated shifts destabilized this prison labor and financial regime. First, technological advancements, new federal laws, and broader global economic shifts made forced prison labor less cost effective than it had been in the past. Second, imprisoned people increasingly threatened the prison system's budget through work stoppages, slowdowns, and strikes. Third, rising incarceration rates led to growing idleness behind bars as the number of prisoners began to outpace the number of available prison jobs. Fearful of increased prison activism, state leaders from across the political spectrum responded to this crisis by passing legislation that disentangled the prison system's budget from prison labor and instead funded it directly through the state's general fund. Legislators also used state funds to create menial prison jobs, including roadwork, that paid small wages and offered sentence reductions to encourage good behavior. Bounds's vision fell by the wayside. State leaders were no longer confident prison labor could rehabilitate imprisoned people, and they were sure it could not—and should not—help finance the prison system. Rather, they viewed prison labor primarily as a tool to tame the politicized prison population.

State leaders' response to the prison labor crisis succeeded in impeding prisoners' organizing efforts. By no longer conditioning any part of the prison system's budget on prison labor, the General Assembly stripped imprisoned people of the power they once held in their labor, a process already set in motion by broader technological and economic shifts. Additionally, the incentives legislators attached to prison labor, although meager, undermined prisoner solidarity, especially as the prison population continued to grow. Despite North Carolina funding make-work programs like road gangs, the number of imprisoned people continued to outstrip the number of prison jobs in the decades following 1975. As a result, some prisoners began to view prison labor, especially labor that came with small perks, as a privilege rather than a part of their punishment—a privilege they were reluctant to jeopardize by organizing. Many understandably saw working outdoors on the roads for $0.10 a day and the promise of a sentence reduction as a better option than wasting away in an over-crowded cell.

In examining the relationship among prison labor, prison finance, and prison organizing, this chapter uncovers the political economy of the pris-oners' rights movement in North Carolina. While recent scholarship has revealed how imprisoned people joined together to challenge conditions behind bars during the 1960s and 1970s, scholars have yet to fully inves-tigate how prison labor and financial practices shaped—and were shaped by—imprisoned people's activism.[3] This gap stems in part from the dearth of scholarship on prison labor after the mid-twentieth century. A vibrant body of historical work has traced the origins and rise of convict leasing practices during the nineteenth and early twentieth centuries.[4] But the work on prison labor then largely jumps ahead to the late 1970s when Congress rolled back New Deal–era restrictions on private companies' access to prison labor, a policy that today impacts less than 1 percent of the prison population.[5] Indeed, the vast majority of imprisoned people continue to labor for the state—if they work at all. In North Carolina, as in many states, at least 10 percent of imprisoned men and women do not work or participate in any prison program, even part time.[6] By over-looking the 1960s and 1970s, then, scholars have missed the role prison labor and financial policy played in the rise—and later suppression—of the prisoners' rights movement. In North Carolina, imprisoned people mobilized during a moment when the prison budget remained tied to their labor. The shared experience of forced prison labor unified racially diverse people. Yet as the prisoners' movement gathered strength and the incarceration rate began to rise, state leaders reshaped prison labor and financial practices in ways that ultimately undermined prisoners' ability to organize. In the process, state leaders laid the groundwork for today's prison labor and financial regime in which prison labor serves the primary purpose of controlling imprisoned people rather than financing the prison system or teaching imprisoned people new skills.

· · · · ·

When Vernon Lee Bounds took office as prison secretary in 1965, he inherited a prison system shaped by the state's long-standing expectation that imprisoned people work to offset the cost of their imprisonment. From 1933 to 1956, North Carolina officials did not provide any funding directly to the state's prisons. Instead, the prison system was a subsidiary of the State Highway Commission, which put nearly all imprisoned people to work on the roads. When the two agencies separated in 1956 under intense pressure from prison reformers, the state passed a series of laws ensuring that the prison system's budget remained inextricably tied to prisoners' labor. To finance the prisons, state law compelled the Highway Commission "to employ as many prisoners . . . fit for road work as [could be] economically used" and then pay the Prison Department for that labor from its budget. Each year, the prison superintendent and the state highway commissioner negotiated a contract, known as the "road quota," that set the number of prisoners who would work on the roads each day and the price the commission would pay for them. The two departments determined the price based on the prison system's budgetary needs and the commission's desire to keep labor costs low. In 1966, for instance, the commission paid the prison department $3.25 per day per man, a price higher than the cost of imprisoning a person but significantly lower than the wage paid to a free laborer. If the prison system ran a deficit, state law dictated that the additional funding come out of the Highway Commission's budget rather than out of the state's general fund. State legislators also expected prison officials to raise additional revenue through the sale of prison-made goods to state and local agencies. By 1965, North Carolina's prison system owned two farms, a series of laundry facilities, a paint plant, a license plate and metalwork plant, a canning operation, and a number of smaller workshops.[7]

Bounds despised the road quota system because it impeded his ability to establish what he viewed as meaningful vocational and educational programs for prisoners. He believed that road labor lacked any rehabilitative value, but he nevertheless had to assign a substantial number of the state's prisoners to the roads in order to receive payment from the Highway Commission. To replace the road quota, Bounds pushed legislators to adopt a new model of prison finance that blended the older, labor-based system with a new commitment to prisoner rehabilitation. First, he urged the General Assembly to fund the further expansion and diversification of North Carolina's prison industries with the goal of increasing the number and kind of prison-made goods available for purchase by government agencies. Recognizing North Carolina's economic roots in agriculture and small manufacturing, Bounds believed that, unlike roadwork, prisoners' labor on state farms and in state factories taught them useful skills. He also thought the profits from the new industries would eventually be so great that the state could abolish the chain gang and pay imprisoned laborers wages for their work at no additional cost to taxpayers.[8] Second, Bounds hoped to expand a program he had pioneered while serving as a professor at the University of North Carolina. In 1957, Bounds, in collaboration with prison staff, introduced a work-release program, the first of its kind in the nation, that enabled imprisoned people to work in their communities for wages during the day and return to prison at night. Prison officials then deducted money from the prisoners' paychecks to cover the cost of housing, food, and transportation in addition to any child support or victim restitution payments they might have owed.[9]

Bounds's rehabilitative vision came with its own set of sexist, racist, and class-based assumptions about the needs of imprisoned men. It was also inherently coercive.[10] Bounds's ideas were shaped by then cutting-edge, social-scientific theory that rooted criminality in alleged "cultural pathologies" within poor communities, especially communities of color. Foremost among those pathologies, according to many social scientists, was the breakdown of the traditional family structure, demonstrated by the large number of women-led households in poor communities. Social scientists reasoned that crime stemmed from men's failure to serve as providers and heads of their households.[11] Following this logic, prison reformers such as Bounds believed that "rehabilitation" required prisons to teach men how to conform to their proper familiar roles. For Bounds, that meant instilling in men the "dignity" of labor by teaching them valuable skills and allowing them to earn a paycheck. With their pay, Bounds argued, prisoners could support themselves and keep their families "off welfare."[12] Those who failed to demonstrate sufficient "progress," however, suffered stark consequences, including the denial of parole, the withdraw of privileges, and time in solitary confinement.

North Carolina legislators supported Bounds's plan in theory, but they proved unwilling to pay for its implementation, even after Congress began to push states to "modernize" their criminal justice systems in the mid-1960s.[13] Long dependent on prison labor to finance the prison system, state legislators were reluctant to grant Bounds the funding he needed to follow through with his ideas. In 1967, after two years of pressure from Bounds, state legislators enacted a series of reforms, but they proved to be largely symbolic. The General Assembly changed the Prison Department's name to the more modern "Department of Corrections" (DoC). It also transferred responsibility for the DoC's budget deficit from the State Highway Commission, then renamed the Department of Transportation (DoT), to the state's general fund. Additionally, legislators approved Bounds's plan to pay imprisoned workers an incentive wage of $0.10 to $1.00 a day, citing other states' adoption of the practice. During budget negotiations, however, the General Assembly failed to fund the incentive wage program or to expand the state's prison industries, leaving the older prison labor system in place.[14]

Disappointed, Bounds responded to the legislature's actions by delaying the new programs and continuing to rely on the DoT for financial support while remaining committed to his vision for the future. In 1968, Bounds sent twenty-five hundred prisoners, approximately 25 percent of the state's prison population, to the roads. To bring in additional funds, he renegotiated the rate the DoT would pay for imprisoned people's labor. Although the DoC estimated it cost $4 per day to house each state prisoner, Bounds persuaded the DoT to pay $6 per day for each maximum-security prisoner, $7 for each medium-custody prisoner, and $9 for each honor-grade prisoner who labored on the roads.[15] Bounds intended to invest the additional funds in expanding the state's prison factories and farms in hopes of both financing the new incentive wage program and eventually persuading the General Assembly to abolish the chain gang.[16]

The General Assembly's decision and Bounds's response to it outraged imprisoned people in North Carolina. The 1967 legislation had raised their expectations only to let them down. Not only did the state refuse to pay the prisoners their promised incentive wages, but the increase in the road quota also prevented many eligible prisoners from earning wages through participation in the work-release program. Imprisoned people expressed their anger through rebellion. By early 1968, Bounds regularly complained to the Prison Advisory Commission, which helped oversee the prison system, about arson in the prison industries and men who threw "bolts and screws in the machinery" on the prison farms.[17] On the roads, DoT officials reported groups of prisoners who "wouldn't get out of the truck" in low temperatures or who simply "refused to work."[18] That April, frustrated prisoners at North Carolina's maximum-security Central Prison went on strike. Nearly half of the facility's one thousand men failed to show up for their jobs in the facility's license plate factory. Soon, an additional three hundred men joined them in the prison yard, refusing to return to their cells until state leaders agreed to meet their demands, including the payment of their incentive wages. Bounds responded with force, underscoring the coercive nature of his rehabilitative vision. At his signal, the police retook the prison, leaving six prisoners dead and seventy-seven injured.[19]

In the wake of the strike, Bounds began to rethink his commitment to financing the prison system through prison labor. Before Bounds suppressed the protest, imprisoned men did $42,000 worth of damage to Central Prison's metal shop and license plate plant, jeopardizing the prison system's budget and Bounds's ability to expand the state's prison industries.[20] In a letter to the governor written soon after the protest, Bounds warned that the state's prison labor and financial regime might give imprisoned people too much power. "What's to prevent them from shutting this operation down?" he asked.[21] Signaling his change of heart, Bounds submitted a budget request the following July that asked for an additional $18 million from the General Assembly—not to pay the prisoners' incentive wages or to expand prison industries but to buy new surveillance equipment, hire additional guards, and modify prison structures to make them more "secure." [22] Bounds remained committed to the abolition of the chain gang, but he became less certain of what should take its place or how to pay for it. As he told the governor, imprisoned people "should perform meaningful labor" but "the security of the prison system" should be the state's "highest priority."[23]

The 1968 strike and imprisoned people's ongoing activism exacerbated the already volatile relationship between transportation and prison system officials. By the end of the 1960s, DoT leaders had joined Bounds in his call to eliminate the road quota, albeit for different reasons. Since the 1950s, DoT officials had complained that North Carolina's system for financing its prisons forced them to take on more imprisoned people than they needed to complete their work. By the mid-twentieth

century, advances in road-building machinery had reduced the number
of men required to perform tasks. In 1954, the DoT hired a consulting
firm that suggested the road quota, by creating an oversupply of labor,
wasted more money than it saved the state.[24] The federal government's
growing involvement in highway construction made the problem worse.
Since the 1930s, federal law had banned the use of state prison labor on
construction projects receiving federal funds.[25] As the federal government
increased the number of grants available for highway building during the
mid-twentieth century, it restricted the number of sites where imprisoned
people could work. DoT officials claimed they only needed a small number of prisoners to perform road labor, but prison officials pushed them
to take on large numbers to keep the prison system solvent. As a result,
DoT officials often found themselves guarding large groups of prisoners
with little to do. Already dissatisfied with the system, DoT officials seized
on the news of the 1968 strike to argue that the state's increasingly politicized prisoners were becoming impossible to manage, putting both DoT
staff and the public at risk. "Nobody benefits from this system," the state's
transportation commissioner told the *Raleigh News and Observer*. "It's got
to end."[26]

Despite the DoT's calls to eliminate the road quota system, state officials kept it in place. It took the prospect of receiving substantial federal
funds for North Carolina officials to act. In 1970, Congress established a
new grant program designed to fund "the construction, acquisition, and
renovation of corrections institutions and facilities, and for the improvement of corrections programs and practices."[27] In hopes of taking advantage of the funding, North Carolina's Democratic governor Bob Scott, at
the urging of Bounds, called on the North Carolina Bar Association in
August 1970 to study and make recommendations for the improvement
of North Carolina's prison system. Many of the Bar Association's suggestions mirrored those put forth by Bounds years earlier. First and foremost,
the Bar Association called for the road quota to be "drastically reduced
and eliminated as soon as possible" and the incentive wage to be put into
effect. While the lawyers believed "a large number of inmates" were not
"suited for anything other than manual labor," they thought all prisoners
should be paid for their labor in order to encourage them to "accumulate
some savings . . . work efficiently . . . and achieve rehabilitative goals."[28]

In seeking to implement its recommendations, the Bar Association encountered the same budgetary issues that had plagued prison reformers in 1967. In the spring of 1971, the Bar Association worked with sympathetic members of the General Assembly to introduce a series of laws designed to reshape the prison system's labor and financial practices. After learning Congress had approved an additional $98.5 million in funding for state correctional programs, North Carolina's General Assembly passed a bill phasing out the chain gang. By July 1973, the legislation dictated, the road quota would be eliminated entirely.[29] Yet a month later, when the General Assembly returned to discuss the state budget, lawmakers failed to allocate funds to close the anticipated $4.8 million funding gap—over 10 percent of the prison system's budget—that would be left when state prisoners came off the roads. The General Assembly also declined to fund prisoners' incentive wages. While the promise of federal funding had succeeded in compelling state leaders to phase out the chain gang, they remained stubbornly opposed to dedicating additional taxpayer dollars directly to the prison system. As the end of the chain gang neared, Bounds's prison budget remained tied to the State Department of Transportation—and thus also to prisoners' labor. In 1971, Bounds reluctantly signed a new contract sending eighteen hundred prisoners to the roads in exchange for $12.50 per day for each man, an increase designed to compensate for the reduced number of laborers in the years to follow.[30]

. . . . .

Bounds's plan to replace the chain gang was a product of its historical moment. His rehabilitative philosophy aligned with the recommendations put forth by the federal government, which in turn reflected best practices in the field of corrections. Yet the years immediately following the General Assembly's passage of the 1971 law phasing out the chain gang witnessed a series of political shifts that reshaped the prison population and destabilized the already shaky consensus concerning the future of prison policy. In North Carolina, voters moved steadily rightward, embracing the "tough-on-crime" rhetoric espoused by George Wallace and Richard Nixon, and leaving state leaders all the more reluctant to dedicate funding to prisoner rehabilitation. The state's incarceration rate, following national trends, also began to rise in 1972, reflecting both an increase in violent crime and "tough" new policies. Subject to increasingly overcrowded and deteriorating conditions, imprisoned workers in North Carolina doubled down on their organizing campaigns, joining a nationwide movement to unionize. By the time the prisoners came off the roads in July 1973, the state's prison system was in crisis.

In late 1972, four white prisoners confined to North Carolina's Central Prison began corresponding with members of the California Prisoners' Union (CPU), which had formed in 1970 in the wake of a nineteen-day strike at Folsom Prison. By 1974, eleven states, aided by the CPU, had formed prisoners' unions.[31] With discussions of prison labor and finance constantly in the news, imprisoned people in North Carolina viewed themselves as uniquely well situated to unionize. They understood that the prison system's budget remained tied in part to their labor on the roads and in the state's prison industries. They also recognized that their work performing maintenance tasks behind bars lowered the cost of the prison system. In flyers encouraging others to join the union, the men at Central noted that prisoners' "slave labor" saved the state "millions of dollars" and "kept the prison system in operation."[32] Drawing inspiration from the broader upsurge of public sector labor organizing during the early 1970s, the union organizers argued that they too should be viewed as public sector workers who labored for the state.[33]

While many of the union's goals aligned with Bounds's plan for the prison system, its members advanced one core demand that was irreconcilable with Bounds's vision: the prisoners wanted a say in the policies that impacted their lives. The union planned to leverage prisoners' labor to win the right to bargain collectively with state leaders. Its members also planned to obtain lawyers to advocate on their behalf. In addition to collective bargaining rights, the union sought a series of policy changes, both sweeping and specific. Similar to Bounds, the prisoners demanded "an end to employment [in prison] without reasonable compensations, wages . . . or benefits." Citing the 1967 law enabling the state to pay prisoners an incentive wage, they sought the "just compensation" for their labor and the same benefits afforded free workers, including workers compensation in the case of injury, social security, and unemployment insurance. The union also wanted an end to brutality and racial discrimination on the part of prison guards, improved medical care, better access to legal materials, changes to sentencing and parole practices, respect for prisoners' procedural rights, and an end to both the construction of large penal facilities and the death penalty.[34]

Bounds opposed the union from the start, telling reporters that, while "a prisoner may claim he is in a union," he would get "no recognition" from him.[35] Yet Bounds's stance was not tough enough to satisfy North Carolina's new governor, James Holshouser. The first Republican to hold the office since Reconstruction, Holshouser, following Nixon's lead, campaigned in 1972 on the promise to get tough on crime and to cut bureaucratic red tape. Once in office in January 1973, he consolidated state agencies by placing the Department of Corrections under the supervision of a newly established Department of Social Rehabilitation and Social Control, which also oversaw probation, parole, and juvenile corrections. To head the new department, Holshouser bypassed Bounds, who had expressed interest in the job, and instead appointed an outsider, David Jones, a TV salesman who had curried favor with Holshouser by working on his gubernatorial campaign. Only days after starting his new job, Jones, who had gubernatorial aspirations of his own, rented a helicopter on the state's dime and traveled to all of the state's prisons to inform imprisoned people that he would not "tolerate any nonsense." Disgusted, Bounds announced his resignation soon after, leaving five months later in July 1973.[36]

Jones had never been inside a prison before taking office, and he was in over his head. Not only was the North Carolina Prisoners' Labor Union hard at work recruiting new members, but the state's prisons were also becoming overcrowded, making it increasingly difficult to monitor the prison population. Since the early 1960s, North Carolina's prison population had hovered around 10,000 people, already at the top of the prison system's capacity. Beginning in 1972, the population, following national trends, steadily began to grow. By the end of 1973, North Carolina's prisons housed over 11,500 people, and the incarceration rate's rise showed no signs of slowing.[37] Prison officials regularly complained to Jones that the overcrowded conditions made it nearly impossible to "maintain order," let alone operate rehabilitation programming. One supervisor reported that some cells were so overcrowded that prison staff could not see inside when they walked past to perform regular checks. At Central Prison, guards simply refused to go inside large, overcrowded prison barracks after dark, leaving imprisoned men to fend for themselves. Jones responded by attempting to recruit additional guards to monitor the growing prison population, but the measly wages paid by the state made it impossible for him to hire enough workers.[38]

Tensions ran high inside the state's prisons, especially because so many men and women spent their days locked inside with nothing to do. There simply were not enough prison jobs or spots in the state's limited rehabilitation programs to occupy prisoners' time. Since the nineteenth century, prison systems had struggled periodically with what corrections experts called "the problem of prison idleness," a problem made worse by the passage of laws, first at the state and later at the federal level, that restricted the sale of prison-made goods on the open market. The "state-use" system, widely adopted in the 1930s, was designed in part to address this issue. By encouraging state and local agencies to use prison labor and purchase prison-made goods, the state-use system aimed to put imprisoned people back to work and, at least in theory, keep the cost of prisons low.[39]After the 1930s, states' prison populations remained relatively small, making it a viable, if imperfect, means to employ most imprisoned people. But when the incarceration rate began to rise in the 1970s, legislators once again had an idle prison population on their hands. Instead of rethinking the state's sentencing practices, they punted, leaving the problem for prison officials who, in their limited policy-making capacity, could address only the symptoms, not the causes, of the problem.

After he took office in January 1973, Jones, concerned by the number of idle prisoners, attempted to renegotiate the road quota and put additional men to work on the highways. When challenged by other prison officials, he offered a one-line response: "Idle hands are the devil's tools."[40] Transportation officials, however, had no desire to put imprisoned people's idle hands to work. Like Bounds, they had viewed the 1971 bill phasing out the chain gang as a victory. Increasing the road quota, they argued, would re-create the problem the DoT first experienced in the mid-1950s: an oversupply of labor. Not only had road technology continued to develop since midcentury, but the DoT had also already hired additional free laborers to make up for the reduction in imprisoned road workers after 1971. The

DoT superintendent told Jones that he "didn't intend to pay for inmates to stand around next to the highways," nor was he willing to "make work when none existed."[41]

For Jones, renegotiating the road quota seemed like the most immediate way to resolve the idleness problem. As the prison population grew, it became increasingly difficult to envision employing most people in prison industries jobs. By design, state-use laws limited the market for prison-made goods and services. North Carolinians, for instance, only needed so many license plates. When Bounds suggested the state put the majority of the state's prisoners to work on state farms and in states factories, he did not foresee the prison population skyrocketing well beyond ten thousand people. North Carolina's prison leaders, like those in most states, attempted to create new jobs by diversifying their industries. In the early 1970s, prison officials used a portion of the profits from prison-made goods, once envisioned as a means to pay for prisoners' wages and rehabilitation programs, to open a print shop and factories that produced furniture and cleaning supplies.[42] Still, the number of new prison jobs fell far short of the number of imprisoned people. As Jones quickly learned, the profits from the state's prison industries only went so far, especially as the prison population, and thus also the cost of the prison system, continued to grow. The tightening budget forced Jones to make hard choices between long-term goals, such as the further diversification of prison industries, and short-term needs, such as providing prisoners with adequate food, clothing, and shelter.

Jones saw work release as a less costly way to relieve prisoners' idleness, but his efforts to expand that program encountered unforeseen obstacles, too. According to the 1957 statute establishing the program, the parole board had to approve imprisoned people's participation in work release. When Governor Holshouser took office, however, he appointed tough-on-crime hardliners to the parole board who approved substantially fewer people for the program than in the past. Parole officials and prison leaders were working at cross-purposes. While Jones and his staff were attempting to get people out of the prison, at least during the day, the parole board was working to keep them behind bars.[43] To further complicate the situation, few business owners proved willing or able to hire incarcerated people, especially with talk of crime constantly in the news. Before the parole board would approve a person's participation in work release, he or she already had to have a job in place. Imprisoned men and women had to write to the few local businesses within driving distance of their often-rural prison facilities and ask for work. Most employers declined the offer, and those few who agreed often revoked their job offers after waiting months for prisoners to obtain permission from the parole board.[44] While the work release program worked well for the relatively small prison population under Bounds's care, it would require a major overhaul to function in the emerging era of mass incarceration.

The leaders of the North Carolina Prisoners' Labor Union took advantage of the prison overcrowding and widespread idleness to do exactly what Jones and his staff feared they would do: they organized. At Caledonia and Odum Prison Farms, union organizers waited until after dark, when guards refused to walk through overcrowded prison barracks, to hold union meetings and pass around union cards. At Central Prison, unemployed men devoted their entire days to filing lawsuits and producing literature on the union's behalf.[45] Their work paid off. By the summer of 1973, internal prison correspondence noted that the union had spread to twenty-five of the state's eighty-seven prisons.[46] Jones was on edge—and he had reason to worry. The movement to unionize prisoners was growing nationally and, in some states, it even seemed to be winning. In Massachusetts, the prisoner union had won limited recognition by prison staff.[47] Given the DoC's tight budget, Jones feared a system-wide strike by the prisoners' union would jeopardize the prison system's finances or, worse, force prison staff to make some concessions—an event Jones believed would surely damage his gubernatorial prospects.[48]

With the abolition of the chain gang looming over the prison system, Jones submitted a 1973–1974 budget proposal requesting additional funds to manage the prison population. State leaders' response made clear that Bounds's vision would never come to fruition. Jones sought to expand prison industries, establish new recreation and rehabilitation programs, and close the budget gap that would result from the chain gang's abolition. He also wanted to hire additional guards and build new prisons to contain the growing prison population. The General Assembly approved only two of the requests. First, it increased the prison system's operations budget by $5.1 million beginning July 1 to replace the money that would be lost from prisoners' roadwork. Second, it approved $17 million for the construction of a prison with single-person cells designed to facilitate the control of the prison population.[49] While state officials ended the practice of tying the prison system's budget to imprisoned people's labor on the roads, they declined to fund the new programs for imprisoned people that Bounds had envisioned taking the chain gang's place. Instead, state leaders seemed to embrace a new plan that emphasized containment over rehabilitation or even cost-cutting efforts.

Imprisoned people assumed that after the chain gang's abolition state officials would attempt to raise additional revenue for the prison system by increasing production on the state's farms and in the state's factories. Soon after the General Assembly finalized the state budget, in June 1973, men associated with the prisoners' union went on strike at Odum Prison Farm. Declaring themselves "in allegiance with the North Carolina Prisoners' Labor Union," three Black prisoners called on all the farm workers to "refuse to do any work . . . unless minimum wages were paid." A group of thirty men heeded the organizers' call. By refusing to work, the imprisoned men hoped to demonstrate the power, albeit dwindling, that they continued to hold in their labor—and prison officials got the message loud and clear. Upon learning of the strike, Jones dispatched Regional Supervisor F. L. Sanders to the farm to "stop the strike before it spread across the river to Caledonia [Prison Farm.]" He rounded up the "known union agitators" who were "influencing or trying to influence others" and transferred each of them to the Central Prison's solitary confinement unit.[50]

Still reeling from the Odum strike, North Carolina's prison system was wholly unprepared to manage the sixteen hundred imprisoned men left without work when the chain gang ended on July 1, 1973. While Bounds had envisioned the men transitioning to new jobs in prison industries, the work release program, or new educational and vocational training courses, the former road workers joined the thousands of other prisoners who spent their days in cramped conditions with little to occupy their time. The *Greensboro Daily News* estimated that 80 to 90 percent of prisoners had nothing to do during the day.[51] With the population nearing two thousand above capacity by 1974, prison officials began converting shared spaces and recreation facilities into cells while they awaited the construction of new facilities. "We have them sleeping in showers. . . . We have them sleeping on pool tables. We have them sleeping on floors and anywhere else we can put them," prison officials told the *Raleigh News & Observer*.[52] Meanwhile, the prisoners' union remained hard at work, recruiting new members and planning future actions.

.   .   .   .   .

Seven months after the chain gang's abolition, in February 1974, Jones wrote a letter to transportation officials making them an offer. For the old rate of $12.50 per day, the DoT could have "as many minimum-custody, honor-grade inmates as [it] could use" on the roads. The prison system, Jones explained, was "not able to utilize the entire work force in any constructive activity" and, as a result, was struggling to "properly control" the prison population.[53] The state's rising incarceration rate, coupled with prisoners' unionizing efforts, had left the prison system in a state of disarray. To make matters worse, the recession that began in late 1973 reduced the demand for prison-made goods, limiting the number of people Jones could employ in the state's factories and on the state's farms. Desperate to put imprisoned people back to work, Jones turned to what he viewed as the only remaining solution to the "idleness crisis": imprisoned people needed to go back on the roads.

Transportation leaders had little sympathy for the prison system's problems. They remained uninterested in resurrecting the practice of using forced prison labor on the roads. "Our personnel feel that their sentences were completed when the use of inmate labor was discontinued," one road engineer wrote in response to Jones's offer. As in 1971, they argued that reestablishing the chain gang would create an oversupply of labor. They also complained that "inmates [had] no real incentive to work" and that "the return of prison labor would decrease [the department's] maintenance standards." Moreover, DoT officials told Jones their agency was "not experiencing any difficulty maintaining its [labor] quota," especially given the recession. The DoT director noted that working prison labor would "put us in a difficult position . . . with free labor looking for work" and that, if prisoners were returned to roads at their pre-1973 rate, the agency would have to "terminate trained and dedicated employees at a time when [the nation was] having an economic slump." The agency estimated that to put prisoners back to work, it would have to fire as many as 383 tempo-rary and 93 permanent employees.[54]

Jones had hoped the DoT would welcome imprisoned laborers, since he could no longer create new prison industries positions without an infu-sion of funds from the General Assembly. During the recession, the profits from the state's prison industries began to dwindle, making it impossible to develop new product lines. Not only were state and local agencies pur-chasing fewer prison-made goods, but the cost of raw materials had also begun to rise, increasing the cost of operation.[55] North Carolina was not alone in experiencing such troubles. The recession also hit the Federal Prison Industries, once the model for the states. Citing the increased cost of materials and its own problems with prison organizing, Federal Prison Industries reported an annual loss in 1973 for the first time since its establishment in 1935. Although Congress had designed Federal Prison Industries to be self-supporting, legislators delegated funds to the agency in 1975 to diversify its industries with the explicit goal of employing a larger percentage of the prison population, even if it meant sacrificing effi-ciency.[56] While North Carolina's prison industries continued to make a small profit in the mid-1970s, it was becoming clear to many lawmakers that employing prisoners might eventually take—rather than make—money, especially if the incarceration rate continued to rise.

Many imprisoned people, including union members, embraced prison officials' efforts to put them to work. They wanted meaningful jobs. They also wanted to be treated fairly. After learning of Jones's efforts to return prisoners to the roads, the prisoners' union sent a letter signed by eighty-seven men to the General Assembly endorsing the idea, so long as they received a decent wage and the state recognized their union. To assure leg-islators of their willingness to compromise, the prisoners adopted many of Bounds's earlier arguments. The union pushed legislators to model all prison labor after the work release system. The prisoners wanted the state to pay them at least minimum wage for their labor, minus the cost of their room and board. Drawing on the language of rehabilitation once used by Bounds, the union members argued that, under their plan, imprisoned people could send money home to their dependents and thus "remove people from the welfare rolls." They also claimed that, by recognizing the union, the state could "minimize overhead cost" by allowing imprisoned people to oversee the prison-labor system, which would in turn "empower men to take responsibility for their actions" and imbue the "convicted class" with "feelings of unity and power that would benefit all prisoners."[57]

After the chain gang's abolition, activists inside and outside of the prison put pressure on state leaders to address prison idleness, unfair working conditions, and overcrowding. In an effort to compel the state to pay them their promised incentive wages, in December 1974, four men affiliated with the union filed a lawsuit complaining that they had been forced to "work in the Central Prison Printing Plant without compensation." Such unpaid labor violated their rights under the state constitution, the prisoners argued, because in 1971 the General Assembly had removed "involuntary servitude" from the constitution's list of acceptable forms of punishment.[58] Meanwhile, prisoners' rights lawyers affiliated with the National Prison Project of the American Civil Liberties Union (ACLU), aided by the US Department of Justice, were expanding their efforts to bring suit against states with overcrowded, decrepit prison conditions. The lawyers also began experimenting with a new set of legal arguments that sought to require state officials to offer imprisoned people meaningful rehabilitation opportunities, including the ability to work or participate in vocational or educational programs. The ACLU's "right to rehabilitation" argument, an extension of the "right to treatment" established for the disabled in *Wyatt v. Strickney* (1971), never fully materialized, but news of its development left state leaders worried that their "prison idleness problem" would result in costly and time-consuming lawsuits.[59]

Fearful of litigation and the intensifying activism behind bars, Republican governor James Holshouser, in early 1974, called on the General Assembly to form a commission to examine the state's sentencing policies, parole practices, and "any other matter it deemed relevant to the problem of prison overcrowding."[60] Chaired by liberal Democratic senator Eddie Knox, a former Charlotte mayor who had long expressed interest in criminal justice reform, the commission began its work by visiting all of the state's eighty-seven prison facilities. Shocked by their findings, the "Knox Commission" issued a "statement of concern" to the General Assembly in August 1974, urging legislators to take "emergency action" on the "potentially dangerous situation" inside the state's prisons. The commission members, drawing on their conversations with prison officials, claimed the overcrowding "hampered custodial control" and endangered prison security.[61] Six months later, in February 1975, the Knox Committee offered a specific set of recommendations to resolve "the problem of prison idleness," most of which echoed Bounds's suggestions from the previous decade: the expansion and diversification of prison industries; a greater emphasis on counseling; the creation of new recreational, vocational, and educational programs; and the expansion of work release.[62]

The Knox Commission's call for additional rehabilitation programs faced immediate pushback from the more conservative members of the General Assembly. To justify their opposition to the Knox Commission's proposal, the conservative legislators pointed to a recent publication, later known as "Nothing Works," by sociologist Robert Martinson. Cited widely in policy-making circles, Martinson's piece, which surveyed a broad swath of studies related to prisoner rehabilitation, suggested that no program reduced the recidivism rate, despite claims to the contrary.[63] In North Carolina, as in many states, legislators used Martinson's article to argue against new rehabilitation initiatives. They claimed that since efforts to rehabilitate prisoners inevitably failed, prisons should simply incapacitate people convicted of crimes by holding them behind bars.[64]

Legislators on both sides of the aisle, however, agreed on one reform: imprisoned people should be put back to work. While not all state leaders viewed prison labor as a path to rehabilitation, they all agreed forced labor could—and should—be used as a means to control the politicized prison population. In 1975, State Senator Lamar Gudger, a member of the Knox Commission, introduced two pieces of legislation designed to "put prisoners back to work." The first compelled the DoT, despite its leaders' protest, to put "as many minimum custody prisoners as [were] available and fit for road work and who [could not] appropriately be place[d] on work release, study release, or other full-time programs" back on the state's roadways. The second empowered the prison superintendent to "enter into contracts to supply inmate labor" to any state or local agency that requested it as long as the proposed projects benefited the citizens of North Carolina as a whole and did not displace free labor.[65]

In putting prisoners to work, legislators drew on the lessons they had learned during the previous decade of prisoners' activism. The 1975 bills and the budget negotiations that followed carefully decoupled prison finance from prisoners' work in ways that further weakened the power imprisoned people held in their labor, a decision likely made easier by the declining profitability of the state's farms and factories. Unlike the prison labor system prior to 1973, the new bills no longer required state agencies to supplement the prison system's overall budget by paying for prison labor. Instead, the 1975 bills offered prison labor to state agencies— including the DoT—in exchange only for prisoners' transportation costs and the cost of the guards who monitored them. Not only did this new financial arrangement lower the cost of prison labor to state agencies, but it also weakened imprisoned workers' bargaining position since the prison system's budget was not contingent on their labor.

After stalling for eight years, the General Assembly also approved the payment of incentive wages of $0.10 to $1.00 a day for imprisoned laborers. Bounds's appeals to prisoner rehabilitation had failed to persuade legislators to make good on their promise in 1967. But as the prisoners' movement grew more powerful and the courts threatened increased intervention, legislators embraced the incentive wage as both a disciplinary tool and as a way to signal the state's adherence to best correctional practices.[66] With the incentive wage in place, those who dared to organize risked time in solitary confinement and the loss of money they could use to buy items in the prison commissary. "Essentially, an Incentive Wage Program would assist the Division of Prisons in the effective management of the offender population," one member of the Knox Committee told her skeptical colleagues in the State Senate.[67] Moreover, by 1975, North Carolina was one of only a few states, along with Texas, Georgia, Arkansas, Mississippi, Maine, and Alabama, that declined to pay imprisoned people for their labor, a status that invited the scrutiny of prisoners' rights lawyers.[68]

To finance the new wages, the General Assembly allocated money from the general fund to the DoT, which in turn paid the wages of imprisoned road workers and those who performed maintenance duties inside prison facilities.[69] It also directed North Carolina's prison industries to use its limited profits to pay the incentive wages of the people who labored on state farms and in the state factories, a move eliminating any remaining hope of expanding the state's prison industries without additional taxpayer funding.[70] By financing prisoners' incentive wages and redirecting prison industries profits, the General Assembly further undermined the power imprisoned people held in their labor. The prison system's budget was no longer tied to prison labor. Instead, the General Assembly paid, albeit a small sum, for prisoners to perform make-work designed to occupy their time. While imprisoned people's labor, especially their work maintaining prison facilities, continued to reduce the cost of the prison system for tax-payers, prisoner work stoppages and strikes no longer created an immediate budget crisis for prison officials. Prior to 1973, protests had threatened the prison system's budget. But after the 1975 legislative session, as State Senator Gudger assured prison officials, "work stoppages . . . only hurt inmates." Protests deprived prisoners of their incentive wage rather than bringing the prison system to its knees.[71]

In addition to funding the incentive wage, the General Assembly expanded its "good time" program, which offered imprisoned people sentence reductions in exchange for good behavior on the job. Similar to the incentive wage program, good time appealed to a wide range of legislators because it served multiple purposes. It dissuaded prisoners from organizing, and it helped relieve dangerous overcrowding by shortening people's sentences. Prior to 1975, imprisoned workers received a small sentence reduction if they labored beyond regular work hours, outside in bad weather, or on the holidays.[72] The 1975 legislature reshaped the program to offer imprisoned workers a one-day sentence reduction for each full day of work, regardless of the circumstance.[73] With the new program in place, imprisoned activists not only ran the risk of spending time in solitary confinement and losing their incentive wages, but they also lost the opportunity to reduce the time they spent in North Carolina's deteriorating and overcrowded prisons.

The Knox Commission also pushed the General Assembly to eliminate the barriers created by the parole board blocking the expansion of work release, a program that, like good time, had broad appeal. While only some legislators viewed work release as an effective rehabilitation program, they all agreed it was a cost effective—and relatively safe—way to reduce prison idleness. Legislators recognized that work release positions, which paid at least minimum wage, were highly sought after by imprisoned men and women, making participating prisoners less likely than other incarcerated workers to join organizing efforts. Even if work release prisoners protested, they reasoned, the financial damage would be limited because the program only covered the cost of the participating prisoners.[74] With widespread support for the program in place, the General Assembly passed a bill bypassing the parole board and allowing sentencing judges to recommend individuals for the work release program.[75] The Knox Commission then worked to address the shortage of jobs for work release prisoners by pressing state agencies to employ them. The Governor's Mansion was one of the first agencies to sign up, employing work release prisoners at minimum wage to serve as chauffeurs and maintenance workers.[76] The scene at the mansion surely conjured images of the Old South as the largely African American, incarcerated workforce waited on the governor and his staff.

In September 1975, after two months of planning, nearly 1,100 of the state's then 12,500 prisoners returned to the roads. Among the imprisoned workers, the new program garnered mixed reviews, suggesting a growing divide within the prison population. Interviewed by the *Raleigh News & Observer* and the *Durham Sun*, some prisoners noted that working on the roads was better than "watching time creep by on the unit clock" or "laying around the unit." Others claimed that the $0.70 a day they made on the roads was "better than nothing." Still others complained that the return of the chain gang harkened back to slavery. "Man, this is supposed to be 1975. It's more like 1905," one man said. "What we have here is forced slavery." Some noted that prison officials removed them from the few available educational programs in order to meet the reinstated road quota, an accusation prison staff did not deny. "Hell, gettin' an education will do me a lot more good than making seventy cents a day sweating out here," one imprisoned man told reporters, "but at least it's something to do."[77] Given the choice to remain confined in a cell all day or work on the highways for a small incentive wage, many imprisoned people chose the latter. The interviews made clear that, to some, enforced idleness was a form of punishment worse than hard labor.

The 1975 legislation ultimately did not solve the prison system's woes. Prison idleness was there to stay. Although the General Assembly financed make-work programs like highway crews, the prison system could never create enough full-time jobs to keep pace with the growing prison population. By 1976, the state's prison population had risen to 13,500 men and women. North Carolina employed only 1,500 people on the roads and

7,885 in some other kind of prison job. Due to the lack of available spots, a mere 1,800 prisoners participated in some form of vocational or educational program. According to prison officials' estimates, over 20 percent of the population continued to sit idle throughout the day.[78] The problem was especially acute for medium- and maximum-security prisoners who were excluded from participating in most jobs and rehabilitation programs beyond the prison gates. In 1977, the General Assembly passed a bill allowing medium- as well as minimum-security prisoners to work on the roads, but with the incarceration rate continuing to rise, the legislation only slightly diminished the number of men and women who spent their days in idleness.[79]

The North Carolina Prisoners' Labor Union keenly felt the effects of the 1975 legislation reshaping the state's prison labor and financial regime. Not only did the power it held in prisoners' labor become less evident than it had been in the past, but with prison idleness continuing to plague the state, many imprisoned people also began to view work, especially work earning them an incentive wage and good time credits, as a privilege rather than as part of their punishment. Instead of uniting imprisoned people, as it had in the past, prison labor began to divide prisoners already struggling to overcome divisions based on race. The dearth of jobs created a new hierarchy behind bars that impeded organizing. Writing to an outside organizer in early 1977, Wayne Brooks, the union's president, reported that the organization was struggling to recruit new members because many imprisoned people worried about jeopardizing their prison jobs. "Many cons [convicts] now believe the dangers outweigh the benefits," the union president wrote, "and how do I persuade them otherwise?"[80]

. . . . .

By disentangling the prison system's budget from prison labor and by creating new incentives accompanying prison jobs, state officials in North Carolina helped undermine prisoners' organizing efforts. During the late 1960s and early 1970s, savvy prison activists recognized the power they held in their labor and sought to use it to push state officials to pay them meaningful wages and to grant them a say in prison policy. State leaders responded by working to suppress the prisoners' activism. Long reluctant to finance the prison system directly from the state's general fund and to pay imprisoned people for their work, legislators finally implemented such reforms to pacify the prison population. In a compromise satisfying both liberal reformers and the "get tough" crowd, the General Assembly revived the chain gang and expanded state agencies' access to prison labor to create jobs that, while menial, offered incarcerated people a way to fill their time, reduce their sentences, and earn a small wage. Such reforms reduced imprisoned people's ability to leverage their labor for change. To be sure, the North Carolina Prisoners' Labor Union continued to organize after 1975. Even as they lost some of the power they once held in their labor, imprisoned people retained another crucial source of leverage: their rights under the US Constitution—rights the federal courts would later curtail, dealing yet another blow to the prisoners' movement.[81] But with the passage of the 1975 bills reshaping the political economy of prison labor in North Carolina, imprisoned people's chances of winning recognition for their union and implementing their alternative, more democratic vision of justice slipped further away.

By the mid-1970s, even Bounds's plan, which never included input from imprisoned people, seemed inconceivable. The entire spectrum of prison policy had narrowed and become more punitive than it had been only a decade earlier. During the 1960s, Bounds wanted to create new jobs for imprisoned people that paid fair wages, taught prisoners meaningful new skills, and kept them tied to their families and communities. To finance such improvements, he had envisioned growing the state's work release program and, most crucially, expanding and diversifying the state's prison industries. Yet Bounds's plan became impossible to implement as the incarceration rate began to rise in the 1970s, prison industries became less profitable, and legislators embraced tough-on-crime political positions. Faced with a prison labor crisis, state leaders created new prison jobs, a solution that proved only partial at best. After 1975, North Carolina's prison population continued to grow. As of 2020, North Carolina houses over thirty-five thousand imprisoned men and women, many of whom continue to perform "make-work" tasks, often for only a few hours a week. Some, especially those in maximum-security facilities, remain idle throughout the day. Alongside the state's highways, incarcerated people still pick up trash and perform routine maintenance duties for a few cents an hour, and, in some ways, they are the lucky ones. Unable to manage imprisoned people's behavior through labor alone, North Carolina, like the rest of the nation, increasingly turned to more brutal tools of control after the 1970s: solitary confinement, long-term lockdowns, and other forms of isolation, a shift already set in motion when Jones requested additional funding for prison construction in 1974.[82]

Today, news about prison labor tends to concentrate almost exclusively on the small number of private companies that profit by employing imprisoned laborers.[83] Such stories tend to obscure the fact that prison labor remains largely unprofitable, including in prison industries, which remain heavily subsidized by the government. While forced prison labor may offset the cost of the prison system by allowing states to avoid hiring additional free workers, it does not raise money for states. On the contrary, prison systems cost taxpayers billions of dollars.[84] When we view today's prison labor system in light of the plans put forth by both Bounds and the union in the 1970s, most striking is not the continued exploitation of imprisoned workers for profit but rather how quickly Americans consented to paying the high costs of mass incarceration. As late as the 1960s, states such as North Carolina remained committed to the older idea that prisons should remain as self-supporting as possible. Yet during the mid-1970s—amid a recession—state leaders pivoted, agreeing to finance the warehousing of thousands of men and women who could have otherwise contributed to their families, society, and the nation's economy.

Focusing exclusively on private companies' exploitation of prison labor also obscures the more central ways that such companies profit from mass incarceration, most notably through selling goods and services to prisons and prisoners.[85] Ironically, much of those profits are extracted from the very people Bounds's plan was designed to help: imprisoned people's families. In North Carolina, as in most states, the incentive wages paid to prisoners have barely increased since the 1970s. Yet states charge imprisoned people high prices for necessary goods from the commissary and burden them with fines and fees stemming from both the courts and their time behind bars. It can take imprisoned workers weeks, for instance, to save up for a $10 phone card or to buy stamps to mail critical legal documents. To cover the cost of imprisonment, incarcerated people turn most often to their families, who often face their own economic struggles.[86] Even

Bounds's deeply paternalistic plan did what today's system of mass incarceration so miserably fails to do: it took into account how the imprisonment of individuals also impacts families and communities.[87]

Prisoners' reliance on their families for income makes their involvement in prison organizing all the more dangerous. Not only do imprisoned activists risk punishment, but they also threaten their families' finances. In 1975, state officials took steps to make imprisoned people think twice before challenging inhumane prison conditions and practices. They reshaped the balance of power between prisoners and the state by passing legislation that ensured prisoners—rather than the prison system—would feel the impact of protests most acutely. Yet as the recent wave of prison strikes has revealed, the legislators' plan was far from perfect. Despite the high stakes, imprisoned people continue to resist. In the fall of 2016 and 2018, thousands of incarcerated men and women in dozens of prisons across the nation, including in North Carolina, participated in work stoppages to call attention to low wages, decrepit conditions, and harsh laws.[88]

Understanding the shifting political economy of prison labor during the 1970s renders the recent strikes all the more impressive. In joining together, imprisoned people subverted work programs designed in part to divide the prison population and suppress organizing behind bars. But this history also underscores prisoners' need for a support system beyond the prison walls to amplify their demands and to put pressure on government leaders. As historian Dan Berger has rightly pointed out, it is doubtful that "withholding labor can topple a system . . . premised on repression, not production."[89] Prison work stoppages no longer clearly threaten prison systems' massive budgets. To make meaningful and lasting reform a reality, outside allies must force elected officials to rethink their sentencing practices and stop investing in the construction of prison facilities that warehouse men and women.

ACKNOWLEDGMENTS

The author thanks Dan Berger, Eladio Bobadilla, Matthew Dimick, and Nate Holdren for their helpful feedback. This chapter also benefited from comments made by participants in SUNY Buffalo's Law Review Workshop.

NOTES

1. Jim Lewis, "Inmate Road Work to End," *Raleigh News & Observer* (*N&O*), June 30, 1971.

2. For more on this thinking, see Elizabeth Kai Hinton, *From the War on Poverty to the War on Crime: The Making of Mass Incarceration in America* (Cambridge, MA: Harvard University Press, 2016); and Naomi Murakawa, *The First Civil Right: How Liberals Built Prison America* (Oxford: Oxford University Press, 2014).

3. Erik Cummings, *The Rise and Fall of California's Radical Prison Movement* (Stanford, CA: Stanford University Press, 1994); Alan Eladio Gomez, "Resisting Living Death at Marion Federal Penitentiary, 1972," *Radical History Review* 96 (Fall 2006): 58–86; Toussaint Losier, "'. . . For Strictly Religious Reasons': *Cooper v. Pate* and the Origins of the Prisoners' Rights Movement," *Souls* 15, nos. 1–2 (Summer 2013): 19–38; Dan Berger, *Captive Nation: Black Prison Organizing in the Civil Rights Era* (Chapel Hill: University of North Carolina Press, 2015); Heather Ann Thompson, *Blood in the Water: The Attica Uprising of 1971 and Its Legacy* (New York: Pantheon Books, 2016); Julilly Kohler-Hausmann, *Getting Tough: Welfare and Imprisonment in 1970s America* (Princeton, NJ: Princeton University Press, 2017); Garrett Felber, *Those Who Know Don't Say: The Nation of Islam, the Black Freedom Movement, and the Carceral State* (Chapel Hill: University of North Carolina Pres, 2019). One key exception is Robert T. Chase's *We Are Not Slaves*, which reveals how imprisoned people in Texas rebelled against the state's plantation-style model of prison labor. See Robert T. Chase, *We Are Not Slaves: State Violence Coerced Labor, and Prisoners' Rights in Postwar America* (Chapel Hill: University of North Carolina Press, 2020).

4. The historical scholarship on prison labor before World War II is rich. See David Oshinsky, *"Worse Than Slavery": Parchman Farm and the Ordeal of Jim Crow Justice* (New York: Free Press, 1996); Matthew Manchini, *One Dies, Get Another: Convict Leasing in the American South, 1866–1928* (Columbia: University of South Carolina Press, 1996); Alex Lichtenstein, *Twice the Work of Free Labor: The Political Economy of Convict Labor in the New South* (New York: Verso Press, 1996); Karin Shapiro, *A New South Rebellion: The Battle against Convict Labor in the Tennessee Coalfields, 1871–1896* (Chapel Hill: University of North Carolina Press 1998); Mary Ellen Curtin, *Black Prisoners and Their World, Alabama, 1865–1900* (Charlottesville: University of Virginia Press, 2000); Rebecca McLennan, *The Crisis of Imprisonment: Protest, Politics, and the Making of the American Penal State, 1776–1941* (Berkeley: University of California Press, 2008); Douglas Blackmon, *Slavery by Another Name* (New York: Anchor Books, 2008); Talitha LeFlouria, *Chained in Silence: Black Women and Convict Labor in the New South* (Chapel Hill: University of North Carolina Press, 2015); and Sarah Haley, *No Mercy Here: Gender, Punishment, and the Making of Jim Crow Modernity* (Chapel Hill: University of North Carolina Press, 2016).

5. See, for instance, Heather Ann Thompson, "Rethinking Working-Class Struggle through the Lens of the Carceral State: Towards a Labor History of Inmates and Guards," *Labor: Studies in Working-Class History of the Americas* 8, no. 3 (2011). Again, for a key exception, see Chase, *We Are Not Slaves*, especially 60–101.

6. Statistics regarding imprisoned people's participation in rehabilitation and job programs are difficult to find. In 2018, the North Carolina Sentencing and Policy Advisory Commission released a report examining the recidivism rate of people placed on probation or released from prison in 2015. It noted that out of the 15,077 people released from prison in 2015, approximately 9 percent of them neither held a job nor participated in a prison program while incarcerated and 13 percent of them only participated in a prison program. These numbers underestimate idleness behind bars because they fail to account for individuals with life or death sentences. They also fail to note that many prison jobs and programs are part-time, leaving imprisoned people without anything to do for much of their days. See North Carolina Sentencing and Policy Advisory Commission, "Offenders Placed on Probation or Released from Prison: Fiscal Year 2015," April 15, 2018, https://www.nccourts.gov/assets/documents/publications/recidivism_2018.pdf ?4VQBsstuyzU5dH1Ap7SJQiMe0zTKYU1G. Some scholars have suggested prisons today function more like warehouses than they do as meaningful sites of production. See Ruth Wilson Gilmore, *Golden Gulag: Prisons, Surplus, Crisis and Opposition in Globalizing California* (Berkeley: University of California Press, 2007).

7. Austin MacCormick, *Osborne Association Survey Report on North Carolina Prison System* (New York: Osborne Association, 1940); "Prison Department to Separate from Highway Commission July 1," *N&O*, December 22, 1956; C. W. Lee to Highway Engineers, "Prison Labor," August 5, 1966, Folder Revised Prisoner Labor 1966, Box 10, Prison Labor Reports and Correspondence Files, Maintenance Unit, North Carolina State Highway Commission Records (hereafter State Highway Commission Papers), Mars 64.43, North Carolina State Library and Archives, Raleigh, North Carolina.

8. V. L. Bounds to Barry Farber, WQR-TV, July 10, 1967, Folder Director of Prisons, Prison Administration, Box 1, Director's Subject Files (hereafter Director's Subject Files), Record Group 53.2, Department of Corrections Records, North Carolina State Library and Archives, Raleigh, North Carolina; V. L. Bounds, "To the Reader," 1970, Folder Commission General: Department of Corrections Division, Director's Subject Files.

9. Ann D. Witte, "Work Release in North Carolina—A Program That Works!" *Law and Contemporary Problems* 41, no. 1 (Winter 1977): 230–51.

10. As recent scholarship has shown, the concept of "rehabilitation" was always partial, repressive, and racist. Thank you to Dan Berger for encouraging me to underscore this point. See especially Gomez, "Resisting Living Death at Marion Federal Penitentiary, 1972"; Berger, *Captive Nation*; Kohler-Hausmann, *Getting Tough*; and Anne E. Parsons, *From Asylum to Prison: Deinstitutionalization and*

the Rise of Mass Incarceration after 1945 (Chapel Hill: University of North Carolina Press, 2018).

11. The clearest example of midcentury liberal thinking rooting criminality in "cultural pathologies" within communities of color can be found in Daniel Patrick Moynihan, *The Negro Family: A Case for National Action* (Washington, DC: Office of Policy Planning and Research, Department of Labor, 1965). For additional scholarship on how midcentury liberal thinkers associated Blackness, in particular, with criminality, see Hinton, *From the War on Poverty to the War on Crime*; Khalil Gibran Muhammad, *The Condemnation of Blackness: Race, Crime, and the Making of Modern Urban America* (Cambridge, MA: Harvard University Press, 2010); and Murakawa, *The First Civil Right*. As historian Jessica Wilkerson notes, experts on poor whites, especially those from Appalachia, also employed this model, albeit in racially specific ways. According to Wilkerson, "They bound a heroic history of Anglo-Saxon mountain culture, forged during the eugenic call for a pure white race in the early twentieth century, to the images of a fallen people— the shiftless hillbilly in popular culture." See Jessica Wilkerson, *To Live Here, You Have to Fight: How Women Led Appalachian Movements for Social Justice* (Champaign-Urbana: University of Illinois Press, 2018), 42–43.

12. Bounds regularly linked the work release program to efforts to keep families off welfare. See, for instance, David Cooper, "State's Work Release Program," *N&O*, July 30, 1965; Laurie Holder Jr., "Work Release Ruling Costs," *N&O*, November 2, 1966; "Prisoners Go Back to Work," *N&O*, December 2, 1966.

13. For federal efforts in the mid-1960s that encouraged states to "modernize" their criminal justice systems, see Hinton, *From the War on Poverty to the War on Crime*, and Murakawa, *The First Civil Right*.

14. "New Prison Setup Becomes Law," *N&O*, September 10, 1967; Jim Lewis, "NC Convicts to Be Paid for Labors," *N&O*, October 20, 1967; "Under the Dome," *N&O*, August 6, 1967.

15. "An Agreement between the State Highway Commission and the State Prison Department Regarding the Number of Prisoner to be Kept Available on the Public Roads and the Amount to Be Paid for This Labor for the Period of July 1, 1968 through June 30, 1969," Folder Revised Prisoner Labor 1968, Box 10, Prison Labor Reports and Correspondence Files, Maintenance Unit, State Highway Commission Papers.

16. Lee Bounds to Prison Managers, December 15, 1967, Folder Enterprises General, Box 3, Director's Subject Files.

17. Prison Commission Executive Minutes, April 4, 1968, Folder: Prison Commission Minutes, Box 11, Director's Subject Files.

18. "Prison Labor Report," March 1968, Folder: Prison Labor Correspondence, Box 15, Prison Labor Reports and Correspondence Files, Maintenance Unit, State Highway Commission Papers; Prison Commission Executive Minutes, April 4, 1968, Folder: Prison Commission Minutes, Box 11, Director's Subject Files.

19. After the strike, Lee Bounds asked all Central Prison guards to write reports concerning what happened during the protest. The North Carolina State Archives has redacted all of the prison personnel's names, but thirty-three individual accounts of the strike can be found in the following location: Folder: Riot at Central Prison, 16–17, Box 8, Director's Subject Files. Bounds used the reports to compile the state's official account of the strike. See V. L. Bounds, *Riot at Central Prison* (Raleigh: North Carolina Department of Correction, 1968). After the strike, imprisoned people filed dozens of lawsuits related to the incident, which contain their versions of the event. See, for instance, *James Robert Castellott v. Gov. Dan Moore, et al.* Folder: James Castellott, Box 6; *Jack Edward Haley v. Lee Bounds, et al.* Folder: Jack Haley Box: 15; *Jerry D. Jarrett v. Lee Bounds* Folder: Jerry Jarrett, Box: 18; Civil Action Case Files (hereafter civil action case files), Department of Corrections Records, North Carolina State Library and Archives, Raleigh, North Carolina.

20. Russell Clay, "Riot Boosts Prison Budget Needs," *N&O*, July 18, 1968.

21. V. L. Bounds to Bob Scott, May 2, 1968, Folder Correspondence, Box 6, Director's Subject Files.

22. Clay, "Riot Boosts Prison Budget Needs.".

23. Bounds to Scott, May2, 1968.

24. "Maintenance Supervisors' Replies to Questionnaire on Comparison between Free and Prison Labor on Road Work," September 1955, Box 1, Prison Labor Reports and Correspondence Files, Maintenance Unit, State Highway Commission Papers, North Carolina; "Highway Operation of Prison Not Economical," Durham *Morning Herald*, November 28, 1954.

25. During the Great Depression, states had to prioritize the employment of free labor to receive funds from the Emergency Relief Act and, later, the Works Progress Administration, thus pushing nearly all imprisoned people off the roads until the economy rebounded in the early 1940s. See McLennan, *The Crisis of Imprisonment*, 462.

26. Frank Mills to V. Lee Bounds, May 24, 1968, Box 6, Prison Labor Reports and Correspondence Files, Maintenance Unit, North Carolina State Highway Commission Records.

27. For a detailed discussion of the Nixon administration's approach to corrections funding, see Interagency Council of Corrections, "Statement of Goals" and "Minutes," Folder Interagency Council of Corrections, November 70–August 71, Box 44, Charles Clapp Papers, Richard Nixon Presidential Library and Museum, Yorba Linda, California. See also Hinton, *From the War on Poverty to the War on Crime*, 163–67.

28. North Carolina Penal System Study Committee of the North Carolina Bar Association, "Interim Report," March 15, 1971 (Raleigh, North Carolina), 8. https://archive.org/details/northcarolinapen00nort/page/8.

29. Charles Clapp to John Erlichman, "Corrections," September 16, 1971. Folder National Conference, Box 15, Speech Files of Velde, 69–71, Law Enforcement Assistant Administration, National Archives and Records Administration, College Park, Maryland.

30. Paul J. Dupree to Division Engineers, "Inmate Labor," August 31, 1971, Prison Correspondence 70–71, Box 13, Prison Labor Reports and Correspondence Files, Maintenance Unit, State Highway Commission Papers.

31. Berger, *Captive Nation,* 185–88; C. Ronald Huff, "Unionization behind the Walls: An Analytic Study of the Ohio Prisoners' Labor Union Movement" (PhD diss., Ohio State University, 1974).

32. North Carolina Prisoners Labor Union, N.D. Folder B-General-1973, Box 4, Director's Subject Files.

33. For a discussion of public sector union's power during the early to mid-1970s, see Joseph McCartin, "'A Wagner Act for Public Employees': Labor's Deferred Dream and the Rise of Conservatism, 1970–1976," *Journal of American History* 95, no. 1 (June 2008): 123–48.

34. "Goals of the North Carolina Prisoners' Labor Union," September 27, 1974, Folder NC Prisoners' Union 74–77, Box 1, T. J. Reddy Papers, University of North Carolina–Charlotte Special Collections, Charlotte, North Carolina.

35. See Folder 11, Box 2407, AFL-CIO of North Carolina Papers, Georgia State; Jack Schism, "Bounds Will Not Recognize Any Union Activity in Prison," *N&O,* March 17, 1973.

36. Ron Aldridge, "Ex-Salesman Makes Prison System Hop," *N&O,* January 22, 1973; Daniel C. Hoover, "Prison System Is Reorganized," *N&O,* August 15, 1973.

37. Jerry Allegood, "Tar Heel Prison Badly Overcrowded," *N&O,* December 17, 1973.

38. David Jones to Honorable Thomas J. White, Chairman of the Advisory Budget Committee, March 10, 1973, Folder Advisory Budget Committee, Box 19, Director's Subject Files.

39. Frank T. Flynn, "The Federal Government and the Prison-Labor Problem in the States I. The Aftermath of Federal Restrictions," *Social Service Review* 24, no. 1 (March 1950): 19–40; McLennan, *The Crisis of Imprisonment,* 193–238, 417–67; and Matthew Pehl, "Between the Market and the State: The Problem of Prison Labor in the New Deal," *Labor* 16, no. 2 (May 2019): 77–97.

40. David Jones to V. Lee Bounds, January 17, 1973, Folder Enterprises General, Box 3, Director's Subject Files.

41. Paul J. Dupree to David Jones, "Inmate Labor," February 6, 1973, Prison Correspondence 72–73, Box 14, Prison Labor Reports and Correspondence Files, Maintenance Unit, State Highway Commission Papers.

42. V. L. Bounds to G. A. Jones, State Budget Office, "Prison Enterprises Fund," December 6, 1972, Folder Enterprises General, Box 3, Director's Subject Files.

43. Linda Williams, "Prison Crowding Role Rejected: Boxley Defends Tougher Parole Policy," *N&O*, June 29, 1974; Associated Press, "Parole Panel Record Defended," *N&O*, July 13, 1974.

44. Commission on Sentencing, Criminal Punishment, and Rehabilitation, January 10, 1975, "Work Release Proposal," Folder Proposed Legislation, Box 23, Director's Subject Files.

45. Chuck Eppinette, outside organizer for North Carolina Prisoners Union, interview with author, September 25, 2014, Durham, North Carolina, interview in author's possession.

46. Ralph Edwards to David Jones, "union activity," Folder General-E-1973, Box 5, Director's Subject Files.

47. Jamie Bissonette, Ralph Hamm, Robert Dellelo, and Edward Rodman, *When the Prisoners Ran Walpole: A True Story in the Movement for Prison Abolition* (Cambridge, MA: South End Press, 2008), 85–122.

48. David Jones to Ralph Edwards, "union activity," Folder General-E-1973, Box 5, Director's Subject Files.

49. Connor Jones, "Money Held Key to Lock Up State Prison Problems, *N&O*, June 24, 1974.

50. F. L. Sanders to Major Fred Briggs, "Attached Classification Referral," June 19, 1973, Folder Johnson, Box 19, Civil Action Case Files.

51. "N.C. Prisons Overcrowded, Understaffed: Money Called Corrections 'Cure,'" *Greensboro Daily News*, February 23, 1975.

52. Jones, "Money Held Key."

53. David Jones to Paul DuPre, "Inmate Labor," February 5, 1974, No Folder, Box 17, Prison Labor Reports and Correspondence Files, Maintenance Unit, State Highway Commission Papers.

54. Summary of Response Made by Division Engineers, Folder Inmate Labor & Correspondence 1975, Box 17: Maintenance Unit: Prison Labor Reports and Correspondence File, 1971–1975, Maintenance Unit: Prison Labor Reports and Correspondence File, State Highway Commission Papers.

55. C. G. Martin to Mr. James Wilson, "Present Status of Industrial Projects," December 5, 1974, Folder Enterprises 2, Box 10, Director's Subject Files.

56. "A Discussion of and Recommendations Concerning the Financial Prospects of Federal Prison Industries for the Period March 1974 to June 1975," Folder 71/18 Justice Prison Industries, Box 71, Collection No. RG1-038, George Meany Archives, University of Maryland Special Collections, College Park, Maryland.

57. NCPLU to Rep. Aaron Plyler, March 21, 1974, Folder 15 NC Prisoners Union 74–77, Box 1, T.J. Reddy Papers, University of North Carolina–Charlotte.

58. Inmate Grievance Commission, Order, January 17, 1975; David Jones, "In the matter of: Donald W. Morgan, Frank Strader, John Lunsford, Vernon Rich," Disposition, Folder: Morgan, Strader, Rich, Box 25, Civil Action Case Files.

59. Larry Yackle, *Reform and Regret: The Story of Federal Judicial Involvement in the Alabama Prison System* (New York: Oxford University Press, 1989), 53–63.

60. Commission on Sentencing, Criminal Punishment, and Rehabilitation, Interim Report, February 1, 1975, p. 1 https://archive.org/stream/2013090601/2013090601_djvu.txt.

61. Commission on Sentencing, Criminal Punishment and Rehabilitation, Folder Knox Commission, Statement of Concern, Folder Knox Commission, Box 4, North Carolina Council of Churches Papers, Rubenstein Library Duke University, Durham, North Carolina.

62. Commission on Sentencing, Criminal Punishment, and Rehabilitation, Interim Report, p. 8.

63. Robert Martinson, "What Works? Questions and Answers about Prison Reform," *The Public Interest* 35 (Spring 1974): 22–54.

64. Commission on Sentencing, Criminal Punishment and Rehabilitation, Folder Knox Commission, Meeting Minutes, March 7, 1975, Box 4, North Carolina Council of Churches Papers (hereafter NCCC Papers), Rubenstein Library Duke University, Durham, North Carolina.

65. "An Act to Make Prisoners Available for Work on the Public Roads," July 9, 1975, https://www4.ncleg.net/enactedlegislation/sessionlaws/html/1975-1976/sl1975-506.html; "An Act to Encourage Useful Work by Prison Inmates Using the Present Power of the Secretary of Correction to Enter into Contracts Involving Inmate Labor," July 19, 1975: https://www4.ncleg.net/enactedlegislation/sessionlaws/html/1975-1976/sl1975-682.html.

66. See "Incentive Wage Program," n.d., Folder Grievance Commission, Box 19, Director's Subject Files.

67. Statement by Kathy Sebo, Testimony on Prison Labor, June 18, 1975, Folder Grievance Commission, Box 19, Director's Subject Files.

68. See "Incentive Wage Program."

69. State officials fought for nearly a year about whether to finance the wages of prisoners who labored as maintenance workers through the profits of North Carolina Prison Enterprises, the DoT's highway maintenance fund, or a direct allocation of taxpayer dollars to the DoC. Eventually, the General Assembly decided to allocate additional funds to the DoT, which it then paid the DoC for prisoners' wages. The General Assembly's decision underscores the degree to which legislators remained reluctant to finance prison programs directly through the general fund. See Folder: Morgan, Strader, Rich, Box 25, Civil Action Case Files. Documents regarding the debates concerning the payment of incentive wages appear here because prisoners challenged the non-payment of their wages in court. Their case was later dismissed.

70. Morgan, Strader, Rich, Box 25, Civil Action Case Files; D. W. Patrick to Division Engineers, "Use of Inmate Labor," September 22, 1975, Folder Inmate

Labor 1975, Box 17, Prison Labor Reports and Correspondence Files, Maintenance Unit, State Highway Commission Papers.

71. Lamar Gudger to David Jones, "Inmate Labor Bills," May 21, 1975, Folder Highway Labor, Box 3, Director's Subject Files.

72. North Carolina Advisory Committee to the United States Commission on Civil Rights, "Prisons in North Carolina," August 1974, Folder Attorney General's Office, Box 1, Legal Correspondence, Department of Corrections Records, North Carolina State Library and Archives.

73. For legislators thinking on "good time" as a managerial tool, see the testimony of State Senator Kathy Sebo before the North Carolina Inmate Grievance Commission, April 12, 1975, Folder Grievance Commission, Box 19, Director's Subject Files.

74. Commission on Sentencing, Criminal Punishment and Rehabilitation, Folder Knox Commission, Meeting Minutes, June 12, 1975, Box 4, NCCC Papers, Rubenstein Library Duke University, Durham, North Carolina.

75. Work Release Senate Bill, Folder Work Release Senate Bill, Box 5, Director's Subject Files.

76. Commission on Sentencing, Criminal Punishment and Rehabilitation, Folder Knox Commission, Meeting Minutes, August 7, 1975, Box 4, NCCC Papers. In putting imprisoned people to work in the Governor's Mansion during the 1970s, state leaders were reinstating an older practice. Imprisoned people also worked in the Governor's Mansion during the 1950s. See "Gold Explains Prison System's New Policies," N&O, October 5, 1950.

77. Bill Noblitt, "Neater Highways Seen with Return of Prisoners to Roads Next Month," N&O, June 23, 1975; David Zucchino, "Jury Still Out on Road Gang," N&O, September 14, 1975.

78. "Inmate Work," Commission on Sentencing, Criminal Punishment, and Rehabilitation, Final Report, January 1977, Folder Corrections Recommendations, Box 57, General Correspondence 1977, Hunt Papers.

79. In 1977, the General Assembly provided the Transportation Department with $500,000 to fund the expenses of using medium-security prisoners on the roads. An Act to Make Appropriations for Current Operations of State Departments, Institutions, and Agencies, and for Other Purposes, July 1, 1977. https://www4.ncleg.net /enactedlegislation/sessionlaws/html/1977-1978/sl1977-802.html.

80. Wayne Brooks to Alan McGregor, February 5, 1977, Box "Archives," North Carolina Justice Policy Archives (Private Collection), North Carolina Justice Policy Center, Durham, North Carolina.

81. In 1977, the US Supreme Court ruled in *Jones v. North Carolina Prisoners Labor Union* that prison administrators could ban prison organizing without violating prisoners' First Amendment rights. The North Carolina Prisoners' Labor Union collapsed soon after the ruling. Jones et al. v. North Carolina Prisoners Labor Union, 433 US 119 (1977).

82. For states' adoption of solitary confinement and other isolation tactics in response to prison activism, see in particular Gomez, "Resisting Living Death at Marion Federal Penitentiary, 1972"; and Keramet Reiter, *23/7: Pelican Bay Prison and the Rise of Long-Term Solitary Confinement* (New Haven, CT: Yale University Press, 2016).

83. Such jobs are often highly sought after by imprisoned people because they are some of the highest-paid behind bars. By law, prisoners employed by private companies must make "prevailing wages" for their particular industries. As with the work release program, the state can then deduct the cost of room and board, victim restitution, and child support from prisoners' pay. State and federal leaders justified the introduction of private industries jobs into the prisons by pointing to the continued problem of prison idleness. Many imprisoned people, including former prisoner union members, welcomed the policy shift in North Carolina. The introduction of private industries, then, was both a tool of control and a source of relief for imprisoned people. See, for instance, NCPLU to Rep. Aaron Plyler, March 21, 1974, Folder 15 NC Prisoners Union 74–77, Box 1, T. J. Reddy Papers, University of North Carolina–Charlotte. In their letter, the North Carolina Prisoners' Labor Union asked for private industry to set up shop behind bars in addition to requesting fair wages and the recognition of their union.

84. The Prison Policy Initiative, for instance, estimates public corrections institutions cost taxpayers over $80 billion a year. Peter Wagner and Bernadette Rabuy, "Following the Money of Mass Incarceration," *Prison Policy Initiative*, January 25, 2017. https://www.prisonpolicy.org/reports/money.html.

85. Wagner and Rabuy, "Following the Money."

86. Stephen Raher, "The Company Store: A Deeper Look at Prison Commissaries," May 2018, *The Prison Policy Initiative*, https://www.prisonpolicy.org/reports/commissary.html; Lauren-Brooke Eisen, "Paying for Your Time: How Charging Inmates Fees Behind Bars May Violate the Excessive Fines Clause," July 31, 2014, *Brennan Center for Justice*, https://www.brennancenter.org/analysis/paying-your-time-how-charging-inmates-fees-behind-bars-may-violate-excessive-fines-clause.

87. Thank you to Martha McCluskey for this point.

88. German Lopez, "We're in the Midst of the Biggest Prison Strike in US history," Vox, October 11, 2016; Mitch Smith, "Prison Strike Aim to Improve Conditions and Pay," August 28, 2018.

89. Dan Berger, "Rattling the Cages," *Jacobin*, November 11, 2016, https://www.jacobinmag.com/2016/11/prison-strike-slavery-attica-racism-incarceration/.

3 The Political Economy of Work in ICE Custody

THEORIZING MASS INCARCERATION AND FOR-PROFIT PRISONS

Jacqueline Stevens

This chapter explains how the work of people held by private prison firms under immigration laws is crucial to the profitability of these enterprises.[1] Using a case study of legal challenges to for-profit prisons' use of detainee labor, the chapter shows how analyses foregrounding practices of kleptocracy—that is, unlawful conduct by private prisons—may succeed in thwarting mass incarceration. To evaluate the advantages of this approach in comparison with other theories of mass incarceration, the chapter addresses the following three questions. First, what sort of work is performed by those in custody under immigration laws, and what is its role in the profitability of private prison firms contracting with federal immigration enforcement agencies since the 1980s? Second, what are the legal differences between the work performed by those held in Immigration and Customs Enforcement (ICE) facilities and that ordered or elicited by those convicted of a crime and held in county, state, or federal prisons? Third, under tests that use "process tracing" (Bennett 2010), do inferences from localized observations of economic exploitation, procurement practices, and prison financing fare better as explanations of mass incarceration than theories emphasizing behaviors, attitudes, and discourses?

This chapter proposes that scholarship debating value-laden theories of the carceral state may improve our understanding of narratives influencing and influenced by political subjectivities and yet contribute little to causal explanations of mass incarceration.[2] A careful review of evidence has falsified key causal claims, a point made previously by James Forman (2012) and Marie Gottschalk (2016) in their critiques of accounts of mass incarceration that emphasize racism or neoliberalism, as discussed below. Although one might simply rely on idiomatic conventions of inference and logic to eliminate popular explanations, along the lines pursued both by Forman and Gottschalk, political scientists have developed a more formal approach. "Process tracing" is a qualitative method that assists scholars in rejecting theories falsified by data and selecting those with strong proximate evidence of validity (Bennett 2010). It is one of the few social science methods consistent with the definition of "science" or knowledge making (*Wissenschaft*) propounded by Karl Popper ([1934] 1959), discussed below. Scholars have quite a bit of relevant evidence of conditions that might drive mass incarceration. This chapter will advance a theory that the term *kleptocracy* best describes the causes of ICE's use of mass incarceration, if not the prison industry more generally.[3]

Discussions of harms wrought through some combination of the Protestant work ethic (PWE) discourse, neoliberalism, and racism by scholars theorizing prison work are helpful for organizing our knowledge of the subjectivities associated with the commitment of resources to locking people up and stigmatizing those who are now or have in the past been in criminal custody. But when it comes to explaining the operational details of the enactment and persistence of the carceral state for purposes of its disestablishment, the three dominant theories of mass incarceration, including prison work, may be less useful. The PWE explanation of US penal policy goes back to early modern England and suggests that those in power thought that disordered populations when locked up could benefit from work (McLennan 2008, 18–27). Erin Hatton has documented the pervasiveness of this discourse among not only ideologues but also those actually incarcerated (2018). Corporate welfare and corruption are both incompatible with this discourse, yet they are hallmarks of how Congress appropriates funding of for-profit prisons and many other programs at the state and federal level, discussed below. If the PWE were truly influential on federal policy, then this would not be the case. Moreover, immigrants have a different profile in public discourse than native-born people of color: "Immigrants, unauthorized or not (in contrast to 'convicts' and 'welfare queens') are generally seen as prototypically diligent. But the high marks assigned immigrants in the neoliberal scale of work ethic and personal discipline have produced only weak protection in recent years against the heavy hand of state and public retribution" (Katzenstein 2012, 990). According to Bennett's four-square taxonomy, the PWE ideology passes the "Straw in the Wind" test but fails the "Hoop Test" (Bennett 2010, 201). In other words, the PWE is a plausible explanation, but it is missing from key contexts in which its proponents suggest it should appear—that is, the halls of popular assemblies on whose appropriations for-profit prisons depend and the discourse on the demographic targeted for mass incarceration.

Some scholars define "neoliberal" policies—the second paradigm for reflecting on the carceral state considered here—as encompassing an insistence on the individualist work ethic. But the two are more usefully disaggregated so as to distinguish a bona fide belief in the virtues of individual effort versus a blind faith in the benefits of the unfettered market. The truly neoliberal framework attributes the explosion of people in custody under criminal laws in the United States since the 1970s to US-based firms moving production outside of the United States, along with hiring non-US citizens for domestic production, a dynamic that has nothing to do with individual subjectivity or effort (e.g., Brown 2005, 2010, 2015; Wacquant 2001, 2009). In her analysis of prison labor Susan Kang insightfully attends to the multifaceted and contradictory views on prison labor, in particular US policy that promotes close monitoring of prison exploitation in China while turning a blind eye domestically (2000, 140). Drawing on work by Loïc Wacquant and others who attribute to neoliberal globalization a causal role in mass incarceration, she writes: "Since the dominant neoliberal political ideology has affirmed the importance of market solutions and marginalized the social provisions of 'big government,' citizens do not demand social guarantees and solidarity from the state. Instead, individual citizens' feelings of economic insecurity have translated into punitive attitudes toward vulnerable segments of the population" (Kang 2009, 140). According to this widely held contemporary analysis (Kang 2010, notes 16–18), the unrelenting market society produces precarity and a sensitivity to exposures of disorder that we treat by building prisons. However, the neoliberal account is falsified if markets are distorted by corruption, as is the case with for-profit prison contracts.

Finally, a third paradigm employed by scholars from W. E. B. Du Bois (1910) to Michelle Alexander (2012) ties US penal practices to the legacy of racialized slavery. Du Bois quotes political scientist John Burgess, "(whom no one accuses of being negrophile) . . . : 'Almost every act, word or gesture of the Negro, not consonant with good taste and good manners as well as good morals, was made a crime or misdemeanor, for which he could first be fined by the magistrates and then be consigned to a condition of almost slavery for an indefinite time, if he could not pay the bill'" (Burgess quoted in Du Bois 1910, 784). Untethered to any specific causal theories except for the metanarrative of racism, Alexander discusses in her section titled "Origins" in *The New Jim Crow* the findings of historians William Cohen and Douglas Blackmon, in particular that vagrancy laws that effected a "system of forced labor," such as those discussed by Du Bois.[4] Alexander devotes her attention to associations between policies that incarcerate a vastly disproportionate number of African American men with racist attitudes and practices mobilized by White US-Americans, as does Wacquant (2001, 2009). And yet when Alexander looks for the proximate mechanism behind mass incarceration, she focuses not on long-standing fears and hate, but the pressures to criminalize behaviors by the private prison industry: "Prison profiteers must be reckoned with if mass incarceration is to be undone" (232). In light of Forman's (2012) and Gottschalk's (2016) falsifications of the racism explanation of criminal mass incarceration—Forman points out the ground-level push for increased sentencing by Black communities and African American political attitudes consistent with this (2012)—a process-tracing study of the causes of mass incarceration should attend to the prison profiteers Alexander highlights.

In sum, using Bennett's typology of four tests of causation (2010, 210) it appears that all three dominant causal explanations of mass incarceration fail the Hoop Test—they are falsified by strong evidence inconsistent with the theories and thus don't make it through "the hoop" necessary for further consideration of probative evidence in their support. Immigrants are in ICE custody because they *want* to work and will work harder and for less compensation than US citizens, even those who arrive with skills and education (Abramitzky and Boustan 2017, 22–23). The racism or xenophobia account also fails the Hoop Test because large portions of communities affected by these policies themselves support them, as discussed below. The balance of this chapter explores the political economy or kleptocracy behind for-profit prisons' exploitation of the labor of those in their custody and lays out an alternative explanation of the mechanisms behind mass incarceration and the tools for their "reckoning," as Alexander puts it.

WORK PROGRAMS FOR THOSE HELD UNDER IMMIGRATION LAWS

This section describes the current practices, protocols, and laws that organize work for those in custody under immigration laws and highlights differences from the laws authorizing this for those convicted of a crime.

Working for CoreCivic, GEO, and County Jails

"Volunteer Work Program," the way I describe it, is basically doing the same as working in the outside world. But with a chip labor with no benefits. For e.g., I am assign as "Dorm Porter," meaning that I do the sweeping and mopping the floors of the dorm we [detainees] are house in or assign to. I clean and scrub the toilets, urinals, showers and sinks, clean tables, windows, and have trash ready for pick-up by "Hall Porters." I perform other tasks, if necessary at the direction of a CCA staff member, such as working both shift, day and nights, although I am assigned to work at nights, only 8 hrs I'm assign to work. . . . During the past 3 month I have been assign to work night shift, stating from 6:00 pm to Breakfast, which is about 4:00 am or at times about 5:00 am. Out of those hrs. I approx work 4 hrs. because I refuse to work the whole 8 hrs. 3 There's many different jobs and hours, but some of them are the same job title, some are call "Hall Porters," "Recreation Porters," "Dorm Porters," "Kitchen Workers" ect. . . . The function of Recreation work is cleaning up the rack room, gather the all balls left out-side, bring-in the water jar (5 gallons), sweep and mop the restroom and other duties directed by the staff. There's also kitchen workers where you prepare food trades for the male detainees, wash dishes, although a machine washes the dishes . . . just as working in a restaurant. You clean-up the kitchen area, by sweeping and moping the floor and other work requested by the staff.

Basically the kitchen work is as working out-side. Hours, I have an under-standing they work from 8:00 am to 2:00 pm, from 2 pm to 7:00 pm and from 3:00 am to 7:00 am. Now there's also "Hall Porters," they work the hall ways, do painting at times, sweep and mop the hall way floors, buffing and waxing, help out with the commissary cards by pushing them to the dorms to be deliver accompanied with staff and any other job as directed by the staff, clean offices, take care of the trash, bring-in cleaning supply, etc. . . . Basically they perform more of the work than any other job mention above. . . . All jobs are paid one dollar/day except Kitchen workers, I believe they get paid differently from the rest of the job. There is also laundry workers, they work in the laundry but are call "Hall Porters," they work 8 hrs and perform the watching of detainee's cloth, (uniforms), sheets, blankets etc. . . . They perform other duties at the direction of staff, e.g., if staff needs the detain to some type of cleaning and that detainee is close by, the staff will ask him to do that cleaning. (Robinson Martinez, on the work he performed for the Correction Corporation of America [now CoreCivic] in 2012 [Stevens 2016, 395]).

In 2019, about fifty-two thousand people each day across the United States were in the custody of Immigration and Customs Enforcement (ICE), up from twenty-seven thousand in Obama's last year in office and a few dozen in the 1970s (Aleaziz 2019).[5] That's about four hundred forty thousand people each year in detention under immigration laws (Greenwold 2016; US ICE 2018).[6] The immigration courts lack the capacity to hear so many new cases. As a result, the average amount of time people spend in ICE custody also is on the rise (Alvarez 2017). The facilities are holding people to insure they are present for their immigration hearings or for government-paid transportation to their countries of origin. ICE custody is legally entirely distinct from punishment.[7] And no one is in ICE custody to serve time for a criminal violation.[8]

Contracts, interviews, reimbursement accounts, e-mail, grievances, and numerous other documents obtained from ICE since 2010 through litigation under the Freedom of Information Act suggest that if Mr. Martinez found himself in a different for-profit prison a few years earlier or later, his narrative would be quite similar.[9] Overall, most of the work in these facilities is undertaken by people who have no one on the outside to fund commissary accounts on which people rely for basic foodstuff, clothes, and hygiene products. Mr. Martinez and others are therefore forced to work for a single employer offering wages of $1 to $5 per day. Furthermore, ad hoc reports, including for one of the facilities now being sued for violating laws against forced labor and unjust enrichment, reveal CoreCivic committing wage theft of the small amounts owed its detained workers.[10]

ICE detention facilities operate without regulations. The Bureau of Prisons (BOP), housed in the Department of Justice (DOJ), has no jurisdiction over ICE.[11] In 1979, in response to a *New York Times* report on conditions in the Port Isabel Service Processing Center, Congress held hearings that resulted in a directive that the Immigration and Naturalization Service (INS) produce policies for managing detention facilities. Over twenty years later, INS implemented this advisal with its first "National Detention Standards," followed by the 2008 Performance Based National Detention Standards (PBNDS) and the 2011 PBNDS.[12] These Standards lack the legal authority of regulations. The PBNDS stipulate the obligations of private and government organizations, typically county sheriffs, that contract with ICE, including Section 5.8, the so-called Volunteer Work Program (VWP).[13] The VWP authorizes people to "volunteer" at a rate to be determined by the facility, but "at least one dollar per day," for shifts of up to eight hours a day, five days a week, for the stated purpose of first, to "enhance . . . essential operations," and second, to reduce through "decreased idleness, improved morale and fewer disciplinary incidents" the "negative impact of confinement."[14]

A 2014 lawsuit filed in a Denver federal court against GEO Corp. by workers held in Aurora, Colorado, tracks Mr. Martinez's observation that some of the labor required was outside the formal work program. Plaintiffs in *Menocal et al. v. GEO Corp.* accused GEO of requiring a rotating crew to perform janitorial work each week dedicated to deep cleaning common spaces, including bathroom facilities.[15] In the privately owned or managed facilities ICE refers to as Contract Dedicated Facilities (CDFs), people in custody, such as Mr. Martinez, provide the labor for all of the facility's operations except guard duties. In contrast, county jails with ICE contracts have their criminal inmates doing the vast bulk of the kitchen work, laundry, and maintenance (Urbina 2014; Stevens 2016, 414–27; Stevens 2019). Among the legal problems of the VWP is that its definition of a "volunteer" contradicts that of the regulation on volunteers Fair Labor Standards Act (FLSA).[16]

In the CoreCivic CDF in Stewart County, Georgia, men may wake up in a large room with rows of metal bunk beds inches apart, as well as the showers, toilets, and tables for their meals. They call this housing section "the chicken coop."[17] The prison conditions are part of the mise-en-scène that normalizes unlawful work and employment conditions by encouraging those in and outside the walls to think of those housed as inmates, not administrative detainees awaiting immigration or deportation processing. In the county jail in Butler County, Ohio, those in ICE custody will wait for their morning meals in stacked, locked rooms until their shift is released to the central area of the pod of ninety-six men or women, where they may eat from trays a cold piece of white bread and a cold, hard-boiled egg. If they want tea or coffee they must pay for teabags or packages of instant coffee, or they may be paid twenty packages per week if they work five days per week, as is the case for those in the rest of the county jail (Stevens 2019).

The processed meat CoreCivic uses in its meals might be moldy, rancid, or otherwise inedible, according to a report by the Office of Inspector General (OIG).[18] The OIG stated: "Multiple detainees at the Hudson County Jail and Stewart Detention Center also complained that some of the basic hygienic supplies, such as toilet paper, shampoo, soap, lotion, and toothpaste, were not provided promptly or at all when detainees ran out of them. According to one detainee, when they used up their initial supply of certain personal care items, such as toothpaste, they were advised to purchase more at the facility commissary, contrary to the PBNDS, which specify that personal hygiene items should be replenished as needed" (US ICE OIG 2017, 10). When meals are inedible or insufficient, then people are forced to purchase food through the commissary maintained by the same firm serving the meals. The commissary sells instant soups, canned chili, or candy bars, as well as hygiene products. A can of chili is $2.25. One must also pay for soap (1 bar, Ivory, $1.10), toothpaste (Colgate 4 oz. $2.20), and any other hygiene product.[19] Yet contracts require hygiene products to be provided at no cost in addition to edible food.[20] The need to pay for such items incentivizes the work performed (Stevens 2016, 396n7, 402–3). A complaint from GEO's Tacoma facility indicated GEO was increasing its commissary prices and speculated this was to recruit people to perform kitchen work required by GEO's contract.[21]

How Administrative Detention Became (Unlawful) Punishment

This section first explains the effective similarity of the custody for people being held under immigration laws with that of convicted criminals. Second, it compares how these current conditions are quite different from those for people held under immigration laws before the 1980s. And finally, it describes how the takeover of immigration custody by for-profit prison firms changed the conditions from those akin to residential dormitories or motels to those of prisons, absent any legal basis for these changes and indeed contracts specifically requiring otherwise. Among the conditions lawful only for those held as a condition of punishment but no one else are the work programs described above. The following section will describe how attorneys in recent years have been filing lawsuits challenging this.

Similar to prisons, the paid staff in ICE facilities are guards or sheriffs. The officials call the facilities "correctional" and refer to those in immigration custody as "inmates" or "prisoners" (Stevens 2019). The warden of the Butler County Jail said that his contract with ICE does not obligate him to treat anyone in civil custody differently from those in the section of the jail reserved for accused or convicted criminals:

> Sheriff Jones had referred to "immigration prisoners" and Chief Wyden said any emphasis on the distinction between ICE and criminal detainees was "an invalid point." He stated that the IGSA [Intergovernmental Service Agreement] with ICE stated that as long as the porters held for ICE are "compensated like anybody else," i.e., the porters convicted of crimes, then the jail had no legal worries. I asked if he could read the portion of the text that stated this. He stated he had seen a picture of this section of the contract but could not read it to me. He reiterated that the "IGSA says we should compensate for whatever you do the same as you do for anyone else in the facility." (Stevens 2019)

These places may sound like a prison, look like a prison, operate based on the same American Correctional Association Handbook (2004) used for a prison, and even be built and owned by for-profit prison firms.[22] But according to statute and Constitutional case law they are not prisons, and those inside are not prisoners (e.g., Stevens 2016; Sinha 2015).

The contract for Butler County emphasizes the difference, along similar lines in all ICE detention contracts: "All persons in the custody of

BICE will be referred to as an 'Administrative Detainee.' This term recognizes that BICE detainees are not charged with criminal violations and are only held in custody to assure their presence throughout the administrative hearing process."[23] Those found guilty of a crime may be punished only insofar as the government adheres to procedures in the Sixth Amendment. Those who are not charged much less convicted of any crimes may not be subject to treatment akin to punishment that is otherwise unlawful.

This means that despite the physical resemblance and often co-location of prisons and ICE facilities, the enslavement and forced labor that are legal for inmates are prohibited for people in administrative custody. The Thirteenth Amendment implements a corollary of the Sixth Amendment: "Neither slavery nor involuntary servitude, except as a punishment for crime whereof the party shall have been duly convicted, shall exist within the United States, or any place subject to their jurisdiction."[24] Case law for the Sixth and Thirteenth Amendments, discussed below, interprets "hard labor" as "punishment" and, along with emerging interpretations of the Trafficking Victim Protection Act (TVPA) protects those in custody under immigration laws from the forced labor required of prisoners. As a result of the jurisprudence elucidating this distinction between criminal and administrative custody, government policy in the first part of the twentieth century was to bestow on those in custody under immigration laws the hospitality befitting guests, and not the suspicion of unwanted trespassers, much less criminals. A 1915 report to Congress states:

> For a satisfactory administration of the immigration laws, the character and condition of immigrant stations at ports of entry are of prime importance. So far, therefore, the Department of Labor is permitted by law and equipped for the purpose, it aims to make these stations as much like temporary homes as possible. While regulation and exclusion and therefore detention, are necessary in respect of immigration laws, it should be understood by all who participate in administering these laws that they are not intended to be penalizing. It is with no unfriendliness to aliens that immigrants are detained and some of them excluded, but solely for the protection of our own people and our institutions.
>
> Indifference, then, to the physical or mental comfort of these wards of ours from other lands should not be tolerated. Accordingly, every reasonable effort is made by the department, within the limits of the appropriations, to

minimize all the necessary hardships of detention and to abolish all that are not necessary. (US Secretary of Labor 1915, 69–70)

A hundred years later, US ports of entry are convenient to ICE holding cells and rented jail space, and it was the policy of President Barack Obama, a Democrat, to mandate harsh detention and the separation of families in order to deter asylum seekers (Dominguez, Lee, and Leisero 2016).

The 1952 law on the conditions of detention are the ones in place today, but the operationalization of work in these facilities is entirely different from current work programs. Before the takeover of immigrant detention by the for-profit prison industry, the US government paid service workers prevailing wages or fees for labor devoted to the care of those detained under immigration laws—including maintenance, food preparation, cleaning, and laundry. A *New York Times* magazine article in 1950 chronicled the delays of days or weeks for those attempting to enter the United States. The headline was: "New Role for Ellis Island: The One-Time Gateway of Hope Has Become a Hotel of Detention" (Raskin 1950).

The "Voluntary Work Program" (VWP) in ICE's PBNDS has its roots in a bill passed in 1950 at the urging of the Department of Justice to respond to World War II prisoner-of-war reforms pursuant to the Geneva Convention (Stevens 2016, 463). Few people in this time frame were in custody under immigration laws. Although immigrants had been held on Angel Island and Ellis Island since the late nineteenth century, their custody was never considered akin to criminals or criminality. The word *detainee* was not used by the federal government until 1941 and was not popularized for arriving immigrants or those in removal proceedings until decades later.[25] In 1950, the *New York Times* magazine described people held in Ellis Island as "newcomers," "travellers," "wayfarers," "persons under detention," or simply "immigrants," but never "detainees" (Raskin 1950), a word that has connotations of criminal inmates or prisoners.

A. H. Raskin's reporting suggested at worst tedium and even malaise, but not the mistreatment and humiliation rampant in the facilities today. Raskin noted that children were receiving milk and cookies and living in dorm-like quarters with their parents. Government employees, not the immigrants, maintained the facility, including cleaning personal quarters. "The authorities do not require any of the immigrants or deportees to make their beds or clean their rooms. Some do. Most don't. When they don't, regular civil service cleaners do the job" (Raskin 1950, 75). Immigrants choosing to work in the kitchen received 10 cents per hour (75).[26] The reporter distinguished the conditions on Ellis Island not only from US adversaries, but also from the conditions reported for US facilities today: "Unarmed guards, freedom of communication, second helpings at mealtime, a school for the children, an excellent hospital for the sick, a constant effort on the part of the officials to make themselves approachable, if not always informative—all these are signs we are not aping Hitler's concentration camp methods. Or Stalin's labor camps, either. No one has to work at Ellis Island" (Raskin 1950, 78). Between 1954 and 1981 there was virtually no detention of those in the interior (Wilsher 2011). The VWP that today makes possible vast profits for the private prison industry (Linthicum 2015) did not emerge until 1983, with the opening of the first INS prison in Port Isabel, Texas, run by the newly formed Correction Corporation of America.[27] The protocols initiated by the prisons entirely changed the circumstances of immigration detention to resemble those of prisons, although Congress authorized no such changes.[28] Arriving immigrants were held for days, weeks, and even years in regular travel lodging adjacent the ports of entry, including land border crossings and airports (Lehman 1992).[29]

The shift from housing families in dorms to ad hoc motels to prisons occurred because the private prison industry opportunistically responded to a sui generis event that occurred outside the control of capitalists or the US government—that is, the arrival of thousands of Cubans and Haitians in 1981, many of them Cubans recently released from prisons (Simon 1998). Congressional hearings reveal that in the wake of these new arrivals, officials tied to each other through the BOP revamped immigrant detention into a program far more punitive and restrictive than had previously been the case at Ellis Island or the casual arrangements of the Immigration and Naturalization Service "processing" migrants with an eye toward most of them arriving and remaining in the United States. It was only in the wake of 1982 testimony by then assistant attorney general Rudy Giuliani that we can see the Reagan DOJ repurposing state prisons and county jails for the purpose of indefinite detention and removal. Giuliani's congressional testimony in 1982 makes it clear that the Department of

Justice, in the same time frame as the emergence of private prisons (see below), was driving an initiative to expand imprisoning asylum seekers and was not considering non-penal alternatives.[30]

FOR-PROFIT PRISON CONTRACTS AS KLEPTOCRACY

In 2016, members of the House and Senate sent letters to the Secretary of the Department of Homeland Security pointing out the direct connection they saw between the poor conditions of the facilities for families seeking asylum and the profiteering of the private prisons.[31] Such letters pointing out the role of prison profiteering in defining an immigration policy that has been increasingly incarcerating people by those with proximity to these policies is akin to what Bennett calls a "Smoking Gun"—that is, direct evidence that a hypothesis of a cause is indeed correct.[32]

Some legal professionals concerned about the harms inflicted by the radical uptick in mass incarceration under immigration laws have attempted specific interventions to deter the cycle of venality wrought by for-profit firms financing groups with political leverage to advance racist and nationalist myths and thus direct billions of dollars into the coffers of for-profit prisons and related industries, especially finance. Since 2014, eight class action lawsuits have been filed against GEO and CoreCivic alleging violations of federal and state employment and labor laws. Before turning to this litigation, the second section discusses the underlying legal and political analyses that made it possible. This includes the federal procurement system. Knowledge of the financial and regulatory context of for-profit prisons allowed one attorney activist to successfully thwart its expansion. This suggests that knowledge of specialized law and regulations may make possible interventions on behalf of precarious communities routinely targeted by attorneys employed on behalf of for-profit prisons, banks, and finance firms, not to mention other industries as well.

To understand these legal and policy dynamics, scholars may need to reconsider conventional causal narratives of mass incarceration. Instead of prison labor revealing one more lawful and inevitable, if abhorrent, consequence of capitalism, neoliberalism, or racism, the successful interventions of these attorneys invite mobilizing against a different framework:

kleptocracy, a form of government based on old-fashioned greed and corruption. According to theories of capitalism, inequality occurs from owners extracting surplus value by exploiting labor.[33] In contrast, a theory of kleptocracy suggests inequality is driven by a relatively small number of elites knowledgeable about gaming government procurement and other payment protocols, corruptly moving large amounts of funds from taxpayers into their private accounts, typically with no accountability (see, e.g., Painter 2009; Ramirez 2012). This is an entirely different critique of prison labor from that of Marxists Georg Rusche and Otto Kirschheimer (1939) as well as Melossi (1978) and Melossi and Pavarini (1981). ICE jails typically do not produce goods for the market, nor do they structure a threat to coerce workers into low-paying jobs. The profit motive behind the thirty-four-thousand-minimum-bed mandate is ad hoc and not specific to capitalism. If government procurement contracting, a key operational linchpin of mass incarceration under immigration laws, is done officially or effectively in secret, and is not simply embodying nativist or racist values by way of legal policies and practices, then articulating the process by which GEO or CoreCivic are paying (or withholding) slaving wages to (or from) those in custody under immigration laws requires new methods for analyzing how the profits from exploitation in particular are possible and how they might be thwarted.[34]

Federal Procurement Procedures and Kleptocracy

Recent scholarship and journalism have suggested that the cause of the increase in detentions is a shift from government to private prisons for holding people accused of violating immigration laws, a change that incentivizes for-profit prisons and financing firms and banks to lobby Congress for these expenditures.[35] The privatization of government operations initiated in the 1950s, pushed by private prisons and finance firms in the 1980s (discussed below), and fast-tracked by President Bill Clinton in the wake of Performance-Based Budgeting signed into law in 1993 meant a pseudo-neoliberal and in fact kleptocratic takeover of government programs; in turn, this facilitated policy making by a community of MBAs and JDs with specialized expertise in illicitly manipulating the system of creating and bidding on federal contracts (Teachout 2014).[36] Hundreds if not thousands of policies designed to assist US residents, from health to transportation, have been eviscerated in the name of "performance" and "efficiency" (Templin 2010; Hill and Painter 2011). Key to attracting funding was the ability of federal contractors to defend expenditures on programs based on self-serving metrics specified to benefit the owners and stockholders of firms producing the targets. Behind the scenes, members of Congress, including the leadership of both parties, signed off on appropriations that kept these firms in business (Templin 2010; Teachout 2014; US GAO 2008). Although privatization is pitched as cost-saving, for decades government audits, including the OIG reports cited earlier in this chapter, reveal widespread failures, while the costs are far higher than government-run facilities.[37] The for-profit prison industry in general and the contracts with components of Homeland Security exemplify this pattern (see, e.g., Michaels 2010).

To thwart federal contractors from using taxpayer funds to buy influence with the government distributing these funds, Congress passed a law prohibiting such firms from "directly or indirectly . . . mak[ing] any contribution of money or other things of value, or to promise expressly or impliedly to make any such contribution to any political party, committee, or candidate for public office or to any person for any political purpose or use" (52 U.S.C. 30119(a)). The law also makes it unlawful for "anyone . . . knowingly to solicit any such contribution from any such person for any such purpose during any such period" (52 U.S.C. 30119(b)). In 2016, GEO Corp. and then-candidate Donald Trump violated this law, in the aftermath of which the Trump administration announced a $110 million contract would be awarded to GEO for immigration detention.[38]

Exacerbating the influence of money on policy is the source of the information on which the agencies and Congress rely, an outcome required by regulations these same firms pushed through.[39] The same firms that are providing the government in-house information technology services have components that seek to benefit from this information (Fang 2013). A former White House ethics attorney writes: "Contracting firms may structure government transactions, or advise the government, in ways that are more helpful to their own interests or private clients' interests than the public interest" (Painter 2009, 153). Richard Painter's focus is on the hedge fund Black Rock's role in managing risk assessments for the 2008 financial bailout (see esp. 153n52); but the observation is on point for firms holding ICE detention contracts as well. For-profit prison firms with multi-year rolling contracts disfavored by procurement regulations easily distort information on their sole-supplier costs.[40] In addition, they, and not government employees, are creating and of course themselves making use of data for potential government detention needs and costs. Firm resources and plans for mergers, and acquisitions, may be shifted by companies with insider access to information in anticipation of new "Requests for Proposals" (RFPs) from the federal government.[41] The firms with the most expertise in federal appropriations and procurement are the ones best positioned to set the policy agenda when it comes to creating federal budgets, a circumstance against which the Obama White House warned, even though President Obama made numerous appointment and signing decisions suggesting he was failing to heed his own advice. Within a year of signing the Executive Order "Economy in Government Contracting," Obama signed a law ordering ICE to house no fewer than 33,400 people daily under immigration laws, shortly after which the United States deported more people in one year than in any prior year in US history.[42] These sorts of laws and contracts do nothing more sophisticated than operationalize narrow programs benefitting repeat visitors to the federal procurement trough. Such Beltway transactions and short-term political maneuvers have little to do with broad ideological commitments of either party much less neoliberalism. They contradict cost-saving and free market commitments of Republicans as well as racial equality norms of Democrats: the worst anti-immigrant laws in recent history were passed with a majority of votes from both parties and signed by Presidents Clinton and Obama, both Democrats.[43]

The effect of these laws is to put immigration detention facilities under the control of for-profit firms, even though for-profit facilities are charging more than twice the rate of county jails or the facilities run by the US Marshals (Table 1). When Congress drafted its first detention policies, tracking those for Ellis Island discussed above, the federal government owned the land and ran the operations. Today, the majority of people detained under immigration laws are in for-profit prisons. According to ICE data collected by the National Immigrant Justice Center, in 2017, 71 percent were in facilities that are operated by privately owned companies.[44] On average,

Table 1   US Government Analysis: Allocation of Funds and People among
ICE Facilities

	Daily Rate	Person-Days/2019	Total Spent	Percent Held
SPC (private operated)	$203.87	1,479,386	$301,602,423	9.1
CDF (privately owned and operated)	$148.43	3,062,683	$454,594,037	18.8
DIGSA (privately operated)	$123.62	4,508,862	$557,385,520	27.9
IGSA (county owned and operated)	$99.99	3,587,693	$358,733,423	22.1
US Marshals (federal)	$89.73	3,358,505	$301,358,653	20.6
Other* (private/govt.)	$155.63	245,370	$38,186,933	1.5
TOTAL		**16,242,499**	**$2,011,860,989**	**100**

Data from DHS, "ICE Budget Overview, FY 2019," Department of Homeland Security, Office of the Secretary (2019).
* This includes juveniles, families, and those in hospitals, the vast majority of whom are in privately operated facilities under contract to the federal government (DHS 2019, O&S, 109).

the cost of the private prison operations is more than 50 percent higher than that of the government-run facilities.[45] The five government-owned and -run "Service Processing Centers" that held arriving immigrants for a few days in the 1970s are now a global sprawl of over six hundred jails, prisons, and holding rooms confining people in harsh conditions up to several years (Simon 1998; Torrey 2015; Misra 2018).

Hacking the For-Profit Prisons' Regulatory System

The project of attorney Bianca Tylek, pursued through various nonprofits over the past several years, has produced results inconsistent with theories of critical legal or critical race scholars that claim government is unfailingly sympathetic to corporate interests, neoliberal priorities, and racist agendas (e.g., Alexander 2012; Brown 2004; Kang 2009; Wacquant 2001, 2009). Relevant to those interested in understanding prison work in the context of larger financial and economic dynamics is a comment Tylek submitted to the Federal Communications Commission (FCC).

Tylek objected to communications procurement giant Securus taking over a competitor with a phone contract for federal prisons on the grounds that the transaction would violate antitrust laws. Tylek's intervention may seem far afield from the plight of those in custody whose labor is exploited by GEO and CoreCivic. However, Tylek's analysis provides an excellent example of the dependence of prison profiteers on anti-capitalist models of accumulation, including the use of forced labor. And her response demonstrates how highlighting one of the numerous unlawful business practices on which these firms depend may be a more effective means of thwarting exploitation than profiles of behaviors, attitudes, or wide-ranging theories of neoliberalism.

In an open comment to the Federal Communications Commission responding to an application by Securus to transfer control of one private firm to another for prison phone services to the federal government, Tylek observed that the transfer of business would "reduce competition and harm consumers of correctional telephone services" (Tylek 2018a, 1). Crucially, she also tied this objection to the larger mission of the Corrections Accountability Project she founded within the Urban Justice Center and on whose behalf she had filed her protest.[46] Her comment indicated that these same concerns had been made public through a report she and her colleagues copublished with the Marshall Project, a tie-in bringing to the attention of the FCC the imprimatur of a respected, independent organization and thus the appeal of Tylek's analysis to other experts in the public arena. Tylek's letter noted Securus's pattern of "swallowing up its smaller competitors"; hoarding and trolling patent rights "to compel smaller companies to sign expensive, bilateral licensing agreements" to end costly litigation; and the specific harms anticipated if the FCC approved the transaction (Tylek 2018a, 2).[47] In a second comment a few weeks later, Tylek responded to Securus's claims in the firm's reply to Tylek's initial comment.[48]

On April 2, 2019, the FCC Chairman issued a statement: "Based on a record of nearly 1 million documents comprised of 7.7 million pages of information submitted by the applicants, as well as arguments and evidence submitted by criminal justice advocates, consumer groups, and other commenters, FCC staff concluded that this deal posed significant competitive concerns and would not be in the public interest. I agree. I'm therefore pleased that the companies have determined that withdrawing their application is the best course."[49] Two days later, Tylek issued a press release with the subject-heading: "VICTORY! A David and Goliath battle against the prison telecom industry."[50] Analyses and criticism from leading theorists of mass incarceration would have predicted Tylek's defeat. The actual outcome, along with the employment class action litigation against private prisons described below, suggests viable responses using the rule of law to counter the kleptocracy in which the for-profit prison firms now operate.

The background and success of Tylek exposes a potential flaw in the causal analysis of critics who blame capitalism and racism for the prison profiteers. Tylek says her "organization is dedicated to ending the exploitation of people targeted by the criminal legal system."[51] But unlike those who find the profiteers as exemplifying capitalism or neoliberalism, Tylek is pointing out that the Securus business model is fundamentally anti-capitalist, and indeed is blatantly violating US antitrust laws.[52] That said, Tylek's campaign very clearly tied her legal attack on the Securus business model to her underlying objective of eliminating mass incarceration by cutting off its profits. Her approach does not fit neatly into traditional social science or law and society analyses of how social movements, interest group lobbying, and strategic litigation change policies. Also of note is that Tylek's intervention was motivated by a personal experience, and her strategy for intervening drew on her professional expertise.[53] In the language of process tracing, Tylek's intervention suggests the causal paths to resisting mass incarceration put forward by Alexander or Wacquant fail the Hoop Test, while her focus on firm misconduct meets the Smoking Gun test for a theory of kleptocracy.

Tylek's interventions that make use of existing laws and procedures to advance larger policy goals that have as their primary target the externalities of illicit arrangements are perhaps best understood as a "forensic intelligence," a process by which a citizen "discovers, elicits, and produces knowledge of law and force with the ultimate objective of thwarting injustice" (Stevens 2015, 725). Tylek's own description of her motives and actions exemplify this. She understood that the work she was doing "could fly under the radar" and how she avoided this: "This might not be something anyone pays attention to. We were writing challenges to the

FCC and Securus is responding. So what? Who's going to know? I thought we needed more public attention on the deal to be successful. The public has the most power. People power matters. We pushed the Marshall Project into writing an op-ed. They picked it up. We drafted that first with the Marshall Project and then followed with a post on our blog that goes into more detail. . . . From there, we were thankful quite a number of outlets picked up the story."[54] The media coverage elicited additional comments to the FCC critical of Securus. Tylek's interventions name and confront the injustice of prison economies through forensic (i.e., legal) analysis that becomes widely publicized.[55] These are, of course, techniques of large corporations that spend tens of millions on public relations firms, lobbyists, and strategic consulting and many others who market their expertise to the highest bidder. According to this analysis, visible injustice serves as a counterweight to well-resourced groups and causes on the other side.

Tylek is of course attentive to the racialized character of the exploitation, but she sees the firms and their unlawful profits, not racist attitudes, as the linchpin to mass incarceration. Tylek explains her goal is to "end the exploitation of people, to work on every private vendor that exists." She says, "The private industry is seeking to use the criminal industry to extract wealth from communities of color and people in poverty disproportionately affected by this system. We strongly believe that it is this industry that is getting in the way of our reforming the system. There's a massive industry that's pushing back."[56] If Tylek is right about this, then criticism of narratives of personal responsibility, neoliberalism, and nativism and racism may be less relevant to implementing reforms than the scholars writing on prisons and prison work believe (Wacquant 2009, xx).[57]

CLASS ACTION LABOR RIGHTS LITIGATION AGAINST PRIVATE PRISONS WITH ICE CONTRACTS

The current litigation against private prisons for violations of state and federal labor and employment laws exemplifies the perspective and strategy explained by Tylek.[58] This section reviews federal litigation of labor, employment, safety, and contracts advanced on behalf of those forced to work by GEO and CoreCivic. The orders in these cases do not preclude a focus on the institutionalization of values of the individualist work ethic, neoliberalism, or nativism and racism. But they should incentivize researchers to consider strategies that have successfully challenged the effects of the policies associated with the broader causal models, and the possibility that these policies may be operationalized in ways only loosely or not at all tied to the attitudes themselves.[59]

Copious scholarship over the past several decades reveals an increasing number of obstacles that prevent plaintiffs in civil cases in general, but especially class action lawsuits regarding employment, from surviving motions to dismiss and going to trial (Berry, Nelson, and Nielsen 2017; Moore 2015, 1205; Staszak 2014).[60] In 2018, .08 percent of all civil cases filed proceeded to a trial (US Courts 2019, Table C4). In this context, the court orders from seven district court judges, one three-member unanimous appellate court panel, and the denials of petitions for review by the Ninth Circuit and the Supreme Court between 2014 and 2019 are truly remarkable. The most legally and economically disadvantaged group in the country has been waging a battle in the courts against firms on the New York Stock Exchange, and the judges are denying almost all the motions to dismiss or deny class certification filed by GEO and CoreCivic.[61]

A Dollar a Day, Forced Labor, and Unjust Enrichment Litigation Highlights

In 2014, attorneys in Denver, Colorado, filed the first lawsuit claiming that a for-profit prison exploited those in their custody to meet contractual obligations to ICE, in violation of both a state minimum wage law, the Trafficking Victims Protection Act (TVPA) (18 U.S.C. § 1589), and common law prohibiting "unjust enrichment."[62] By 2019, eight lawsuits— seven brought by plaintiffs represented by private attorneys and one in 2017 brought on behalf of the State of Washington by the attorney general— were alleging over a dozen violations of state and federal labor, employment, and occupational safety laws by CoreCivic or GEO.[63] None of the lawsuits named ICE as a defendant. The most common claims across the lawsuits were violations of the minimum wage laws, the TVPA, and state common law prohibiting "unjust enrichment," the last being the only one that was in all eight complaints.[64] One suit in New Mexico alleges minimum wage law violations but does not have a TVPA claim.[65] A 2015 complaint filed in San Diego also alleges violations of occupational health and safety laws.[66]

In the first case filed, in October 2014, the claim based on the Colorado Minimum Wage Order (CMWO) was dismissed, but the TVPA and unjust enrichment allegations were ordered to proceed.[67] Federal District Court Judge John Kane's order focused on differences between case law in litigation brought by criminal inmates and those awaiting criminal trials alleging working conditions in violation of the Thirteenth Amendment, on the one hand, and the case law of the TVPA, on the other. Cases brought based on the Thirteenth Amendment require allegations of physical coercion. In contrast, the TVPA has a lower threshold for inducements and harm prompting culpability:

> Whoever knowingly provides or obtains the labor or services of a person by any one of, or by any combination of, the following means—(1) by means of force, threats of force, physical restraint, or threats of physical restraint to that person or another person; (2) by means of serious harm or threats of serious harm to that person or another person; (3) by means of the abuse or threatened abuse of law or legal process; or (4) *by means of any scheme, plan, or pattern intended to cause the person to believe that, if that person did not perform such labor or services, that person or another person would suffer serious harm or physical restraint.* 18 U.S.C.§ 1589(a) (Emphasis added.)

"Serious harm" is further elaborated: "any harm, whether physical or non-physical, including psychological, financial, or reputational harm, that is sufficiently serious, under all the surrounding circumstances, to compel a reasonable person of the same background and in the same circumstances to [render labor] . . . to avoid incurring that harm." 1589(c)(2).[68] Plaintiffs argued that the threats of solitary confinement and the implicit threat of force inherent in their being under the physical control of their employer, if proven, were in violation of the TVPA.[69] Judge Kane agreed.

Kane's historic order noted that the factual allegations underlying the unjust enrichment claim, the third of the three laws the suit alleged GEO violated, tracked those made under the CMWO, which was dismissed (Phillips 2017).[70] Nonetheless, Judge Kane's order held that the plaintiffs' minimum wage claim was distinct from their unjust enrichment claim.

Unjust enrichment could include profits from practices that may not violate the CMWO but are nonetheless illegal under Colorado common law. Further, if the damages for unjust enrichment track the plaintiff's claims for compensation based on the Service Contract Act (SCA), they will be owed "prevailing wages" for specified occupations such as laundry workers, barbers, and kitchen staff. This pay is considerably higher than the minimum wage.[71] Judge Kane also rejected GEO's claim that the plaintiffs' suit must be thrown out under the "government contractor defense." GEO asserted that the dollar-per-day voluntary detainee work program was established at the behest of the federal government, but the court found that the contract between GEO and the federal government only establishes guidelines for the government's reimbursement of the so-called Voluntary Work Program (VWP), and even for this program, "does not prohibit Defendant from paying detainees in excess of $1/day in order to comply with Colorado labor laws. In fact," Kane continues, "the contract specifically contemplates that the Defendant will perform under the contract in accordance with '[a]pplicable federal, state and local labor laws and codes'; and the contract is subject to the SCA."[72] In sum, the order held that if a jury finds that the facts in the complaint are as alleged, GEO Corp. will need to remediate the damages it caused by its violation of the TVPA and its failure to pay prevailing wages and benefits.

In 2016, the attorneys for Menocal and eight other plaintiffs named in the initial complaint filed a motion requesting the judge certify a class of plaintiffs and allow litigation to proceed on behalf of all those who were forced to work in GEO's Aurora facility and whose exploitation unjustly enriched GEO over the past ten years, the outermost reach for filing charges based on the TVPA.[73] Kane granted the motion. In his order authorizing up to sixty thousand people held in GEO's Aurora facility alone over the last decade to have a jury decide whether GEO's policies violated the TVPA and Colorado's common law prohibiting unjust enrichment, Judge Kane states: "Although Representatives and putative class members have diverse backgrounds, their circumstances are uniquely suited for a class action. All share the experience of having been detained in the Facility and subjected to uniform policies that purposefully eliminate nonconformity. The questions posed in this case are complex and novel, but the answers to those questions can be provided on a classwide basis. Appreciating that the class action is a 'valuable tool to circumvent the barriers to the pursuit of justice,' [citation omitted], I GRANT the Motion for Class Certification."[74] Judge Kane's order emphasizes the precarity of the proposed class as key to his rationale for supporting class action litigation: "The putative class members reside in countries around the world, lack English proficiency, and have little knowledge of the legal system in the United States. It is unlikely that they would individually bring these innovative claims against GEO."[75] The plaintiffs had a resounding round-one victory.

GEO then appealed the class certification. On February 9, 2018, the Tenth Circuit in a three-person published opinion unanimously affirmed the class certification.[76] On January 11, 2019, Judge Kane approved the plaintiffs' proposed announcement about the litigation and attorneys began using a list supplied by GEO to inform up to sixty thousand potential class members of the litigation and that they were by default represented but could choose to opt out.[77]

GEO and CoreCivic in their briefs repeatedly emphasized that their exploitation of those in their custody was contractual.[78] The firms also pressed ICE behind the scenes and through Congress to support their cause (January 2018),[79] to enter the litigation as an intervenor,[80] and to reimburse the firms for the costs of litigation as well as payments if they lose.[81] To date, ICE has not entered as an intervenor and has refused GEO's requests for incur fee increases for the litigation or coverage for potential damages.[82]

On April 1, 2019, the US government for the first time weighed in on the litigation. For the purpose of a review by the Eleventh Circuit appellate court of Judge Clay Land's order denying CoreCivic's motion to dismiss a lawsuit alleging its labor policies for those in its custody violated the TVPA and unjust enrichment,[83] the solicitor general filed an amicus brief "in support of neither party."[84] The brief addresses itself primarily to the question raised by CoreCivic and GEO: "Whether the forced labor provision of the Trafficking Victims Protection Act, 18 U.S.C. §§ 1589, 1595, applies to work programs in federal immigration detention facilities operated by private contractors." The solicitor general affirmed the TVPA analysis of the district court judge—that is, that a for-profit prison is not categorically excluded from TVPA coverage, while also claiming that work performed consistent with the PBNDS did not violate the TVPA.[85] The

Georgia case did not allege minimum wage violations and the analysis does not address any potential conflict between the PBNDS—which are internal agency guidelines—and the FLSA or other wage laws. The US government is essentially supporting the legal pleadings of the plaintiffs in response to the motion to dismiss.

Challenging the illegal externalities of the work assigned to those in their custody, on which the private prisons rely for profits, disregards claims about paternalism, neoliberalism, and civil as well as Constitutional rights, but could bring down the for-profit sector's support for mass incarceration of noncitizens. According to GEO's appeal to the Tenth Circuit, if the class action lawsuits prevail, the firm will no longer be able to do business with ICE: "The district court's novel certification of a class comprising all people detained at the Facility over the past ten years poses a potentially catastrophic risk to GEO's ability to honor its contracts with the federal government. And the skeleton of this suit could potentially be refiled against privately operated facilities across the United States, causing GEO and other contractors to defend them even though GEO firmly believes that policies give the Plaintiffs no legal claim."[86] If GEO and the other firms cannot honor their contracts to detain people under immigration laws, then the logistical challenge is likely to lead to the removal from the prison industry of the for-profit players and, as Tylek hypothesizes, and end the legislative support for funding them and thus mass incarceration more generally.

Although the legal strategy described above is directly useful only for those in custody under civil and not criminal law, the admission by GEO reveals the fundamental centrality of the work by prisoners to the economic viability of prison operations and is therefore relevant to analyzing any facility whose population is forced to work while in custody, including county jails. If those locked up stopped working, prisons would need to pay market wages and these costs would be prohibitive.[87]

CONCLUSION

The process-tracing method for analyzing the mass incarceration of people under immigration law discredits arguments that the Protestant work ethic, neoliberalism, or racism/nativism are the primary drivers of mass incarceration: none of these can pass the Hoop Test—that is, the absence of these conditions alongside the flourishing of mass incarceration, especially in the context of ICE jail contracts. The Hoop Test is the equivalent of Popperian falsification, a test he claims to be the sine qua non of knowledge. It is not surprising that social scientists do not rely on this methodological test, with which regressions are incompatible (Stevens 2009, 227–31). According to Popper ([1934] 1959), a theory of gravity is plausible only when every single time one drops the apple it falls toward the ground. If one released an apple 999 times, and on the 1,000th identical drop it flew to the ceiling, the theory of gravity explaining the 999 bruised apples would be falsified. Such a test is clearly incompatible with the study of society, as Popper himself avers: "Long term prophecies can be derived from scientific conditional predictions only if they apply to systems which can be described as well-isolated, stationary and recurrent. These systems are very rare in nature, and modern society is surely not one of them" (Popper [1948] 1972, 339). Katzenstein implicitly relies on this framework in her critique of the multi-method Racial Classification Model put forward in *Disciplining the Poor: Neoliberal Paternalism and the Persistent Power of Race* (Soss, Fording, and Schram 2011): "A broad overarching theory of neoliberal discipline is inevitably in some tension with the attempt to recognize variability" (Katzenstein 2012, 990). Katzenstein references a similar critique of European mass incarceration theorization by Nicola Lacy (2008).

Judge Kane's order basing the class certification on the precarity of those represented seems further evidence challenging the framework of Wacquant (2001, 2009). Meanwhile, the hypothesis that kleptocratic incentives from federal procurement policy make possible the for-profit industry appears to pass the Hoop Test and perhaps the Smoking Gun test as well. The timing of the expansion of private prisons leading to the infrastructure for mass incarceration coincides with two separate activities that push kleptocrats toward the vicious cycle of lobbying state legislatures and Congress to pay for private prisons. The first is the near-contemporaneous analysis shared by a researcher commissioned by the House Judiciary Subcommittee on Courts, Civil Liberties, and the Administration of Justice in 1985. In testimony for a hearing on "Privatization of Corrections,"

Professor Ira Robbins notes that privatization of prisons developed in response to counties failing to pass prison bonds, a situation that proved perilous to the finance industry and thus provoked banks and other financial firms that profited from issuing the bonds to seek new customers, namely state and federal legislatures.[88] "The corporation can build the institution and the government can lease it" (Robbins 1985, 77).[89] Robbins points out in a written response added later to the Committee Report that the finance firm E.F. Hutton was pushing private prison investments in its promotional brochures (US House Judiciary Subcommittee on Courts 1985, 103, quoting Robbins).

Robbins also points out a concern by critics of privatization in the 1980s. Its relevance to contemporary debates warrants quoting it at length: "They claim that it is inappropriate to operate prisons with a profit motive, which provides no incentive to reduce overcrowding (especially if the company is paid on a per-prisoner basis), nor to consider alternatives to incarceration, nor to deal with the broader problems of criminal justice. On the contrary, the critics assert that the incentive would be to build more prisons and jails. And if they are built, we will fill them. This is a fact of correctional life. The number of jailed criminals has always risen to fill whatever space is available" (Robbins 1985, 75). These hearing statements suggest, first, that finance firms misrepresenting the nature of the industry sold investors and legislatures on private prisons based on protocols of financing that were anti-democratic and anti-capitalist, but also had little relation to instrumentalizing ideas about personal responsibility, the market, or race. At the very least, this suggests the kleptocracy theory passes the Hoop Test. Meanwhile, GEO's 2018 petition vowing it will be unable to honor its contracts with the government if it must cease practices that several federal judges and an appellate court say are unlawful indicates the profiteering from illegal actions keeps them in business and thus passes the Smoking Gun test.

In the wake of the Black Lives Matter protests of 2020, it is possible that county, state, and federal representatives will change police, arrest, and prison-funding policies for those alleged of criminal wrongdoing. But inasmuch as the communities ICE is targeting do not fit the logic of mass incarceration, nothing will change for noncitizens. And because firms and individuals use lobbyists to direct taxpayer funds to private interests, the distribution of power and resources will continue to impose exorbitant opportunity costs on the 99 percent in the form of under-resourced public schools, transportation, and housing from which grand theories of mass incarceration direct our attention.

ACKNOWLEDGMENTS

Portions quoted from Robinson Martinez, as well as some laws, cases, and descriptions of the work required by private prisons have been published previously (Stevens 2016). I am indebted to attorneys Andrew Free and Nicolette Glazer for their representation of my litigation under the Freedom of Information Act and to Mr. Free and other attorneys suing GEO and CoreCivic in the cases discussed below for their insights and persistence in testing and advancing the rule of law. I want to thank Mark Lyttle for bringing to my attention in 2009 the existence of a work program in then Correction Corporation of America Stewart Detention Facility in Lumpkin, Georgia. Without the detailed descriptions of his shifts and payments during his months of unlawful detention, this research would not have been possible. Thanks also to Robinson Martinez for contemporaneous documentation of his experiences at facilities in Texas; Andrew Free and Nicolette Glazer for legal representation in FOIA litigation; and research assistants Matthew Casler, Daisy Conant, Matthew Marth, Khadijah Milhan, and Caleb Young for assistance obtaining and tracking records from the FOIA litigation on which I relied for analysis in this chapter. Funding was provided by Northwestern University's Weinberg College for Arts and Sciences Posner Fellow program and the Political Science Department Farrell Fellow program, as well as the Buffett Institute for Global Affairs.

NOTES

1. It is tempting to simply refer to these populations as "noncitizens," but for decades the US government has been unlawfully detaining and deporting US citizens under immigration laws (Balderrama and Rodriguez 2006; Stevens (2011, 2017a, 2017b Olsen 2017). ICE's work program came to my attention in 2009 through a US citizen, Mark Lyttle, who had just returned from Guatemala after

having been unlawfully deported to Mexico, despite being born in North Carolina, speaking no Spanish, and having no relatives in Mexico (Stevens 2011). He explained that the Correction Corporation of America (CCA), now CoreCivic, had been paying him one dollar each day for his midnight-to-8 a.m. shift buffing floors, and also kitchen work. He was concerned that CCA owed him $32. (Interview with author, Kennesaw, Georgia, June 22, 2009.)

2. This is an extremely large body of literature. Exemplary of the frameworks I am engaging is work by David Garland (2002), Loïc Wacquant (2001, 2009), and Michelle Alexander (2012). I am especially concerned with evaluating whether theories of ideology (as expressed in attitudes, behaviors, and statements to interviewers) provide robust causal accounts of incarceration. That said, much of the literature on mass incarceration focuses on the racialized effects and not causes of mass incarceration (e.g., Western 2006, 23–34). While producing knowledge of one strain of mass incarceration, the long-standing dependence of this literature on racialized incarceration—and its disregard of the effects on democracy of federal procurement systems that concentrate wealth among kleptocrats—may itself unwittingly contribute to the inertia of mass incarceration.

3. The American Heritage Dictionary definition of *kleptocracy* is "a government characterized by rampant greed and corruption." https://www.ahdictionary.com/word/search.html?q=kleptocracy.

4. Alexander also cites Cohen to describe how laws banned "insulting gestures" and thus "opened up a tremendous market for convict leasing in which prisoners were contracted out as laborers to the highest bidder" (31).

5. TRAC, Syracuse University, "Immigration and ICE Detainees Snapshot," June 30, 2018, https://trac.syr.edu/phptools/immigration/detention/. Reliable figures are elusive. Data provided by ICE to Congress on March 6, 2019, indicated 50,049 people in ICE custody, even though Congress had appropriated funds to pay for the detention of no more than 40,520 (Ackerman 2019).

6. Annual arrest "book-ins" to detention by ICE and Customs and Border Control (CBP) for 2016—ICE: 108,372, CBP 244,510. For 2017—ICE: 134,553, CBP: 184,038. For 2018—ICE 153,670 CBP 242,778 (ICE 2018, 8).

7. Not a single person in ICE custody is held for punishment. See Wong Wing v. United States, 163 U.S. 228 (1896). A study by the state of California notes: "Individuals held in custody before trial on criminal charges, cannot be subjected to punishment at all. Their confinement is governed by the constitution's Due Process Clause, which requires that restrictions on liberty not be "excessive in relation to" their purpose" (Becarra 2019, citing Youngberg v. Romeo 457 U.S. 307, 322 [1982]). The official policy rationale is to ensure people show up for the immigration court hearings and comply with final orders of removal. Data show that the flight risks are quite low. In 2013–2017, 92 percent of asylum seekers were present for their final hearings (Cepala 2019).

8. Under the 1996 Illegal Immigration Reform and Immigrant Responsibility Act (IIRRA), those in mandatory detention due to a criminal conviction have served their prison sentences prior to being released into ICE custody.

9. That said, there is some facility-to-facility variation in the amount of work incentivized through nonmonetary carrots, ranging from extra pieces of chicken, and more flexible visiting arrangements to aversive sticks, most commonly threats of solitary confinement and additional restrictions, stated or implied, though threats of physical force were made as well. Records were obtained through records requests and litigation under the Freedom of Information Act. The litigation that many of the documents are quoted from in this chapter is *Stevens v. ICE*, 1:17-cv-02853 (2014). See links on Source Information, Deportation Research Clinic, https://deportationresearchclinic.org/FOIA-Litigation.html. For original source material, including contracts and litigation, see http:deportationresearchclinic .org. And see Stevens (2016, 426–27).

10. A "Report of Investigation" by the Office of Professional Responsibility states, "On January 24, 2008, the Joint Intake Center (JIC), Washington, D.C. received telephonic notification from Detainee [REDACTED] Stewart Detention Center (SDC), reporting he had not been paid for services rendered while working in the kitchen at SDC. Detainee [REDACTED] claims that he has been in the SDC for three years and has never received compensation for his kitchen duties." FOIA Case 2013-00445, 1. The record shows the complaint was closed the same day it was received and was not investigated.

11. 28 C.F.R. § 5. The current BOP definitions have been in use since 1979.

12. PBNDS, 2011, https://www.ice.gov/detention-standards/2011. For the legislative history with citations, see Stevens (2016, esp. 436). The analysis used for the minimum wage litigation highlights Congress's failure to appropriate funds for the VWP since 1978, despite this being required in the authorizing statute. Without such appropriations, the program might be operationally similar to that on the books in 1978 but nonetheless lack the force of law and thus cannot supersede federal and state wage and employment laws.

13. The PBNDS detail obligations to ICE of the contracting private firms and state and local law enforcement officials running jail space rented out. Violations may result in contracts being severed but the standards alone provide no rights or redress for respondents in ICE custody.

14. PBNDS, 2011, https://www.ice.gov/doclib/detention-standards/2011/5-8.pdf.

15. Menocal et al. v. GEO Group, Inc., 1:14-cv-02887 (D. Colo. Oct 22, 2014). Likewise, in the wing of Arizona's Pinal County Jail rented out to ICE, seven people were detailed each day to clean the showers and could be punished with solitary confinement for refusing (Stevens 2016, 41). The media have noted it was the research of this author "about the volunteer work program [that] prompted the lawsuit" (Phillips 2017; and see Holpuch 2018).

16. 29 C.F.R. § 553.101(a)—"An individual who performs hours of service for a public agency for civic, charitable, or humanitarian reasons, without promise, expectation or receipt of compensation for services rendered, is considered to be a volunteer during such hours."

17. Barrientos v. CoreCivic, Order of Judge Clay Land, Middle District of Georgia, 4:18-cv-00070-CDL Doc. 38, 08/17/18, p. 1. Stewart has been assailed for its numerous violations of the PBNDS for several years (pp. 2–4). In 2016 a spokesperson for Rep. Yvette Clarke (D-NY) called the Stewart Detention facility "inhumane" (Glawe 2016).

18. "We observed several problems with food handling and safety at four facilities, some of which did not comply with the [Performance Based National Detention Standards] for food operations and could endanger the health of detainees. We observed spoiled, wilted, and moldy produce and other food in kitchen refrigerators, as well as food past its expiration date. We also found expired frozen food, including meat, and thawing meat without labels indicating when it had begun thawing or the date by which it must be used" (US ICE Office of Inspector General 2017, 8). Stewart was among the six facilities OIG inspected for its report (appendix A, 10).

19. See FOIA Case No. 2015-ICLI-00026-Supp-83. This and other FOIA documents cited in this chapter are available at https://deportationresearchclinic.org. *See* "Source Material on ICE Private Prisons," http://deportationresearchclinic.org/DRC-INS-ICE-FacilityContracts-Reports.html.) A DOJ OIG report also highlights the inferior record of private prisons for federal prisoners (US DOJ Office of Inspector General 2016), https://oig.justice.gov/reports/2016/e1606.pdf.

20. The median wage inside these facilities for jobs available is $1 per day; so, a can of chili requires eighteen hours of labor.

21. FOIA Case No. ICE 2013-32547, released March 21, 2019, http://government illegals.org/Stevens-FOIA-ICE-2015-ICLI-00026_03-20-2019.pdf.

22. The Trump administration has discussed new protocols authorizing detention conditions for those in custody under immigration laws identical for those in criminal custody (Dickerson 2017).

23. County governments also turn to for-profit contracts to defray local costs for jails (Regester 2010). The Folkston facility will gross GEO $1.6 million per *month*. It is attractive to the local county because of property taxes and other small perks, including community donations and "buying supplies from vendors in the county" (Redmon 2018), support that is not based on the PWE, market values, or racism/nativism, but local profits.

24. The Supreme Court has held since 1896 that immigration violations are decided without juries by government officials; the lack of protections the Sixth Amendment requires means their custody is only because of findings that they are flight risks or a danger to the community. Wong Wing v. United States, 163 U.S.

228 (1896) (overturning 1892 law authorizing "hard labor" for violating immigration policies).

25. In 1941 the Immigration and Naturalization Service coined the word *detainee* to refer to Italians and Nazis held in US prisoner of war camps (*New York Times* 1941).

26. Ten cents per hour was 13 percent of the federal minimum wage in 1950 (Elwell 2014, 2), and also less than the rate authorized by Congress in its appropriations act (Stevens 2016). The one dollar/day payments now paid are .8 percent to 1.7 percent of the minimum pay mandated by the Fair Labor Standards Act, depending on the state in which the facility is located. And the minimum wage itself has not kept pace with the cost of living.

27. "The CCA Story: Our Company History." https://web.archive.org/web/2016 0208192833/https://www.cca.com/our-history.

28. For details on the legislative history of the work program under INS, see Stevens (2016, esp. 458–65).

29. Indeed, ICE still holds small numbers of people in this fashion, such as the Comfort Suites Hotel in Miami, the Red Roof Inn in Seattle, and the Best Western Dragon Gate Inn in Los Angeles. See http://trac.syr.edu/immigration/detention /trans.html.

30. For the legislative history and citations, see Stevens (2016, 468). On balance, immigration law since 1952 has increased the possibilities for people to become legal residents or US citizens while, since 1996, providing more triggers for their deportation and mandatory detention. A description of the bills increasing family-based legal residency can be found in Kandel (2018, 2). The 2000 Child Citizenship Act (Pub. L. 106–395) bestowed US citizenship automatically on foreign-born children. For children born prior to 1999, children adopted by parents who were US citizens were not citizens unless their parents applied for this by submitting a form to the US Citizenship and Immigration Services. As a result, adult foreign-born adopted children who grew up in the United States with parents who are US citizens are deported for minor crimes (Stevens 2017a). This is important because it shows policy preferences of loosening admissions criteria for those who are foreign-born are inconsistent with those implicit in the policies that benefit those who have a financial stake in private prisons.

31. "Payne, Jr. Leads Letter Urging Department of Homeland Security to Consider Ending Use of Private Prisons," October 6, 2016, https://payne.house .gov/press-release/payne-jr-leads-letter-urging-department-homeland-security -consider-ending-use-private. September 26, 2016, Letter from Senator Leahy (D-VT) to Jeh Johnson, signed by delegation of Senators. https://www.leahy .senate.gov/press/leahy-leads-senators-in-demanding-answers-from-dhs-on-use -of-private-prisons. The letter initiated by Senator Leahy (D-VT) states: "In addition to the record profits the private prison industry is reaping from American

taxpayers, we are troubled by the pivotal role the industry has played in institution-alizing mass family detention and increasing detention of asylum seekers. Starting in 2014, mass family detention facilities were erected in a matter of months, in order to detain children and mothers fleeing brutal violence and persecution in Central America. ICE managed to stand up these mass detention facilities with alarming speed because the nation's two largest private prison companies were ready and eager to make this happen through no-bid, fixed-price contracts that were negotiated without Congressional or public input, resulting in an enormous windfall to the prison industry."

32. "A smoking gun in the suspect's hands right after a murder strongly impli-cates the suspect, but the absence of such a gun does not exonerate a suspect" (Bennet 2010, 211–12; citing van Evera 1997).

33. "He creates surplus-value which, for the capitalist, has all the charms of a creation out of nothing. This portion of the working day, I name surplus labour-time, and to the labour expended during that time, I give the name of surplus labour" (Marx [1867] 1887, 152).

34. In the fall of 2019 Rep. Lauren Underwood (D-IL) invoked the suffering of immigrants to push through a Customs and Border Protection database that immigrant rights groups did not support and that would benefit contractors such as General Dynamics Information Technology (Washington and Stevens 2020).

35. The latter responded to communities refusing to pass bonds for new state and county prisons and jails by lobbying state legislatures and Congress to use their budgets for this purpose. Private prison firms gave more than $1.6 million to candidates running for Congress in 2018 (Goodkind 2018). For the influence of private prisons on legislative authorization of contracts, see Cohen (2015), Sul-livan (2010), Justice Policy Institute (2011), Hodai (2010) and West and Baumgart (2018).

36. Jacob Hacker and Paul Pierson describe the Republican Party's top-down ideological push for privatization by figures such as Karl Rove and Grover Norquist and also discuss the passage of laws for the benefit of small minorities at the expense of the US public, ranging from regressive tax policies to laws that benefit Big Pharma (Hacker and Pierson 2006). For more on interest-group lobbying, see Bartels (2018).

37. In a meta-review of research analyzing organization delegation, the author writes: "It is only in the case of privatization that most of the reviewed articles that present empirical evidence point to a decrease in performance" (Overman 2016, 1239). His review showed that "Privatization . . . has a plethora of negative political associations. . . . These negative associations are not counterbalanced by any evi-dence for positive political effects associated with privatization in the reviewed articles" (1251). None of the eight articles reviewed indicated a single positive outcome from privatization, in contrast with the three other forms of delegation Overman reviewed (1252). See also Sagers (2007).

38. Campaign Legal Center v. Federal Election Commission, Case 1:18-cv-00053-TSC, Complaint, Doc.1, 01/10/18 https://campaignlegal.org/sites/default/files/CLC%20v.%20FEC%20Complaint%20GEO%20Delay%20ECF%20No.%201.pdf. In 2016, the Campaign Legal Center (CLC) sued the FEC for failing to penalize GEO for its contribution. In 2018, a federal district court judge relied on precedents from administrative law and granted FEC's motion to dismiss. The court did not claim that GEO's contribution adhered to the letter of the law but reasoned the FEC had "prosecutorial discretion" and had not abused this (p. 158).

39. For instance, "1.102-2. Performance standards . . . (4) The Government must not hesitate to communicate with the commercial sector as early as possible in the acquisition cycle to help the Government determine the capabilities available in the commercial marketplace. The Government will maximize its use of commercial products and services in meeting Government requirements." https://www.acquisition.gov/content/part-1-federal-acquisition-regulations-system #id1617MD00E7S.

40. "Excessive reliance by executive agencies on sole-source contracts (or contracts with a limited number of sources) and cost-reimbursement contracts creates a risk that taxpayer funds will be spent on contracts that are wasteful, inefficient, subject to misuse, or otherwise not well designed to serve the needs of the federal government or the interests of the American taxpayer. Reports by agency inspectors general, the Government Accountability Office (GAO), and other independent reviewing bodies have shown that noncompetitive and cost-reimbursement contracts have been misused, resulting in wasted taxpayer resources, poor contractor performance, and inadequate accountability for results." "Memorandum of the President of the United States," March 4, 2009, 74 F.R. 9755. https://www.federalregister.gov/documents/2009/03/06/E9-4938/government-contracting.

41. 40 C.F.R. § 3.104-1 prohibits disclosing information related to government procurement, but it is impossible to enforce if the information is actually being generated by a firm bidding on the contract. A firm that exemplifies this pattern is General Dynamics Corporation (GD). In fulfilling its contract to meet the information technology needs of Citizenship and Immigration Services, GD is acquiring non-public data and policy priorities that give GD unique access to agency planning that is useful for shifting to provide a broad range of services. GD's market niche in this sector (Empower LLC 2018, 15, 30, 33, 35, 40, 66) incentivizes its campaign contributions to those who will support increasing deportation and detention operations and thus distorts government policies (Brown 2018). In the last decade it has substantially increased the share of its sales in information technology services to the federal government in general and Homeland Security in particular (General Dynamics 2018, 31, 73).

42. In 2015, a group of Democrats wrote a letter to the Office of Management and Budget requesting it oppose the thirty-four-thousand-bed mandate in its budget for 2016: "No other law enforcement agency is forced to operate

under a quota for the number of people it must keep in jail each day." https://
foster.house.gov/sites/foster.house.gov/files/FINAL%20Letter%20to%20OMB
%20on%20Detention%20Bed%20Mandate%20in%20the%20FY16%20Budget
%20Request.pdf.

43. In addition to the 2010 minimum bed mandate law, I have in mind the 1996
Illegal Immigration Reform and Immigrant Responsibility Act (IIRRA) and the
1996 Antiterrorism and Effective Death Penalty Act (AEDPA). https://www.law
.cornell.edu/wex/illegal_immigration_reform_and_immigration_responsibility
_act. IIRRA in particular was pushed through Congress on wheels greased by
Democrats in the leadership who wanted the anti-immigrant law to push back in
the 1996 reelection bid for the votes of Californians who had passed Proposition
187 and were feared to be amenable to nativist overtures by the Republican candidate Senator Bob Dole. Clinton's political team, led by Rahm Emmanuel, pushed
the enormous bill through Congress too quickly for staff and members to thwart
its harmful provisions, some of which were later overturned by courts.

44. Using data obtained from ICE through FOIA litigation, researchers from
the Sentencing Project in 2017 put the figure substantially higher, at 73 percent
(Gotsch and Basti 2018). For an interactive map of the facilities see Misra (2018).

45. The average cost of the three different rates for the privately run facilities
(SPCs, CDFs, DIGSAs) is $158.64 per day. The average cost of the county and
federal facilities (IGSAs and USMS IGAs, respectively) is just $94.86 per day.

46. Tylek noted the small group's mission was "eliminating the influence of
commercial interests in the criminal justice system . . . [and] expos[ing] the
harms caused by the commercialization of justice." (Tylek 2018a, 1)

47. "If the deal is approved, forty-seven state prison systems will now contract
with a telephone provider that is owned by one of just three national companies:
Securus, GTL, or CenturyLink" (Tylek 2018a, 2).

48. Tylek's second comment provides concrete evidence falsifying Securus's
denial of patent trolling: "This Statement also conflicts with a 2016 press release
in which the company threatened to "outspend" competitors on patent litigation"
(Tylek 2018b, 2). She also highlights the anti-competitive effects of Securus's frequent patent fights, and provides evidence refuting Securus's claim the transfer
will not reduce competitive bidding (Tylek 2018b, 2).

49. "Chairman Pai Statement on Decision by Inmate Calling Services Providers to Withdraw Merger Application," FCC, April 2, 2019, https://www.fcc.gov
/document/chairman-pai-statement-withdrawal-inmate-calling-merger.

50. Tylek writes: "Spurred by our comments and those of our advocacy partners,
the FCC demanded that Securus and ICSolutions turn over nearly one million
documents. Ultimately, the FCC agreed with our objections, citing the "arguments and evidence submitted by criminal justice advocates" in concluding that
this merger was not in the public interest. . . . We won a David-and-Goliath-type
victory against a massive prison profiteer. It's impossible to overstate the impact

that the Securus-ICSolution merger would have had on incarcerated people and their loved ones had it succeeded. Securus, whose exorbitant call rates have led the predatory industry, would have wielded its power to further increase call rates in its existing and acquired contracts—a cost that would have been borne disproportionately by women in communities of color and poverty (Bianca Tylek email to Listserve, April 3, 2019, on file with author).

51. Telephone interview, April 11, 2019, on file with author.

52. Tylek said she learned about the planned merger from a "footnote of a Moody's report behind a paywall." She then "saw merger application go to the FCC" and thought, "We can challenge it at the FCC. We have a good argument to challenge it on the merits, that it's against the public interest." Tylek had never done this before and had "no idea" if she would succeed. "We realized they had to go to the FCC. Every communications deal has to. . . . We knew there was going to be an approval period. We had never challenged a deal. Our legal summer interns were on it. . . . It's a new strategy hadn't tried before. We don't expect Securus to try to acquire more companies in the near term. This one took them for a spin." The work behind the challenge was done by her and a summer law school intern (telephone interview, April 11, 2019, on file with the author).

53. In response to a question about the origin of her interest in prisons, Tylek said she had been "concerned since childhood" and prisons had affected her "very personally" (telephone interview, April 11, 2019, on file with author).

54. Telephone interview, April 11, 2019, on file with author.

55. Forensic intelligence consists of "explaining that which was previously unseen; narrating locations of time and place that may seem distant to reveal their contiguities with injustice of this moment"; improving "access to information from government and elite institutions"; and finally, legal analyses that change the objects of their inquiries (Stevens 2015, 726). Tylek describes how in the wake of the Marshall op-ed, other groups also wrote comments: "Getting public attention in the media is important. . . . It gets people outraged, talking about it, and potentially recruits more folks to challenge the deal" (telephone interview, April 11, 2019, on file with author).

56. Telephone interview, April 11, 2019, on file with author.

57. Tylek explains that the FCC intervention was a one-off and that most of her work targets city councils and state legislatures to end the practice of charging prisoners for phone calls. Telephone interview, April 11, 2019, on file with author.

58. For a discussion of historical changes affecting workers choosing legal strategies of labor versus employment law, see Galvin (2019).

59. Wacquant acknowledges that *Punishing the Poor* is "one-sided and overly monolithic" (2009, xix). He notes in particular that he excludes from his analysis policy fights among elites as well as efforts at resistance from below. Wacquant's explicit dismissal of facts and dynamics inconsistent with his hypotheses means he is at best ignoring outliers that falsify not only his predictions but his worldview.

(There has been little scholarship on the effect of comments on rule making. It is not clear if Tylek's victory is an outlier or if the intervention is unusual.) By failing to consider any mechanisms and outcomes other than those of a neoliberal, racist state that is monolithically hostile to those who are not rich, White men, Wacquant loses valuable information about causal mechanisms other than those predicted by his theory. For data showing Americans' decreasing concern about immigrants' impact on the labor market inconsistent with Wacquant's scapegoating framework, see Rainie and Brown (2016).

60. The opening sentence of Sarah Staszak's book on the closing of courts to plaintiffs describes the 2011 Supreme Court decision overturning class certification by women employees suing Walmart (2014, 1). The rigidity of prison operations allowed plaintiffs in the ICE litigation to overcome the hurdles the precedent poses for groups that are not under custodial control of their employers.

61. The narrative of the litigation and its iterative revelations draws on documents obtained from ICE since 2010, including four thousand pages of correspondence between ICE and the private firms after the cases were filed. On file with author.

62. Portions of the litigation narrative are from Stevens (2018). For a legislative history of the laws, practices, and canons of interpretation behind the litigation, see Stevens (2016, Part III). For an overview of litigation against private prisons in general under the Trafficking Victims Protection Act, see Levy (2018). For case filing details in the litigation against private prisons contracting with ICE see Stevens (2017b). For related legal research on work programs under immigration laws in private prisons see Marion (2009), Sinha (2014), and Garfinkel (2017).

63. Key filings in these lawsuits and many of the contracts are available at "Private Prison Source Material and Litigation," https://deportationresearchclinic.org. Key legal arguments extracted from these cases appear in a 2018 law review article (Stevens 2018).

64. Unjust enrichment is a common law doctrine that is incorporated into state case law and permits suit for civil damages if a party is found to have induced the transfer of value without payment.

65. In addition, the lawsuits in the Eleventh and Fifth Circuits include only the TVPA and unjust enrichment claims. The lawsuit with the most charges is *Owino v. CoreCivic*. For an overview of the litigation, see Stevens (2018). Filings are periodically updated on the source materials website for the Deportation Research Clinic, https://www.deportationresearchclinic.org/.

66. The variation in charges reflects variation in the work programs, state laws and precedents, and attorney litigation strategies.

67. Menocal v. GEO Group, Inc., 113 F. Supp. 3d 1125, 1132 (D. Colo. 2015). According to the Federal Rules of Civil Procedure, plaintiffs may appeal the dismissal of the CMWO after the trial on the two other claims.

68. Kane's order highlighted the defendants' reliance on the holding in *United States v. Kozminski*, which is limited to the Thirteenth Amendment, and, unlike the TVPA, prohibits only "physical or legal, as opposed to psychological, coercion." The court also rejected the inferences the defendants drew from *Channer v. Hall*, a decision the court understood to hold that threats of solitary confinement used to compel an immigration detainee to perform kitchen work do not constitute a violation of the Thirteenth Amendment's prohibition against involuntary servitude (*Menocal*, 113 F. Supp. 3d at 1132). See also Channer v. Hall, 112 F.3d 214,219 (5th Cir. 1997), holding "that the federal government is entitled to require a communal contribution by an INS detainee in the form of housekeeping tasks, and that Channer's kitchen service, for which he was paid, did not violate the Thirteenth Amendment's prohibition of involuntary servitude." (*Menocal v. GEO Group, Inc.*, 113 F. Supp. 3d at 1125).

69. In one of its filings CoreCivic itself conceded that Congress passed 18 U.S.C. § 1589 to make it easier to sue and convict individuals for psychological and not just physical coercion. "CoreCivic does not disagree that Congress enacted § 1589 in response to Kozminski, or that § 1589(a)(4) includes a psychological-coercion component" (Case 4:18-cv-00070-CDL Document 37 Filed 08/02/18, Reply in Support of Defendant Motion to Dismiss).

70. In rejecting the CMWO claim, Kane cited a Fifth Circuit decision that came out of a Fair Labor Standards Act (federal) minimum wage claim against then Immigration and Naturalization Service, *Alvarado*, 902 F. 2d at 396, internal citation omitted. However, three other judges for four additional cases have noted that *Alvarado* is not precedential for the Ninth Circuit and have denied motions to dismiss the minimum wage claims. See orders for Nwauzor, et al. v. The GEO Group, Inc., 3:17-cv-05769 (2017); State of Wash. v. The GEO Group, Inc., 17-2-11422-2 (2017); Sylvester Owino and Jonathan Gomez et al. v. CoreCivic, case no. 3:17-cv-01112-jls-nls; and Raul Novoa, et al. v. The GEO Group, Inc., 5:17-cv-02514 (2018).

71. GEO claimed that undocumented immigrants are not eligible for protections under the SCA. Judge Kane's order, however, found that the SCA mandates the contractor (or subcontractor) to provide fringe benefits beyond those mandated by the state or federal minimum wage laws.

72. *Menocal*, 113 F. Supp. 3d at 1125.

73. "Motion for Class Certification under Rule 23(b)(3) and appointment of Class Counsel under Rule 23(g)," Doc. 49, No. 14-CV-02887-JLK, May 6, 2016.

74. Document 57, at 2.

75. Document 57, at 2.

76. Appellate Case: 17-1125 Document: 01019942810. Here, the claims of all the class members—including the representatives—share the same theory: that GEO knowingly obtained class members' labor by means of the Sanitation Policy, which threatened—or was intended to cause them to believe they would suffer.

77. The advertisement to which the parties stipulated begins: "If you were detained at GEO's Detention Facility in Aurora, Colorado, between October 22, 2004 and October 22, 2014, please read this notice. A class action lawsuit may affect your right." Case 1:14-cv-02887-JLK-MEH Document 162-1 Filed 01/11/19. EXHIBIT A Proposed Announcement.

78. This argument could fail because the FLSA and the SCA obligate the federal government and contractors. Congress expressly foreclosed one employer evading responsibility because its contractor (or subcontractor) was violating these wage laws (Stevens 2016, 444–48).

79. See, e.g., email from GEO law firm Holland and Knight to ICE, "Subject: Great talking to you—Menocal v. GEO Items," April 10, 2017, "It was great talking to you and catching up with you. You are a good man—there is a lot going on in Menocal, and any help and guidance ICE can provide before Thursday would be immensely helpful." See https://deportationresearchclinic.org/04-10-2017GEOEmail_ICE -2018-ICLI-00052.pdf, release March 8, 2019, p. 2499; on February 16, 2018, Holland and Knight shared with ICE a draft of their en banc appeal, *id.*, 863.

80. In an email dated February 15, 2018, with the subject heading "RE: Menocal—10th Cir Affirms class cert," an ICE official writes: "GEO's general counsel has been calling Mike Davis and their executives have also reached out to Tom Homan [ICE, Acting Director] asking us to intervene in the VWP litigation." See https://deportationresearchclinic.org/02-16-2018GEOEmail_ICE-2018-ICLI -00052.pdf, pp. 5163–64.The names of the sender and recipient are redacted.

81. In a letter dated February 14, 2018, GEO requested $2,057,000 Equitable Adjustment to its contract for legal fees anticipated in the Menocal litigation. See https://deportationresearchclinic.org/GEO_2-14-2018_ICLI00052.pdf, p. 2752.

82. Letter from Peter Edge, Homeland Security Investigations, to George Zoley, CEO/President, GEO, July 9, 2018. See https://deportationresearchclinic .org/DenialRequestEquitableAdjustmentContract3999-END_ICE-2018-ICLI -00052.pdf, p. 6062.

83. Wilhelm Barrientos et al. v. CoreCivic, Inc., 4:18-cv-00070 (CDL), Doc. 38, 8/17/2018.

84. Shoaib Ahmed, et al. v. CoreCivic, Inc., Eleventh Cir.,18-15081, solicitor general, amicus brief, filed April 1, 2019.This is the same case as cited in note 83, but with a different lead plaintiff.

85. "As the district court correctly recognized, there is no basis for reading this broad provision to categorically exclude from its coverage facilities operated by private entities that contract or subcontract to provide immigration detention services to the federal government, particularly in light of Congress's repeated efforts to ensure that federal contractors do not provide goods and services to the government through reliance on forced labor. . . . The TVPA, however, does not bar a facility from operating the work program that Congress has authorized for aliens held in immigration detention." *Id.*, 5

86. The GEO Group, Inc.'s Petition for Permission to Appeal Class Certification, *Menocal v. GEO Grp., Inc.*, No. 1:14-cv-02887 (D. Colo. Mar. 13, 2017), at 30.

87. ICE PBNDS § 3.1 states: "Encouraging others to participate in a work stoppage" may lead to "[d]isciplinary segregation up to 30 days." However, this and other standards are based on the American Correctional Association rules, developed for those punished for a crime. The standard conflicts with other laws and Federal Acquisition Rules and if used against those in ICE custody might be subject to litigation for these violations.

88. Robbins (1985, 77) writes, "In Jefferson County, Colorado, for example, the voters twice rejected a jail-bond issue before E.F. Hutton underwrote a $30 million issue for private jail construction."

89. An additional motive for privatization was the desire to avoid liability. E.F. Hutton informed potential investors: "A final—and significant—anticipated benefit of privatization is decreased liability of the government in lawsuits that are brought by inmates and prison employees" (Robbins 1985, 74). Robbins points out later that courts soundly rejected this analysis (84–87).

REFERENCES

Abramitzky, Ran, and Leah Boustan. 2017. "Immigration in American Economic History." *Journal of Economic Literature* 55 (4): 1311–45.

Ackerman, Spencer. 2019. "ICE Is Detaining 50,000 People, an All-Time High." *Daily Beast*, March 9. https://www.thedailybeast.com/ice-is-detaining -50000-people-a-new-all-time-high.

Aleaziz, Hamid. 2019. "More Than 52,000 People Are Now Being Detained by ICE, an Apparent All-Time High," *BuzzFeed.* May 20. https://www.buzzfeed news.com/article/hamedaleaziz/ice-detention-record-immigrants-border.

Alexander, Michelle. 2012. *The New Jim Crow: Mass Incarceration in the Age of Colorblindness.* New York: The New Press, 2012.

Alvarez, Priscilla 2017 "What the Spike in Immigration Arrests Might Mean for Detention Centers," *Atlantic*, May 20. https://www.theatlantic.com/politics /archive/2017/05/ice-arrests-increase-nearly-forty-percent/527427/.

American Correctional Association. 2004. *Performance-Based Standards for Adult Local Detention Facilities.* Lanham, MD: Department of Standards and Accreditation, 4-ALDF-5C-06, 5C-08, 5C-11(M), 6B-02 (4th ed.)

Balderrama, Francisco E., and Raymond Rodríguez. 2006. *Decade of Betrayal: Mexican Repatriation in the 1930s.* Albuquerque: University of New Mexico Press.

Bartels, Larry. 2018. Unequal Democracy: The Political Economy of the New Gilded Age. New York: Russel Sage Foundation.

Becarra, Xavier. 2019. "Immigration Detention in California, February 2019." California Department of Justice. https://oag.ca.gov/sites/all/files/agweb/pdfs/publications/immigration-detention-2019.pdf.

Bennett, Andrew. 2010. "Process Tracing and Causal Inference." In *Rethinking Social Inquiry: Diverse Tools, Shared Standards*, edited by Henry Brady and David Collier, 207–20. Lanham, MD: Rowman & Littlefield.

Berry, Ellen, Robert Nelson, and Laura Beth Nielsen (2017) *Rights on Trial: How Workplace Discrimination Law Perpetuates Inequality*. Chicago: University of Chicago Press.

Brown, Daniel. 2018. "These Are the 20 Defense Companies Donating the Most Money to American Politicians, *Business Insider*, October 24. https://www.businessinsider.com/the-top-20-defense-companies-donating-the-most-cash-to-us-politicians-2017-11/?op=1.

Brown, Wendy. 2005. *Edgework*. Princeton, NJ: Princeton University Press.

———. 2010. *Walled States, Waning Sovereignty*. London: Verso.

———. 2015. *Undoing the Demos: Neoliberalism's Stealth Revolution*. Cambridge, MA: MIT Press.

Cepala, Zuzana. 2019. "Fact Sheet: U.S. Asylum Process." National Immigration Forum, https://immigrationforum.org/article/fact-sheet-u-s-asylum-process/.

Cohen, Michael. 2015. "How For-Profit Prisons Have Become the Biggest Lobby No One Is Talking About," *Washington Post*, April 28. https://www.washingtonpost.com/posteverything/wp/2015/04/28/how-for-profit-prisons-have-become-the-biggest-lobby-no-one-is-talking-about/.

Dickerson, Caitlin. 2017. "Trump Plan Would Curtail Protections for Detained Immigrants," *New York Times*, April 13. https://www.nytimes.com/2017/04/13/us/detained-immigrants-may-face-harsher-conditions-under-trump.html/.

Dominguez, Lee, Adrienne Lee, Elizabeth Leiserso. 2016. "U.S. Detention and Removal of Asylum Seekers: An International Human Rights Law Analysis," Allard K. Lowenstein International Human Rights Clinic Yale Law School. https://law.yale.edu/system/files/area/center/schell/human_rights_first_-_immigration_detention_-_final_-_20160620_for_publication.pdf.

Du Bois, W. E. B. 1910. "Reconstruction and Its Benefits," *American Historical Review* 15: 781–99.

Elwell, Craig. 2014. "Inflation and the Real Minimum Wage: A Fact Sheet," Congressional Research Service, Washington, DC. https://fas.org/sgp/crs/misc/R42973.pdf.

Empower LLC. 2018. "Who's Behind ICE: The Tech and Data Companies Fueling Deportations." https://mijente.net/wp-content/uploads/2018/10/WHO%E2%80%99S-BEHIND-ICE_-The-Tech-and-Data-Companies-Fueling-Deportations-_v1.pdf.

Fang, Lee. 2013. "How Private Prisons Game the Immigration System," *The Nation*, February 27, https://www.thenation.com/article/how-private -prisons-game-immigration-system/.

Forman, James Jr. 2012. "Racial Critiques of Mass Incarceration: Beyond the New Jim Crow." *New York University Law Review* 87: 101–46.

Galvin, Daniel. 2019. "From Labor Law to Employment Law: The Changing Politics of Workers' Rights." *Studies in American Political Development* 33: 50–86

Garfinkel, S. H. 2017. The Voluntary Work Program: Expanding Labor Laws to Protect Detained Immigrant Workers. *Case W. Res. L. Rev.*, 67: 1287.

Garland, David. 2002. *The Culture of Control: Crime and Social Order in Contemporary Society*. Chicago: University of Chicago Press

General Dynamics. 2018. Annual Report. https://s22.q4cdn.com/891946778 /files/doc_financials/2019/GD-2018-Annual-Report_708854_002_Web _CLEAN.PDF.

Glawe, Justin. 2016. "Immigration Detention Facilities Are Allegedly Denying Inmates Humane Conditions, *VICE*, November 25. https://www.vice.com/en _us/article/avajjj/immigration-detention-facilities-are-allegedly-denying -inmates-humane-conditions.

Goodkind, Nancy. 2018. "ICE Used Taxpayer Money to Pay Private Prisons $800 Million to Detain Migrants in 2018," *Newsweek*, December 12. https:// www.newsweek.com/ice-trump-migrants-800-million-private-prisons -asylum-seekers-1272804.

Gotsch, Kara, and Vinay Basti. 2018 "Capitalizing on Mass Incarceration: U.S. Growth in Private Prisons," Sentencing Project. https://www.sentencing project.org/publications/capitalizing-on-mass-incarceration-u-s-growth-in -private-prisons/.

Gottschalk, Marie. 2016. *Caught: The Prison State and the Lockdown of American Politics*. Princeton, NJ: Princeton University Press.

Greenwold, Robert. 2017. "A Look Inside Our Abusive Immigrant Prisons," *The Nation*, October 18. https://www.thenation.com/article/a-look-inside-our -abusive-immigrant-prisons/.

Hacker, Jacob, and Paul Pierson. 2006. *Off Center: The Republican Revolution and the Erosion of American Democracy*. New Haven, CT: Yale University Press.

Hatton, Erin. 2018. "When Work Is Punishment: Penal Subjectivities in Punitive Labor Regimes," *Punishment & Society* 20: 174–91.

Hill, Claire, and Richard Painter, "Compromised Fiduciaries: Conflicts of Interest in Government and Business," *Minnesota Law Review* 95, no. 5: 1637–91.

Hodai, Beau. 2010. Corporate Con Game: How the Private Prison Industry Helped Shape Arizona's Anti-immigrant Law. *In These Times*, June 21. http://inthesetimes.com/article/6084/corporate_con_game.

Holpuch, Amanda. 2018. "Private Prison Companies Served with Lawsuits over Using Detainee Labor," *The Guardian*, November 25. https://www .theguardian.com/us-news/2018/nov/25/private-prison-companies-served -with-lawsuits-over-usng-detainee-labor.

Jan, Tracy. 2018. "These GOP Lawmakers Say It's Okay for Imprisoned Immigrants to Work for a $1 a Day." *Washington Post*, March 16. https://www .washingtonpost.com/news/wonk/wp/2018/03/16/republican-congressmen -defend-1-a-day-wage-for-immigrant-detainees-who-work-in-private -prisons/.

Justice Policy Institute. 2011. "Gaming the System: How the Political Strategies of Private Prison Companies Promote Ineffective Incarceration Policies, June. http://www.justicepolicy.org/uploads/justicepolicy/documents/gaming _the_system.pdf.

Kandel, William. 2018 "U.S. Family-Based Immigration Policy," Congressional Research Service, February 9. https://fas.org/sgp/crs/homesec/R43145.pdf.

Kang, Susan. 2009. "Forcing Prison Labor: International Labor Standards, Human Rights and the Privatization of Prison Labor in the Contemporary United States." *New Political Science* 31: 137–61.

Katzenstein, Mary. 2012. "Neoliberalism, Race, and the American Welfare State: A Discussion of Joe Soss, Richard C. Fording, and Sanford F. Schram's Disciplining the Poor: Neoliberal Paternalism and the Persistent Power of Race." *Perspectives on Politics* 10: 989–92.

Lacey, Nicola. 2008. *The Prisoner's Dilemma: Political Economy and Punishment in Contemporary Democracies*. Cambridge: Cambridge University Press.

Lehman, Susan. 1992. "Waiting." *New Yorker*, 68 (30): 23.

Levy, Alexandra. 2018. "Fact Sheet: Human Trafficking & Forced Labor in For-Profit Detention Facilities," The Human Trafficking Legal Center; 2018. http://www.htlegalcenter.org/wp-content/uploads/Human-Trafficking -Forced-Labor-in-For-Profit-Detention-Facilities.pdf.

Linthicum, Kate. 2015. "Private Prison Companies Profit from Immigration Detention Boom," *Los Angeles Times*, April 24. http://www.latimes.com /local/california/la-me-immigrant-detention-20150424-story.html.

Marion, Ryan. 2009. "Prisoners for Sale: Making the Thirteenth Amendment Case against State Private Prison Contracts," *William and Mary Bill of Rights Journal* 13: 213–47.

Marx, Karl. (1867) 1887. *Capital: A Critical Analysis of Capitalist Production*. Vol. 1. Translated by Samuel Moore and Aveling. London: Swan Sonnenschein, Lowery.

McLennan, Rebecca. 2008. *The Crisis of Imprisonment: Protest, Politics, and the Making of the American Penal State, 1776–1941*. Cambridge: Cambridge University Press.

Melossi, Dario. 1978. "Review of Rusche and Kirschheimer's *Punishment and Social Structure.*" *Crime and Social Justice* 9: 73–85.

Melossi, Dario, and Massimo Pavarini. 1981. *The Prison and the Factory.* Totowa, NJ, Barnes and Noble.

Michaels, Jon. 2010. "Deputizing Homeland Security," *Texas Law Review* 88: 1435–74.

Misra, Tanvi. 2018. "Where Cities Help Detain Immigrants," City Lab, July 10. https://www.citylab.com/equity/2018/07/where-cities-help-detain -immigrants-mapped/563531.

Moore, Patricia Hatamyar. 2015. "The Civil Caseload of the Federal District Courts," *University of Illinois Law Review* (April 30): 1177–238.

New York Times. 1941. "Detainee Coined for Use," July 2: L13.

Olsen, Lise. 2017. "Hundreds of Citizens End Up in Deportation Proceedings Each Year, Immigration Court Data Shows," *Houston Chronicle*, July 30. http://www.houstonchronicle.com/news/houston-texas/houston/article /Hundreds-of-citizens-end-up-in-deportation-11719324.php.

Overman, Sjors. 2016. "Great Expectations of Public Service Delegation: A Systematic Review." *Public Management Review* 18: 123–262.

Painter, Richard. 2009. "Bailouts: An Essay on Conflicts of Interest and Ethics When Government Pays the Tab," *McGeorge Law Review* 4: 131–60.

Phillips, Kristin. 2017. "Thousands of ICE Detainees Claim They Were Forced into Labor," *Washington Post*, March 5. https://www.washingtonpost.com /news/post-nation/wp/2017/03/05/thousands-of-ice-detainees-claim-they -were-forced-into-labor-a-violation-of-anti-slavery-laws/?utm_term =.0f654ce70b2a.

Popper, Karl. (1934) 1959. *The Logic of Scientific Discovery.* London: Hutchinson.

———. (1948) 1972. "Prediction and Prophecy in the Social Sciences." In *Conjectures and Refutations*, 336–46. London: Routledge and Kegan Paul.

Rainie, Lee, and Anna Brown. 2016. "Americans Less Concerned Than a Decade Ago over Immigrants' Impact on Workforce." Pew Research Center, October 7. http://www.pewresearch.org/fact-tank/2016/10/07/americans -less-concerned-than-a-decade-ago-over-immigrants-impact-on-workforce/.

Ramirez, Mary. 2012. "Criminal Affirmance: Going beyond the Deterrence Paradigm to Examine the Social Meaning of Declining Prosecution of Elite Crime," *Connecticut Law Review*, 43: 865–931.

Raskin, A. H. 1950. "New Role for Ellis Island," *New York Times*, November 12, 20, available via *New York Times* online archive.

Redmon, Jeremy. 2018. "ICE, GEO Weigh Expanding Immigration Detention Center in South Georgia," *Atlanta Journal Constitution*, July 18, https:// www.ajc.com/news/state--regional-govt--politics/ice-geo-weigh-expanding -immigration-detention-center-south-georgia /AehVKtuHbFigT9POmeN8AJ/.

Regester, Yasmine. 2010. "Old Jail to become For-Profit Detention Center," *Carolina Peacemaker*, August 11. https://beyondcagesandwalls.blogspot.com /2010/08/old-jail-to-become-for-profit-detention.html.

Robbins, Ira. 1985. Testimony. "Privatization of Correction," House Rept. House Judiciary Subcommittee on Courts, Civil Liberties and the Administration of Justice, 99th Congress, November 13, 1985 and March 18, 1986, H-521-32. Washington, DC: GPO.

Rusche, Georg and Otto Kirchheimer. 1939. *Punishment and Social Structure*. New York: Columbia University Press.

Sagers, Chris. 2007. "The Myth of 'Privatization.'" *Administrative Law Review*, 59: 37–78.

Simon, Jonathan. 1998. "Refugees in a Carceral Age: The Rebirth of Immigration Prisons in the United States." *Public Culture* 10 (3): 577–607.

Sinha, Anita. 2015. "Slavery by Another Name: Voluntary Immigrant Detainee Labor and the Thirteenth Amendment," *Stanford Journal of Civil Rights & Civil Liberties*, 11, 1–44.

Soss, Joe, Fording, Richard, and Sanford Schram. 2011. *Disciplining the Poor: Neoliberal Paternalism and the Persistent Power of Race*. Chicago: University of Chicago.

Staszak, Sarah. 2014. *No Day in Court: Access to Justice and the Politics of Judicial Retrenchment*. Oxford University Press.

Stevens, Jacqueline. 2010. *States without Nations: Citizenship for Mortals*. New York: Columbia University Press.

——. 2011. US Government Unlawfully Detaining and Deporting US Citizens as Aliens, *Virginia Journal of Social Policy and the Law* 18: 629–30.

——. 2015. "Forensic Intelligence and the Deportation Research Clinic: Toward a New Paradigm." *Perspectives on Politics* 13: 722–38.

——. 2016. "One Dollar per Day: The Slaving Wages of Immigration Jail, 1943 to Present." *Georgetown Immigration Law Journal* 29: 391–500.

——. 2017a. "The Alien Who Is a Citizen." In *Citizenship in Question: Evidentiary Birthright and Statelessness*, ed. Benjamin Lawrance and Jacqueline Stevens. Durham, NC: Duke University Press.

——. 2017b. "United States Citizens in Deportation Proceedings, Immigration Court "Code 54" Adjournments, January 1, 2011 to June 9, 2017, posted July 31, http://deportationresearchclinic.org/USCData.html.

——. 2018. "One Dollar Per Day: A Note on Recent Forced Labor and Dollar-Per-Day Wages in Private Prisons Holding People under Immigration Law." *Valparaiso University Law Review* 52: 343–71.

——. 2019. "New FOIA Release—Butler County ICE Detainees Paid in Coffee Packets, ICE Punishes Hunger Strikers in Tacoma," *States without Nations* (blog), March 25. http://stateswithoutnations.blogspot.com/2019/03/new -foia-release-butler-county-ice.html.

Sullivan, Laura. 2010. "Prison Economics Help Drive Arizona Immigration Law," National Public Radio, October 28. http://www.npr.org/2010/10/28 /130833741/pris-on-economics-help-drive-ariz-immigration-law.

Teachout, Zephyr. 2014. *Corruption in America*. Cambridge, MA: Harvard University Press.

Templin, Benjamin. 2010. "The Government Shareholder: Regulating Public Ownership of Private Enterprise," *Administrative Law Review* 62: 1127–216.

Torrey, Philip. 2015. "Rethinking Immigration's Mandatory Detention Regime: Politics, Profit, and the Meaning of 'Custody.'" *University of Michigan Journal of Law Reform* 48: 879–927.

Tylek, Bianca. 2018a. Comment for WC Docket No.18-193, Application for Transfer of Control of Inmate Calling Solutions to Securus Technologies, Inc., July 16, 2018, https://ecfsapi.fcc.gov/file/10717225630127/2018.07.16%20-%20 Corrections%20Accountability%20Project%2018-193%20Comment%20.pdf.

———. 2018b. Ex Parte Comment for WC Docket No. 18-193, Application for Transfer of Control of Inmate Calling Solutions to Securus Technologies, Inc., July 30, 2018. https://ecfsapi.fcc.gov/file/10731500622310/2018.07.30 %20-%20FCC%20Reply%20Comment%20vFinal.pdf.

Urbina, Ian. 2014. "Using Jailed Migrants as a Pool of Cheap Labor," *New York Times*, May 24, A1.

US Courts. 2019. Civil Litigation, Federal Judicial Caseload Statistics. March 31, https://www.uscourts.gov/statistics/table/c-4/federal-judicial -caseload-statistics/2019/03/31.

US Department of Homeland Security, Office of the Secretary. 2019. Budget Justification, fiscal year 2019. https://www.dhs.gov/sites/default/files /publications/Office%20of%20the%20Secretary%20and%20Executive %20Management.pdf.

US Department of Justice, Office of Inspector General. 2016. https://oig.justice .gov/reports/2016/e1606.pdf.

US Department of State. 1915. *Report of the Secretary of Labor*. Available via Proquest.

US General Accountability Office. 2008. Defense Contracting: Additional Personal Conflict of Interest Safeguards Needed for Certain DOD Contractor Employees. https://www.gao.gov/new.items/d08169.pdf

US House Judiciary Subcommittee on Courts, Civil Liberties the Administration of Justice, "Privatization of Correction," House Rept. House Judiciary Subcommittee on Courts, Civil Liberties, and the Administration of Justice, 99th Congress, November 13, 1985, and March 18, 1986, H-521-32. Washington, D.C.: GPO.

US Immigration and Customs Enforcement. 2018. *ICE Enforcement and Removal Operations Report*. https://www.ice.gov/doclib/about/offices/ero /pdf/eroFY2018Report.pdf.

US Immigration and Customs Enforcement, Office of Inspector General. 2017. *Concerns about ICE Detainee Treatment and Care at Detention Facilities,* https://www.oig.dhs.gov/sites/default/files/assets/2017-12/OIG-18-32 -Dec17.pdf.

Van Evera, Stephen. 1997. *Guide to Methods for Students of Political Science.* Ithaca, NY: Cornell University Press.

Wacquant, Loïc. 2001. "The Penalisation of Poverty and the Rise of Neo-Liberalism," *European Journal on Criminal Policy and Research* 9: 401–12.

———. 2009. *Punishing the Poor: The Neoliberal Government of Social Insecurity.* Durham, NC: Duke University Press.

Washington, John, and Jacqueline Stevens. 2020. "Democratic Representative Pushed to Create a Massive Migrant Health Database That No One Wants," *The Intercept,* January 4. https://theintercept.com/2020/01/04/border -patrol-cbp-migrant-health-database/.

West, Geoff, and Alex Baumgart. 2018. "'Zero-tolerance' Immigration Policy is Big Money for Contractors, Nonprofits," June 21. https://www.opensecrets.org /news/2018/06/zero-tolerance-immigration-is-big-money-for-contractors -nonprofits/.

Western, Bruce. 2006. *Punishment and Inequality in America.* New York: Russell Sage.

Wilsher, Daniel. 2011. *Immigration Detention: Law, History, Politics.* Cambridge: Cambridge University Press.

4 The Carceral Labor Continuum

BEYOND THE PRISON LABOR/FREE LABOR DIVIDE

Noah D. Zatz

Prison labor is persistently scandalous. Incarcerated workers are at once sharply distinguished from "free labor" by their incarceration and yet intertwined with it through their work. For incarcerated workers to receive the pay, protections, and status accorded to free citizen-workers would violate the political demand of "less eligibility" (Melossi 2003); that principle requires that the state impose on those suffering criminal punishment conditions that visibly and viscerally convey degradation relative to those marked as "law abiding." Yet imposing that degradation also threatens free labor (McLennan 2008). It creates an alternative source of cheap, subordinated labor power, and it contradicts the notion that productive work engenders claims to citizenship.

To contain this scandal, the United States constructed a legal and institutional framework for prison labor that purported to carve "a wide moat between the sphere of the market and that of legal punishment" (McLennan 2008, 5). This framework simultaneously denies that incarcerated workers are workers at all (Zatz 2008) and constrains their use as economic substitutes for free labor (McLennan 2008; Thompson 2011).

This settlement has always been incomplete and potentially unstable. Incarceration without work, or productive work, invites its own less-eligibility challenges to state-supported "idleness" (McLennan 2008; McBride 2007). Penal institutions and private capital alike have financial interests in tapping this captive labor pool. Recent decades have laid the groundwork for a resurgence in prison labor (Thompson 2011; Weiss 2001). Simultaneously, movements against contemporary racialized mass incarceration, including those led by incarcerated people claiming the mantle and tactics of striking workers (Bonsu 2017), have treated prison labor as symptomatic of the "New Jim Crow" (Alexander 2012), a broader betrayal of freedom's promise.

This chapter questions a constant in the preceding sketch: the sharp distinction between prison labor and the free labor market outside. In contrast, I argue for a more capacious conception of "carceral labor" that sweeps in an array of work arrangements directly structured by the state's power to incarcerate. Prison labor—work performed by those currently incarcerated—is carceral labor of a distinct and important kind. Nonetheless, scholars and critics rightly speak of a "carceral state" anchored by penal incarceration but reaching far beyond it (Beckett and Murakawa 2012; Lynch 2012). So, too, should we situate prison labor within a more capacious analysis of how criminal law shapes and compels contemporary work, including ways that are integrated with that abstraction "the labor market," not fundamentally apart from or opposed to it.

The threat of state violence can hover over a worker's head even if the worker is not in state custody, let alone custody as punishment for a crime. For instance, a traffic ticket spawns fines and fees, and the debtor unable to pay gets a choice: go to jail or "work off" the debt doing "community service" (Herrera et al. 2019). Or a "diversion" program allows a defendant to avoid prosecution, conviction, or punishment in exchange for compliant participation in "services" offered as an alternative (McLeod 2012), such as working at a poultry processing plant as a purported method of drug rehabilitation (Harris and Walter 2017). Or a parent who owes child support faces prosecution for quitting a job or remaining jobless (Zatz 2016).

Such phenomena arise at a moment when the carceral state itself is changing. After decades of growth, incarceration rates have leveled off or even declined. In tandem, however, state capacity has expanded for other forms of surveillance and control through diversion, probation, debt, and other techniques of supervision "in the community" (Phelps 2016; Lynch 2012). Enforcing work often appears as a means to impose accountability without incarceration. This dovetails with labor's centrality to the increasingly prominent "reentry movement" (Petersilia 2003; Travis 2005), which not only focuses on employment for formerly incarcerated or convicted people but also, with that in mind, constructs institutional continuity between inside and out (Taliaferro, Pham, and Cielinski 2016). Meanwhile, employers seek to pay less and control more. They do so at a time when nationalist mobilizations in the United States against both immigration and trade make employers more dependent on existing domestic workforces. All this occurs while organized labor—which drove what sequestration of prison labor did occur (Thompson 2011; McLennan 2008)—is in decline, state strategies of labor discipline are building on their triumph in welfare reform (Mead 2011), and the intertwined racist libels of laziness and criminality are as vital as ever.

Much is at stake in breaching the institutional separation between punishment and the economy. That separation lies at the foundation of "neoliberal penality" (Harcourt 2011), a specific iteration of the laissez-faire notion of a self-regulating economy operating on its inner market logic apart from state action (Polanyi 2001). Although scholars have long conceptualized incarceration as a regulator of total labor supply and as a means to manage or exploit unemployment (Rusche and Kirchheimer 1939; Wacquant 2009; Gilmore 2007; Western and Beckett 1999; cf. Parker in this volume), its capacity for forced labor has been assumed to operate outside the labor market and *inside* the prison (Melossi 2003). Carceral labor *outside* the prison suggests a need to revise accounts of how the criminal legal system operates as a labor market institution (Zatz 2020). Vice versa, it suggests the potential for critical accounts of "free labor" to go beyond attention to how markets are structured by criminal enforcement of property law (Harcourt 2011; Hale 1923)—which underwrite the "economic" pressure to "work or starve"—to more direct criminal regulation of work behavior (cf. Hatton 2018b). Such developments offer potentially powerful weapons for suppressing labor standards and labor movement. However, by breaching the prison's stark separation between "criminal" and "worker," they also offer a potential material basis for new solidarities between the subjects of criminal law and the subjects of labor markets, now rendered together as subjected to a new, more integrated racialized political economy.

Carceral labor outside the prison may be new, but it is not novel. This chapter first motivates its contemporary account by reprising briefly the "old" Jim Crow era's admixture of criminal law and labor exploitation structured by and in the service of white supremacy. Convict leasing and chain gang systems were integrated with peonage, vagrancy laws, and other criminal legal regulation of work (Du Bois 1935; Hartman 1997; Haley 2016; Lichtenstein 1996; Daniel 1972; Blackmon 2008; Goluboff 2007; Childs 2015). These provide a foil for today's carceral work, even though critical scholarship of contemporary racialized mass incarceration tends to sequester that legacy in today's prisons (Davis 2000; Childs 2015; Alexander 2012). I then sketch the specific legal and institutional basis for the post–New Deal sequestration of carceral work in prisons and the further separation of that prison labor from the conventional labor market. Both are grounded in a hierarchical distinction between the citizen-subjects of "free labor" and the degraded threat of incarcerated people.

This separation, however, has always been incomplete. The reasons arise both from fissures within "free labor" and from the fallacy of treating non-market institutions as noneconomic. Conversely, the boundary between incarceration and freedom is itself indistinct. For this reason, parole and work release provide sites to study how carceral work moves beyond incarceration. Turning to criminal legal debt then shows how carceral work can operate without any prior sentence of incarceration. This illustrates how, once viewed through the lens of carceral labor beyond the prison, what is often termed the "new debtors' prison" may be more fully understood as a "new peonage." Both parole and criminal legal debt suggest how keystones of progressive criminal justice reform—"reentry" policy and "alternatives to incarceration"—may accelerate carceral labor beyond the prison. They may do so uncritically just insofar as such efforts are viewed exclusively through the lens of criminal justice policy and not as forms of labor market regulation. By judging working conditions relative to the brutality of incarceration, and by treating work as an unalloyed good independent of its conditions, the door opens to new forms of labor subordination that reproduce the dilemmas and hierarchies of prison labor on a grander scale.

JIM CROW CARCERAL LABOR INSIDE AND OUTSIDE CUSTODIAL CRIMINAL SENTENCES

The Jim Crow era both stimulates imagination of grim possibility and operates as a touchstone for critical analysis of contemporary configurations of race, labor, and state power. In the period stretching from the abolition of chattel slavery to World War II, the Southern race/labor system was transformed into a regime often referred to as "neoslavery" for African Americans (Du Bois 1935; Hartman 1997; Blackmon 2008; Childs 2015; Haley 2016). Rather than any single practice, there was an interlocking, evolving set of practices that subjected Black workers to violent exploitation benefiting a range of white actors and upholding white supremacy more generally.

The best-known elements of Jim Crow carceral labor were the convict lease and the chain gang, both forms of custodial "hard labor" pursuant to a criminal sentence. As such, they have been incorporated into the history of punishment in the United States generally (McLennan 2008) and analyzed as a prehistory of contemporary mass incarceration specifically (Davis 2000; Childs 2015; Alexander 2012). The early twentieth century saw road work on the chain gang succeed the convict lease throughout much of the South (Lichtenstein 1996; Blackmon 2008). This substituted public for private control (Haley 2016; Childs 2015) but otherwise maintained many essential features: brutal working and living conditions, extreme racial targeting of African Americans, and operation outside any permanent state facility. Both privatized prison labor and public chain gangs functioned in the North and West as well (Lytle Hernández 2017; McLennan 2008), but in qualitatively different ways that mitigated their harshness, productivity, and racialization.

The productive outputs of convict leasing and the chain gang were deeply integrated into the Southern economy. Its coal mines, steel mills, and turpentine camps all sold convict-produced goods, and Southern industry (and public finance) relied on convict-produced public infrastructure (Haley 2016; Lichtenstein 1996; Blackmon 2008). Such integration into product markets became the main target of the prison labor regulation recounted below, but it leaves out another dimension.

Jim Crow carceral labor also was thoroughly integrated into Southern *labor markets*, contrary to any sharp divide between penal custody and free labor, or between emancipation and enslavement (Hartman 1997). The institution of the criminal surety illustrates this continuity. Many sentences to hard labor were not directly imposed but were, instead, the consequence of being unable to pay criminal fines and fees, often for minor crimes (Blackmon 2008; Haley 2016). As an alternative, a local employer acting as a "surety" could pay off the worker's criminal legal debts. In exchange, the worker became bound to the employer in a long-term labor contract to pay off the debt now held in private hands (Blackmon 2008; Daniel 1972; cf. Lytle Hernández 2017). Employer control was backed up by the force of criminal laws that specifically punished failure to perform the surety contract. Thus was created the functional equivalent of the convict lease without any formal criminal sentence (Childs 2015).

The surety system straddled formal punishment on one side and the more general system of debt peonage on the other. Wage advances tied to labor contracts were a routine part of economic life structured to preserve Black agricultural laborers' desperate economic dependence in a state of "indebted servitude" (Hartman 1997). Debts could easily be manufactured (Kelley 1990; Blackmon 2008) based on a white landowner's claims of a broken tool or stolen crop. If denied by the worker, such charges might then be taken up by the local sheriff as accusations of criminal theft. From Reconstruction through World War II, Southern states criminalized workers' failure to complete labor contracts when those contracts were in part a mechanism of debt repayment (Du Bois 1935; Goluboff 2007; Blackmon 2008; Daniel 1972). Private employers thus could trigger public violence—arrest, prosecution, and the threat of the convict lease or chain gang—against workers who sought to leave.

While peonage prevented workers from quitting, other laws criminalized unemployment and labor mobility (Blackmon 2008; Daniel 1972; Goluboff 2007). The most general and notorious was the crime of vagrancy for being out in public "with no visible means of support," again not confined to the South (Stanley 1998; White 2004; Lytle Hernández 2017), but elsewhere seemingly less pervasively utilized to coerce and discipline labor.

These interlocking forms of racialized labor coercion structured by criminal law are well known as descriptions of the period. Nonetheless, they recede—or are sequestered in the prison—when Jim Crow is used as a prism through which to view contemporary life (Dawson and Francis 2016). Perhaps the most common reduction simply writes labor coercion out of civil rights narratives in which racism at work is understood exclusively through the anti-discrimination framework developed through and after *Brown v. Board of Education* (Goluboff 2007; Frymer 2008). Even resolutely structural accounts of racial hierarchy emphasize *exclusion* from good work, leaving Black workers suspended between bad jobs and unemployment. In this vein, Michelle Alexander deploys the "New Jim Crow" to understand how today's carceral state "permanently locks a huge percentage of the African American community out of the mainstream society and economy" (2012, 13). This framework likewise animates reentry scholarship and advocacy focused on criminal records and debt as "barriers to employment" (Bushway, Stoll, and Weiman 2007; Bannon, Nagrecha, and Diller 2010). There is no peonage and forced labor in that story.

This sidelining of subordination *through* labor—not only exclusion from it—can occur even when Jim Crow carceral labor provides the bridge between slavery and contemporary mass incarceration (Davis 2000). Dennis Childs uses physical brutality and confinement to trace an arc from slavery through "convict leasing, peonage, the 'fine/fee system,' and criminal surety" (2015, 8) and into the "coffin-simulating boxcar cells of today's prison-industrial complex (PIC)" (2015, 2). He defends this continuity as consistent with "those entombed within the modern penitentiary . . . not actually producing goods for corporations" because "the mass warehousing of today's PIC" updates the "cargoing of human beings that took place during chattel slavery. . . . The object of commodification in today's neoslavery is therefore not the neoslaves' *labor* but their warehoused *bodies*" (Childs 2015, 190n9). Thus, not only is the contemporary referent incarceration alone rather than a wider racialized labor regime, but even within incarceration, prison labor is sidelined.

Focusing on brutal confinement aligns Childs's account with the influential "warehousing" characterization of the contemporary carceral state (Wacquant 2009; Simon 2007; Lytle Hernández 2017). There, prison labor is understood to have ceased to play any significant role (McLennan

2008; McBride 2007) and to have been replaced by a brutal "idleness" or isolation, epitomized by solitary confinement and the super-max (Simon 2007; Childs 2015). Any integration with the broader political economy operates not through inmates' labor but through the capitalization, construction, and operation of prisons and jails (Gilmore 2007); these complement the integration of policing with gentrification (Stuart 2011), on the one hand, and the carceral state's management of a deteriorating labor market and safety net on the other (Wacquant 2009).

Against the warehousing notion, Heather Ann Thompson describes "a new era of forced labor for America's inmates," one that "eerily echoes the previous exploitative and brutal era of prison labor that flourished in America from 1865 through the New Deal" (2011, 35). Thompson thus highlights carceral labor in the present but confines it to the prison; the resulting historical lineage runs through the convict lease but leaves aside its integration with vagrancy, peonage, and the criminal surety. These are similarly absent from McLennan's incorporation of the Southern convict lease and chain gang into her history of prison labor (2008). In such narratives, carceral work occurs distinctly outside the labor market but then interacts with it when prison labor's output comes into product market competition with market labor's output.

THE LEGAL CONSTRUCTION OF THE PRISON LABOR/FREE LABOR DICHOTOMY

Although the Jim Crow era illustrated the potential economic integration of carceral labor, scholarship has treated carceral labor as largely a relic of the past and at most sequestered within incarceration, walled off from contemporary labor markets. That view mirrors a historically specific sociolegal project of institutionalizing a separation between criminal justice and the economy. This section traces the development of the legal and ideological infrastructure undergirding that apparent separation; subsequent sections turn to the permeability of these boundaries and the contemporary practices that traverse them.

Relative to a baseline like the pre–World War II Jim Crow South, erecting a barrier between spheres of penality and economy requires several distinct, complementary efforts. With regard to prison labor, this separation operates through two prongs: first, allowing prison labor only insofar as its products are isolated from the "the market" where they could compete with the products of free labor; second, separating the legal status of prison labor from that of free labor so as to make them legally and institutionally incomparable (Hatton 2017). Both prongs, however, take for granted a clear distinction between those in carceral custody and those working in the "free" world; in other words, they take for granted the absence of carceral labor beyond the prison. Indeed, the introduction in the South of state-run chain gangs and penal farms was itself part of constructing this boundary, a shift from the convict-leasing era when criminal defendants were placed in the custody of private firms and no large-scale prison infrastructure existed (Haley 2016; Lichtenstein 1996; McLennan 2008).

The sequestration of carceral labor in the prison thus required not only a transformation in convict labor but also the decline or erasure of carceral labor beyond the prison, in noncustodial contexts. All three components—separating prison labor from product markets, distancing remaining incarcerated workers from rights-bearing free workers, and establishing the free labor market as devoid of carceral influence—work together to affirm and create prison labor's distinction from free labor, a freedom incompatible with carceral labor outside the prison.

The Constitution of Free Labor

Unlike the transformations in prison labor discussed in the next subsection, the mid-twentieth-century decline in peonage, vagrancy, and other structures of carceral labor outside the prison is more assumed than understood. Their suppression, however, is essential to the construction of a market in "free labor" apart from penal coercion. Blackmon treats these practices as having been abruptly abolished when wartime geopolitical considerations prompted the Franklin Delano Roosevelt administration to turn against Southern peonage (2008). That turn spurred newly vigorous enforcement of federal anti-peonage laws (Goluboff 2007). This included securing the Supreme Court's reaffirmation in *Pollock v. Williams* (1944) of its Thirteenth Amendment peonage jurisprudence from the 1910s, which had become a dead letter in the interim (Daniel 1972; Blackmon 2008).

The essence of that peonage jurisprudence was to define labor freedom as the absence of criminal sanction. Thus, the Supreme Court in *Bailey v. Alabama* held "involuntary servitude" to arise under any law that would "compel the service or labor by making it a crime to refuse or fail to perform it" (1911, 243). With this rationale, the Court struck down a "false pretenses" law that had criminalized quitting an employer to whom a worker was indebted for a wage advance. Several years, later, it struck down a functionally similar criminal surety law (*United States v. Reynolds* 1914).

The post–World War II years also saw a rewriting and broadening of the statutory scheme enforcing the Thirteenth Amendment, including the direct criminalization of involuntary servitude without reliance on the element of debt that had been critical to peonage prosecutions.[1] Less clear is how these changes persisted after the wartime effort faded and attention turned to antidiscrimination frameworks (Goluboff 2007). Indeed, at least some traces of peonage continued into the 1960s (Daniel 1972).

Vagrancy law and its kin suffered no similar frontal assault on free labor grounds. Instead, by the time vagrancy fell into constitutional disgrace during the 1960s, its association with labor discipline already had faded (Goluboff 2016). In 1967, New York's highest court sidestepped the Thirteenth Amendment issue because "vagrancy laws have been abandoned by our governmental authorities as a means of 'persuading' unemployed poor persons to seek work" (*Fenster v. Leary* 1967, 429–30). Such "persuasion" would be incongruous "in this era of widespread efforts to motivate and educate the poor toward economic betterment of themselves, of the 'War on Poverty' and all its varied programs" (429).[2]

By the time the US Supreme Court struck down vagrancy laws in 1971, the Thirteenth Amendment was not even mentioned (*Papachristou v. City of Jacksonville* 1971). The criminalization of unemployment had dissolved into a question of cultural nonconformity: "If some carefree type of fellow is satisfied to work just so much, and no more, as will pay for one square meal, some wine, and a flophouse daily, but a court thinks this kind of living subhuman, the fellow can be forced to raise his sights or go to jail as a vagrant" (1971, 170). None of the 1,624 subsequent cases citing *Papachristou* discuss vagrancy's history as labor regulation or its connection to neoslavery.[3]

It appears, then, that the postwar era saw a marked retreat in the actual practice of carceral labor outside the prison and a legal infrastructure at least partially suited to compel that retreat. Yet rather than being the object of iconic struggles, peonage, vagrancy, and the like also faded from legal anti-canon of Jim Crow practices to be avoided and distinguished.

Isolating the Products of Prison Labor from "the Economy"

In the pre-WWII era, the market integration of production by incarcerated people posed practical problems for "free labor": the constant wage and strike discipline from the threat of substituting carceral labor (Blackmon 2008; Thompson 2011; Lichtenstein 1996). A series of midcentury federal laws attempted to insulate "free labor" (racialized white [Roediger 1999])—and the firms employing it—from such competition with enterprises that could draw on a captive labor force (Thompson 2011). These developments nationalized a legislative strategy that organized labor had deployed with increasing success at the state level since the late nineteenth century (McLennan 2008).

The first federal volley came in 1929 when Congress passed the Hawes-Cooper Act, which explicitly authorized states to apply their own regulations restricting sales of goods produced by prisoners in other states. Hawes-Cooper thereby removed the otherwise serious threat that such state restrictions would be struck down for improperly intruding on Congress's jurisdiction over interstate commerce (McLennan 2008). In *Whitfield v. Ohio* (1936), Ohio convicted a man for selling shirts manufactured in an Alabama prison in violation of Ohio's 1912 law against selling prisoner-made goods "on the open market in this state" (434). The Supreme Court upheld the conviction and Hawes-Cooper's legitimation of it. The Court explained the underlying policy that "free labor, properly compensated, cannot compete successfully with the enforced and unpaid or underpaid convict labor of the prison" (439).

Congress then repeatedly built on Hawes-Cooper's foundation. The Ashurst-Sumners Act of 1935 directly criminalized under federal law the interstate transportation of inmate-produced goods for sale or use in violation of the receiving state's law. *Kentucky Whip & Collar Co. v. Illinois*

Central Railroad Co. (1937) upheld application of the statute to a railroad, with the Court reciting *Whitfield*'s "free labor" rationale. Next, the Sumners-Amherst Act of 1940 made it a federal crime to conduct interstate commerce in prisoner-produced goods, regardless of state policy. The basic terms and structure of Sumners-Amherst were preserved during a reorganization of federal criminal statutes in 1948.[4] They persist to the present day (18 U.S.C. § 1761–62), with some important modifications discussed below.[5]

These state and federal laws made no attempt to outlaw prison labor altogether. Rather, their prohibitions on market access were coupled with the affirmative construction of a system of "state use" (McLennan 2008) under which government entities could freely purchase and use goods manufactured by incarcerated people. Sumners-Amherst, for instance, has always exempted "commodities manufactured in Federal or District of Columbia penal and correctional institutions for use by the Federal Government," as well as "commodities manufactured in any State penal or correctional institution for use by any other State, or States, or political subdivisions thereof."

State-use regimes preserve prison labor while attempting to separate it from the market. That effort inevitably stumbles over governments' role as economic actors that hire labor and purchase goods and services. This point plagued the chain gang, a "state use" innovation. Although public roads are not sold, they still can be built with private contractors employing "free labor" (Lytle Hernández 2014; Lichtenstein 1996), and so those interests unsurprisingly preferred to suppress the chain gang in favor of the penitentiary.

Congress eventually federalized protections against chain gang displacement of private contractors and their (white) "free labor" workforce. This time it used the leverage of federal spending and, in 1932, barred the use of convict labor on any federally funded state road project (Myers and Massey 1991).[6] The sponsor, New York representative Fiorello LaGuardia, argued in terms familiar from *Whitfield* and *Kentucky Whip and Collar*: "Every convict working in this way takes a place of a free laborer or an unemployed man who obeys the law and wants to live and support a family honestly. Every convict used displaces an unemployed worker."[7] LaGuardia's restriction was renewed annually and eventually codified.[8] It remains in place today (23 U.S.C. § 114(b)). These road-building restrictions extended an older patchwork of prohibitions on federal agencies' and contractors' use of state prisoners (McLennan 2008).[9] The Walsh-Healey Act of 1936 more generally prohibited use of prison labor to fulfill federal contracts for goods.

Isolating Incarcerated Workers from "Free Labor"

These efforts to protect "free labor" in the "free market" have been complemented by the legal degradation of incarcerated workers. As I have shown elsewhere (Zatz 2008), courts largely have rejected incarcerated workers' claims to basic statutory employment rights. They do so on the theory that those rights were meant to constrain only the contractual relationships of the free labor market. They do not apply to work organized through the distinct penal logics of the "separate world of the prison," where "[p]risoners are essentially taken out of the national economy" (*Vanskike v. Peters* 1992, 810).

The prison labor cases often cite Sumners-Amherst and related laws to demonstrate both that this separation exists and that it protects "free world" workers from being undercut by unprotected incarcerated workers (*Hale v. Arizona* 1993). Thus, the working conditions of incarcerated workers already are severed from those of "free labor," rendering superfluous the "fair competition" rationale for employment protections (Harris 2000). Even when Sumners-Amherst and its ilk do not apply, however, courts nonetheless insist upon—and construct—prison labor's separation from market work by denying employment rights on the "separate world" rationale. For instance, incarcerated workers performing data entry and telemarketing for private corporations have lost claims on this basis, notwithstanding that these services fall outside Sumners-Amherst's rule for goods (*McMaster v. Minnesota* 1994; *George v. SC Data Center, Inc.* 1995).

THE INCOMPLETENESS AND EROSION OF PRISON LABOR'S ISOLATION

Notwithstanding these efforts at separation, the boundaries between the criminal legal system and the labor market were always porous and have become more so. This section focuses on how even conventional prison labor is not truly sequestered.

First, the structures described above do not even purport to hermetically seal off prison labor from all conventional market activity. Sumners-Amherst from the beginning and through today applies only to manufactured goods, explicitly exempting agricultural products. Similarly, services lie beyond the statute's reach (Office of Justice Programs 1999, 17,009), escaping even textual mention. Likewise, the Service Contract Act of 1965 (41 U.S.C. § 6703), which governs federal services contracts, contains no convict labor provisions and never has, in direct contrast to Walsh-Healey's provisions governing purchases of goods; the two procurement statutes contain analogous labor protections in other respects. This emphasis on the manufacturing sector mirrors the pattern of New Deal employment laws that focused on protecting workers in sectors dominated by and associated with white men (Palmer 1995; Mettler 1998). Thus, the prison/market dichotomy appears to be substantially bolstered by the specific race/gender configuration of "free labor" and the labor movement campaigns to protect it.

Second, as noted earlier, even where a state-use regime is enforced, it cannot fully isolate prison labor from "the economy" because the state itself engages massively in economic activity. Even the most extreme version of state use—"prison housework" (Zatz 2008) like cleaning, cooking, and laundry used directly in prison operations without sale or benefit to another government agency—interacts with "outside" labor markets. That is because "there is presumably someone in the outside world who could be hired to do the job" instead (*Vanskike v. Peters* 1992, 811). This is how prison officials are able to tout prison labor as saving taxpayers money, as with California's claim that its incarcerated firefighters annually save the state about $100 million that would otherwise be spent to hire civilian firefighters (Helmick 2017). Private prisons also blur the line between prison labor and the "private" market because even prison housework contributes to private profit (Thompson 2011; Stevens in this volume). Nonetheless, courts confronting such cases remain committed ideologically to the separate, unprotected status of incarcerated workers (*Vanskike v. Peters* 1992; *Bennett v. Frank* 2005).

The general boundary problem can be seen in efforts to define the scope of prohibitions on convict labor in federally funded road projects.

An early regulation barred not only convict labor directly on the road site but also installation of prison-made goods such as drain tiles, signage, and waterworks. This regulation was eventually struck down as beyond the statutory prohibition on using convict labor "in construction."[10] Congress then reinstated the prohibition by clarifying that it covered "materials produced by convict labor."[11] Several cycles of repeal, reinstatement, and modification have ensued.[12] Nothing, however, would seem to prevent using prison labor to produce the uniforms worn by "free labor" road crews, and so on.

The separation between prison labor and the market appears better understood as an ideological assertion than a descriptive reality. It provides through distinction an occasion for chest-thumping about how in the ordinary case "labor is exchanged for wages in a free market" (*Hale v. Arizona* 1993, 1394). Meanwhile, large swaths of the conventional labor market are not, in fact, shielded from competition with enterprises reliant on incarcerated workers. By virtue of the prison labor employment doctrine, such enterprises may utilize inmate labor without restraint by employment law.

Third, even these partial barriers have begun to recede since the 1970s (Thompson 2011). Most prominently, Sumners-Amherst was amended in 1979 to create the Prison Industry Enhancement (PIE) program.[13] This amendment authorized pilot programs to employ incarcerated workers in production for sale to, or managed by, for-profit, private sector firms. An additional amendment in 1996 broadened the "state use" exception to include sales to nongovernmental, not-for-profit organizations.[14] Meanwhile, in the states, prominent efforts have been underway to expand prison labor programs (Travis 2005) in tandem with the expanding prison population, worsening prison conditions, and retrenchment in education and supportive services.

Thus, the idea that productive labor has been banished from contemporary US prisons is overstated, as is the corollary that today's prisoners are left either "idle" or engaged in purely punitive make-work (McBride 2007). One Louisiana sheriff recently made news by complaining about new laws that would reduce his jail's population of state prisoners, objecting that this would include "some good ones that we use every day to wash cars, to change oil in our cars, to cook in the kitchens, to do all that where we save money" (Miller 2017). California has made similar, if less vivid, arguments about the tension between decarceration and its reliance on incarcerated labor to fight wildfires.

The overall scale of contemporary prison labor is more difficult to assess. Looking solely at the number of workers employed in "prison industries" engaged in sales to outside entities, the percentages appear quite modest compared to the pre-WWII heydays of convict leasing and the Northern contract system (McLennan 2008). One recent analysis of the federal Survey of Inmates in State and Federal Correctional Facilities found that, in the early 2000s, only about 3 percent of inmates worked in prison industries (Crittenden, Koons-Witt, and Kaminski 2016). Another source puts the combined percentage in prison industries and farms at 11 percent (Camp 2003). But by casting a wider net including work on institutional maintenance, public facilities, and agricultural production, the same study puts prison labor participation at about 50 percent (Camp 2003; cf. Stephan 2008). That is only modestly smaller than what Gresham Sykes found in his classic study of a New Jersey prison in the 1950s (1971), where about half worked in some kind of direct state-use activity and more worked in institutional upkeep. Although these figures do not capture the intensity or hours of work, they suggest that the contrast between the post-WWII and earlier periods is less stark than often asserted.

Beyond the character and scale of prison labor itself, the robustness of its separation from market labor also turns on a more neglected question: the absence of any carceral character from the market labor conventionally deemed "free." The next section returns to labor under the demands and supervision of the criminal legal system *among those not currently incarcerated.*

PAROLE, WORK RELEASE, AND THE BOUNDARIES OF INCARCERATION

The previous section provided a glimpse of the ongoing sociolegal negotiation of the spherical boundaries that structure "neoliberal penality" (Harcourt 2011), particularly the designation of when convict labor production crosses into "the market" and triggers a crackdown. That such production *originates outside the economy* in the penal sphere is never in question, reflecting the notion that the exercise of state power is fundamentally noneconomic. This section turns to the converse problem. Here, the firms doing the buying and selling are anchored in "the market" and thus their activities are deemed forthrightly economic from the outset. In this context, policing violations of the economy/penality distinction proceeds against the backdrop notion that market ordering operates autonomously from state power, and so it becomes problematic for workers in "the economy" to be under penal control. Roughly speaking, the previous section concerns keeping prison production in the prison, outside the economy, while this section concerns grounding market production in labor markets, away from the prison and its workforce. Again, however, the boundary is troubled, here because criminal legal supervision itself is more varied than an all-or-nothing contrast between incarceration and freedom.

Work on Parole

Employment while on parole provides a simple example of carceral work both beyond the prison and yet firmly located within the labor market. Similar points apply to probation and supervised release. Together, these forms of criminal legal supervision pursuant to a criminal sentence, but outside incarceration, currently affect nearly five million people beyond the over two million incarcerated at any one time (Kaeble and Glaze 2016).

For the purpose of doctrines related to prison labor, parolees generally are treated as members of "free labor." Since Hawes-Cooper in 1929, almost all the previously cited federal prohibitions on integrating convict labor into "the market" include an explicit exception for people currently serving a criminal sentence while on probation or parole. So, too, did the state laws like the Ohio prohibition at issue in *Whitfield*, laws that preceded and prompted their federal counterparts. Indeed, such exceptions were essential to the structure of parole, which initially was limited to prisoners who had a specific outside job offer that parole would allow them to accept (Simon 1993). Without this parole exception, however, extending such job offers typically would have been a federal crime once Sumners-Amherst criminalized commerce in goods produced with convict labor.

In some cases, the parole exception amplified the previously noted exclusion of inmate-provided services from prohibitions centered in manufacturing and construction. Thus, Sarah Haley describes how Georgia's creation of parole alongside its elimination of the convict lease led to the parole of incarcerated Black women into domestic service in the homes of white families (2016). Unlike the contemporaneous expansion of the chain gang, this practice would lie beyond the reach of the subsequent federal restrictions on convict labor; it presented only continuity with Black women's domestic work from slavery onward and not in competition with sectors claimed by white men for free labor.

More generally, though, the parole exception challenges the divide between criminal regulation and market freedom. The exception's textual structure shows the practical difficulty. Sumners-Amherst, for instance, applies to work performed by "convicts or prisoners, except convicts or prisoners on parole, supervised release, or probation" (18 U.S.C. § 1761(a)). These forms of criminal legal supervision are aspects of a criminal sentence, and so they operate by virtue of someone's status as a "convict." Strikingly, the Thirteenth Amendment's textual exception applies to "punishment for crime whereof the party shall have been duly convicted," and so there is a plausible textual argument that these forms of supervised release fall within the penal exception alongside actual incarceration (but cf. Pope 2020). Sumners-Amherst and other prison labor sequestration statutes, however, take the contrary approach. They incorporate people under noncustodial supervision into the body of "free labor"—at least for the limited purpose of allowing employers to use that labor without penalty or restriction.

For the workers under noncustodial supervision, however, that freedom looks rather different. Work requirements are ubiquitous conditions of parole, probation, and supervised release, following only general injunctions to "obey all laws" and procedural requirements to maintain contact with supervising officers (Petersilia 2003; Doherty 2015; Travis and Stacey 2010). This means that, in principle, parolees can be incarcerated for failing to find a job, for quitting or refusing a job, or for working at a job that fails to maximize earnings (Zatz 2020). Deciding whether someone is responsible for these outcomes immediately opens the door to a vast set of personal and political judgments about the causes of unemployment and the suitability of jobs (Gurusami 2017). Such judgments are most familiar in the administration of work requirements in social welfare programs (Williams 1999) and are profoundly shaped by race, gender, immigration status, and a host of other differentiating considerations (Soss, Fording, and Schram 2011; Roberts 1996; Waldinger and Lichter 2003).

We know strikingly little about how these work requirements operate in practice. In his classic book twenty-five years ago, Jonathan Simon argued that employment's historical centrality to parole had withered over the twentieth century, to the point that not only was a job offer no longer necessary for initial release but also that post-release work requirements went unenforced (Simon 1993, 164–65). More recent treatments largely ignore work requirements (Petersilia 2003; Travis 2005), though there is some evidence that their prevalence has rebounded and apply almost universally, at least on paper (Travis and Stacey 2010).

The limited available evidence suggests that work requirements are hardly a dead letter. As of the early 2000s, at any one time about nine thousand people nationally were held in prisons or jails on the basis of parole or probation revocations for failure to comply with work requirements (Zatz et al. 2016); those findings are consistent with earlier data showing that about 1 percent of parole revocations nationally are based on nonwork (Petersilia 2003, 151). Those figures enlarge substantially, but still within the same order of magnitude, after incorporating revocations for failure to pay fines, fees, and child support; these are tightly intertwined with work requirements as discussed further below. A recent Kentucky case, for instance, upheld a parole revocation based technically in nonpayment of child support but substantively in the defendant's responsibility for having gotten fired from his job (*Batton v. Com. ex rel. Noble* 2012). Moreover, work requirements can operate indirectly, where suitable employment is deemed evidence of rehabilitation or its potential, and such judgments then shape whether some other violation becomes the basis for revocation (Gurusami 2017; Simon 1993, 221).

Even if work requirements are an infrequent basis for (re)incarceration, the credible threat of incarceration may still shape labor market participation among those *complying* with the mandate, or attempting to (Augustine 2019; Purser in this volume). Susila Gurusami's recent ethnographic study of Black women under probation or parole supervision in

Los Angeles found that their employment status was a mainstay of inter-actions with parole and probation officers (2017). Agents pressured them to work longer, more regular hours; avoid informal work; and prioritize immediate service sector work over efforts to improve skills or health that might sustain longer-term economic security. A recent investigative report detailed how an Oklahoma court-ordered residential drug treatment pro-gram was structured around mandatory work assignments at a poultry processing plant (Harris and Walter 2017); although the report profiles one worker who was incarcerated after becoming unable to work due to on-the-job injury, hundreds more abided brutal conditions and no pay.

Pressure from criminal justice actors also can become a resource for employers (Simon 1993). A brochure advertising a New Orleans reentry employment program touts the benefits of hiring through the program: "Oversight: Probation Officers and Case Managers are your HR Depart-ment" and "Motivation: Gainful employment is their ticket to Freedom and a changed life."[15] As a judge in a Syracuse, New York, drug court explained to a defendant, "When [your employer] calls up and tells me that you are late, or that you're not there, I'm going to send the cops out to arrest you" (Nolan 2002, 32). Gretchen Purser's contribution to this volume explores in depth how the threat of a parole violation for job loss creates a situation in which "you put up with anything" from the employer.

There are some indications that such pressures affect aggregate labor market outcomes. One prominent study of post-incarceration employ-ment found an *increase* in employment during the immediate post-release period relative to the pre-incarceration baseline (Pettit and Lyons 2007); this runs contrary to the notion that recent criminal legal involvement functions primarily as a "barrier to employment," though in this case there also were subsequent reductions in employment. The authors speculate that the initial increase could be attributed to employment services pro-vided through parole, but they fail to consider that it might instead reflect the pressures of work enforcement, recently termed "parolefare" in another study finding similar post-release employment increases (Seim and Hard-ing 2020). The latter would be consistent with evidence that parole often offers more "hassle" than "help" (Gurusami 2017), to use the distinc-tion from the welfare work requirements literature (Mead 2007). It also coheres with evidence from the same study that parolee wages fell even as employment grew (Pettit and Lyons 2007), consistent with evidence that mandatory work programs in the related child-support enforcement and welfare contexts lower rather than raise wage rates (Schroeder and Doughty 2009; Cancian et al. 2002; Zatz and Stoll 2020); such findings suggest that the programs raise employment by pushing people into worse jobs, not by opening doors to better ones.

Work Release and the Incarceration-Parole Continuum

The previous section showed how parole troubles the notion of a sharp boundary between carceral labor in the prison and free labor in the market. Parolee labor operates in the shadow of carceral threat even while workers and their employers stand outside the legal regimes that restrict commerce in prisoner-produced goods and that strip inmates of the protections of standard labor and employment law. This section further shows how the boundary between prison labor and parolee labor is itself far from clear. In other words, prison labor and parolee labor are legally very different, yet not always easy to tell apart.

In principle, quite a lot is at stake in distinguishing work performed by "convicts or prisoners" generally from that performed by "convicts or prisoners on parole, supervised release, or probation" (18 U.S.C. § 1761(a)). Employers selling goods produced by the former commit a federal crime; those selling goods produced by the latter do not. Despite this, I have not been able to locate any litigation about where to draw this line.

The only known dispute was an administrative one concerning the closely related prohibition of convict labor on federally funded roads projects, again with an exception for "convicts who are on parole, supervised release, or probation" (23 U.S.C. § 114(b)(1)). In 1996, South Dakota sought to use incarcerated workers for a variety of "transportation enhancement projects," including landscaping, as part of a "Community Service Program for Minimum Risk and Low/Medium Risk Inmates" (Federal Highway Administration 1996). The work would be done through a community partner and was characterized as a form of "work release." South Dakota sought to include this program under the statutorily exempted term "supervised release," thereby rendering it permissible to utilize this labor source on a federally funded highway project.

The Federal Highway Administration rejected the state's request. It reasoned that the 1984 addition of "supervised release" to the long-standing parole/probation exception was not meant to be a substantive expansion; instead, it simply accounted terminologically for the federal government's adoption of "supervised release" as the name for post-release supervision of federal prisoners. The agency limited the exemption to "supervision after imprisonment," as opposed to "convicts on inmate status." Therefore, the South Dakota work release program fell outside the exception and was therefore prohibited. The US Department of Labor has provided the same interpretation of analogous language in Sumners-Amherst (Office of Justice Programs 1999, 17,008).

What if these South Dakota workers had challenged their working conditions? Where, in other words, does the boundary lie between the legal regime stripping incarcerated workers of employment rights and the one governing "free labor"? It is hard to say.

On the one hand, and unlike Sumners-Amherst, the prison labor employment cases generally *do* treat work release differently than other forms of work by currently incarcerated workers. Unlike other forms of prison labor, worker protections do apply to "work release" programs that operate outside the prison and involve employment by a separate entity that is not catering to the prison's institutional needs. Several cases have allowed workers' claims to proceed under those circumstances (*Watson v. Graves* 1990; *Barnett v. Young Men's Christian Ass'n* 1999; *Walker v. City of Elba* 1994).[16] Courts rejecting inmate claims typically distinguish them from the work release cases because in the latter, "those prisoners weren't working as prison labor, but as free laborers in transition to their expected discharge from the prison" (*Bennett v. Frank*, 2005, 410).

On the other hand, work release easily could be characterized as *not* involving a "free labor" arrangement but instead as possessing those features that courts have found indicative of non-employee status for incarcerated workers. Work release programs often involve some mandatory aspects, including sanctions for refusing to participate at the outset (Drake 2007, 5) and returns to prison from community-based (but still custodial) facilities for failure to maintain employment (Jung 2014; Turner and Petersilia 1996). In some prison labor cases, mandatory work participation has been deemed sufficient to take workers outside the protected realm of "free labor" even when, as is typical of work release, they could choose particular jobs or work assignments (*Burleson v. State of California* 1996); indeed, that analysis would seem to reach parolees, too.

Furthermore, the rationale for work release programs (and, again, parole work requirements) is replete with the language and practice of rehabilitation. This includes integration with services such as drug treatment (Martin et al. 1999; Jung 2014). Courts often have held that prison-structured work was not employment because "the purpose of the program is to prepare inmates upon release from prison to function as responsible, self-sufficient members of society" (*Reimonenq v. Foti* 1996); that is also precisely the stated purpose of most work release programs.

During a prior wave of interest in work release in the early 1970s, program design established a sharp distinction between prison labor, on the one hand, and affirmative connection to the labor market, on the other. Maintenance of labor standards on a par with nonincarcerated workers was widely cited as a core feature of program design (Waldo, Chiricos, and Dobrin 1973; Jeffery and Woolpert 1975). President Nixon updated President Theodore Roosevelt's original executive order barring use of prison labor in federal contracts to include an exception for work release ("work at paid employment in the community") so long as that work did not displace other employees or undercut local labor standards.[17] These concerns have since receded. None of the prominent discussions of work release of the past two decades even mention this design consideration.

Just as the boundary between prison labor and work release is porous, so, too, is that between work release and parole. Work release has been described as a "mid-point between incarceration and probation" (Jeffery and Woolpert 1975) and as "analogous to parole" (Austin and Krisberg 1982). Studies of work release outcomes vary as to whether they use incarcerated people or parolees as the relevant comparison set (Duwe 2015; Turner and Petersilia 1996). This ambiguity, or continuity, is only heightened by considering work release alongside day reporting centers, electronic monitoring, and home confinement (Jung 2014; Petersilia 1997), as well as residential reentry centers, including "halfway back" houses for people with parole violations (Routh and Hamilton 2015), and so-called "restitution centers" (Wolfe and Liu 2020).

A recent case in Los Angeles illustrates this ambiguity. Under California law, the local sheriff is authorized to substitute "work release" for someone sentenced to incarceration in county jail (Cal. Penal Code § 4024.2). Functionally, the resulting arrangement is quite like court-ordered community service for someone on probation or parole; the worker is free to go home at night after completing the day's work rather than returning to a custodial facility. However, the arrangement proceeds under the sheriff's authority over defendants sentenced to jail time, not under a court's authority to substitute probation for incarceration. Nor is it subject to the supervisory arrangements of the Corrections or Probation Departments that manage parole or probation. Nonetheless, a California court recently ruled that, for the purposes at issue, a defendant's noncompliance with his work assignment had to be treated like a probation violation (In re *Barber* 2017). Even more strikingly, a New Jersey Supreme Court decision from the late 1960s characterized an inmate's assignment to perform prison labor in order to "work off" a fine as a form of "cell parole" functionally equivalent to paying off the fine with wages earned on "street parole" (*State v. Lavelle* 1969).

FROM THE NEW DEBTORS PRISONS TO THE NEW DEBT PEONAGE

All the labor associated with prison, work release, parole, and probation arises through a criminal sentence and bridges the supposed divide between punishment and economy. But this intermingling goes further still, because carceral labor also can arise without any extant criminal sentence to incarceration, even one held in abeyance, as with parole or probation. For instance, courts increasingly charge criminal defendants both with fines and with some of the costs of their own prosecution and punishment (Harris 2016). The resulting demands for work are not incidents of a carceral sentence (as with prison labor) or its suspension (as with parole or probation); rather, they are an extension of demands for payment, and incarceration enters as a potential future sanction for nonpayment. The forthrightly economic nature of fines and fees thus offers fertile ground for examining how the criminal justice/economy boundary is breached.

As was the case for criminal surety schemes under Jim Crow and other historical examples where criminal legal debt was converted into forced labor (Lytle Hernández 2017), contemporary fines and fees often originate with minor offenses, such as petty misdemeanors or even speeding tickets (Bingham et al. 2016; Natapoff 2015). Defendants who do not pay become subject to incarceration via either contempt of court or additional criminal charges like "failure to pay." Current constitutional doctrine allows such incarceration only for a *willful* failure to pay (Colgan 2014)—not the bare fact of nonpayment—but in practice courts often fail to make any meaningful, or even nominal, inquiry into ability to pay (Colgan 2017).

Such incarceration has been widely condemned as the "criminalization of poverty" and reintroduction of "debtors prisons" (American Civil Liberties Union 2010). In conjunction with the thoroughly racialized character of the policing, prosecution, and judicial practices at issue, the overall phenomenon exemplifies the confluence of racialized state violence and racialized economic exploitation (Murch 2016) characteristic of racial capitalism (Robinson 2000; Dawson 2016).

This system's labor dimensions, however, have received little attention. Instead of seeing a three-way bind among payment, work, and incarceration (Zatz 2016; Herrera et al. 2019), analysis focuses on the payment/incarceration dyad alone. Even a prominent law review article analyzing the phenomenon as "The New Peonage" divorces that characterization from forced labor (Birckhead 2015). Instead, labor enters the picture, if at all, either through prison labor imposed during incarceration for debt (Southern Poverty Law Center 2017) or as something that lies on the other side of the "barriers to employment" erected by criminal legal debt.

In fact, labor is central to the system of fines and fees. Indeed, this is likely to become more explicit and extensive as critical scholarship and advocacy make "ability to pay" a central concept (Colgan 2017). Scrutinizing ability to pay leads to scrutinizing employment because future wages provide a potential source of funds for those who cannot currently pay. Scrutinizing ability to pay thus can quickly convert into scrutinizing ability to work and the voluntariness versus involuntariness of unemployment (Zatz 2020), just as it does in means-tested welfare programs that assess the ability to pay for household needs (Zatz 2012).

This conversion of demands of "pay or jail" into "work or jail" has already been thoroughly formalized and institutionalized in the closely related domain of child support enforcement (Zatz 2016). For criminal legal debt, analogous dynamics already operate informally as prosecutors and judges make judgments about ability to pay (Harris 2016). In the child-support context a judge may assume that almost anyone can get a job "flipping hamburgers"—and therefore deem unemployment voluntary, and therefore nonpayment willful (*Moss v. Superior Court* 1998). Similarly, Harris found that some judges considering sanctions for criminal legal debt nonpayment "would explicitly assess whether defendants were trying hard enough to secure employment" (2016, 138).

The direct evaluation of responsibility for unemployment—in the context of assessing ability to pay—can easily become institutionalized in an apparatus of monitored job search, job readiness, and related work programs. The duty to work (in order to pay) becomes operationalized as a duty to participate in such programs, or face incarceration. New Jersey's pilot program in this vein was named MUSTER, for Must Earn Restitution (Weisburd, Einat, and Kowalski 2008). Although such programs often are cast as supportive services designed to help workers find employment, in practice they may operate primarily to "hassle" workers into accepting marginal employment that they already could get but elect to avoid. Work programs can achieve this both by confronting people with opportunities for such work and by degrading the value of time spent not working. Thus, we see the Obama administration's child-support work strategy explicitly embracing the "work first" strategy of "rapid labor force attachment" over "services to promote access to better jobs and careers" (Office of Child Support Enforcement 2014, 68558). Although the latter might be appropriate in "other contexts," not so for "unemployed noncustodial parents with child support responsibilities." In the criminal legal debt context, too, it seems likely that the moral weight of indebtedness and conviction, as well as the state's financial incentives for collection, could create a powerful push toward "any job is better than no job."

Criminal legal debt enforcement already has drawn one arrow from the established quiver of welfare work programs. Most jurisdictions make some provision for substituting "community service" work for criminal legal debt payments, especially where defendants lack funds to pay (Harris 2016).

As with "workfare" assignments, such programs generally involve unpaid work for a nonprofit or governmental agency and can be understood as efforts toward several distinct goals (Turner and Main 2001): improving employability (hence the moniker "work experience programs" common in the welfare context), hassling people into taking paying jobs instead, or enabling in-kind payment through valuable labor in lieu of cash.

Little is known about the scope and operation of court-ordered community service. In Los Angeles County, for instance, courts assigned roughly one hundred thousand people to community service in a one-year period in 2013–14 (Herrera et al. 2019). Detailed records on the nearly five thousand people assigned to community service through one neighborhood nonprofit intermediary show a typical assignment of about one hundred hours of work. Based on the work actually completed, and extrapolating to the county level, this would amount to about eight million hours of work annually, or about five thousand full-time, full-year jobs. To be sure, this does not represent a large proportion of the entire low-wage labor market in Los Angeles. However, this form of carceral labor in this one county roughly equals the approximately five thousand incarcerated people working for private companies in the entire national PIE program (Prison Industry Enhancement Certification Program 2020). Moreover, it easily exceeds in full-time, full-year equivalents the number of California inmates statewide who work to fight the state's wildfires, a practice that receives substantial journalistic attention each fire season (Fang 2017).

CARCERAL LABOR AS PROGRESSIVE REFORM

Court-ordered community service programs generally involve forced labor for no pay. This might seem an inauspicious formula for policies designed to counteract the carceral state's toll on racial and economic equality. And yet, such programs are widely touted as progressive solutions to debtors prisons, an "alternative to incarceration" (Bannon, Nagrecha, and Diller 2010; American Civil Liberties Union 2010). Until recently, critical treatments have focused narrowly on how community service can disrupt paid employment or fail to provide a meaningful alternative because of difficulties complying with its requirements (Birckhead 2015; Harris 2016;

but cf. Herrera et al. 2019). Similarly, carceral labor outside the prison is often touted as part of a progressive reentry strategy that can overcome otherwise formidable barriers to employment.

These reformist embraces of carceral labor outside the prison have not seriously considered how critiques of prison labor might apply. Here, too, the state uses its power to incarcerate to deliver up a pool of vulnerable unpaid or low-paid labor, consisting disproportionately of low-income people of color, to cash-strapped government agencies, contractors, or the "private" sector. Instead of triggering such criticisms, these reform programs repeat the dynamics of welfare reform in which "work" becomes an intrinsic good. This role for work operates independently of the *kind of work* at issue and ignores how such programs can degrade the quality of work available both to participants *and* to other workers (Zatz 2020).

Carceral Work as an Alternative to Incarceration

Community service programs carve out a degraded labor market tier operating below conventional labor standards. In Los Angeles, court-ordered community service workers must sign forms declaring themselves to be "volunteers," not employees, and thus to fall outside the protections of workers' compensation, not to mention the minimum wage and rights to organize (Herrera et al. 2019). This reprises conflicts over the employee status—and associated protections—of participants in the unpaid "work experience" programs many jurisdictions introduced as a means to comply with welfare work requirements (Diller 1998; Goldberg 2007; Zatz 2008; Hatton 2018a).

A federal court in New York recently held similar community service assignments to fall outside the employment relationships covered by the federal minimum wage (*Doyle v. City of New York* 2015). The work in question was a condition of a City diversion program. The judge reasoned that community service was noneconomic in nature because the defendants were not motivated by "monetary compensation." Instead, they sought the opportunity to "resolve cases involving minor offenses in a way that provides more substantial consequences than outright dismissal of the charges but allows defendants to avoid the risks and anxieties associated with further prosecution and the 'criminal stigma' that attaches to convictions" (487). The court thus placed the work at issue within a domain of criminal justice policy thought to operate apart from "the labor market," precisely the reasoning animating the caselaw excluding prison labor from employment protections (Zatz 2008); indeed, *Doyle* relied explicitly upon that caselaw.

Despite this effort to separate carceral work from the labor market, the court also drew upon the interconversion among payment, wages, and work. It explained that the program allows defendants to "pay for their offense through community service" when they "do not have money to make restitution" (487). Nothing could better illustrate the conceptual hopelessness of the penality/economy distinction. Moreover, this passage suggests the way that, as in the Obama administration's analysis of child-support work programs, the stigmatized position of the worker—someone whose transgression created a state of moral indebtedness (Joseph 2014)—functions to validate a labor arrangement that would otherwise be illegal (Hatton 2015): a worker with a conventional financial debt would not be permitted, let alone required, to pay off that debt through subminimum wage work.

Doyle also illustrates how carceral labor sweeps even further than formal punishments, stretching not only from prison to parole to fines, but also into the burgeoning world of "diversion." Here, the "alternative to incarceration" operates as a substitute for conviction itself, not only (as in the fines/fees example) as a substitute for a post-conviction carceral sentence (Lynch 2012; McLeod 2012). Mandatory work is a pervasive feature of such programs. For instance, San Francisco's widely touted "Back on Track" (Rivers and Anderson 2009), implemented by then city attorney and now US vice president Kamala Harris, featured both general work requirements and mandatory assignments to work for Goodwill Industries. Other programs are similar (McClanahan et al. 2013), as are some influential approaches to diminishing money bail and substituting supervision (Steinberg and Feige 2015). In conjunction with the intensive, if selective, use of "order maintenance policing," the result can approximate the old regime of vagrancy laws. Forrest Stuart suggests as much in his account of Skid Row policing and its funneling of residents into low-end labor through diversion (2011).

Key features of "community service"—mandates to work at specific assignments, not just to "get a job" generally, and creation of a segregated category of carceral labor operating outside conventional labor protections—also can be integrated into the operations of conventional for-profit employers. A shocking series of recent exposés by journalists Amy Julia Harris and Shoshana Walter began by documenting how what was nominally a drug rehabilitation program was in practice a forced labor camp (2017), an extreme variant of the "therapeutic community" model analyzed in depth by Caroline Parker's chapter in this volume. The workers were ordered into the program by the Oklahoma criminal legal system—either as a condition of probation or as a pre-sentence "drug court" diversion program—and forced to work full-time without pay in poultry processing plants or face imprisonment. The workers' role in the program was deemed to be that of "clients," not employees.

Carceral Work as a Reentry Employment Strategy

Reentry employment "services" also have the potential for integrating carceral work mandates in ways that incorporate features associated with prison labor into programs framed as overcoming "barriers to employment." Within reentry policy, parole and probation have been identified as potential institutional frameworks for offering services (Rhine, Petersilia, and Reitz 2017; Travis and Stacey 2010), but necessarily accompanied by supervision and the potential for coercion.

"Work" is generally treated as a core reentry objective, both because of its obvious connection to economic support through wage income but also as a form of community integration and discipline essential to law-abidingness, self-respect, and flourishing across multiple domains of life (Travis 2005; Uggen 2000). In this regard it recalls the multifaceted and often mystical paeans to work that were characteristic of welfare reform (Bumiller 2013; Gurusami 2017; Zatz 2006) and easily disconnected from questions about the *quality* of work.

Instructive here are Lawrence Mead's writings calling for a "mandatory work policy for men" (2007; 2011). Mead was a leading conservative academic voice for welfare work requirements, and he draws a straight line from its rationales and institutions to those of criminal legal work programs, with child support enforcement regimes providing the bridge in between. According to Mead's "cultural approach," the problem of un(der) employment, including or perhaps especially for formerly incarcerated or convicted people, is that these "dysfunctional" (2011, 14) "nonworking men fail to take advantage even of the jobs they can get," reflecting "a breakdown in work discipline," particularly among Black men (2011, 16). Gurusami identifies similar attitudes, and even more direct connection to the Black women targeted by welfare reform, in her research on Black women under supervision (2017).

In the early 1990s, Mead wrote an entire book attacking the idea that welfare-to-work policies should focus on overcoming "barriers to employment"—in that context, childcare, race discrimination, disability, and lower educational attainment (1992). The recurring form of argument is that while barriers may block access to *some* jobs, there is always some other *worse* job that remains available, and that other people with similar barriers are able and willing to take. The failure or unwillingness to take those worse jobs demonstrates personal incompetence or malingering. The "distinctive purpose of workfare has never been to raise earnings for clients, although this is desirable, but rather to cause more adult recipients to work or prepare for work as an end in itself" (Mead 1992, 167). Once work—divorced from job quality—becomes an end in itself, then working for pennies per hour under brutal conditions can seem a policy success.

An analysis tracing unemployment to poor work discipline or weak "soft skills" invites a policy response grounded in coercion and focused on process characteristics of work—obedience, timeliness, unassertiveness—disconnected from the rewards and protections of conventional employment. According to Mead, "If poverty means disorder, the chief solution to it is to restore order. Government must provide some of the pressure to work that today's poor have not internalized" (2011, 22).

Similar ideas are reflected across the political spectrum regarding reentry, as they were with welfare reform (Zatz 2006). Bruce Western, for instance, traces the employment struggles of recently incarcerated people to a lack of "the rudimentary life skills of reliability, motivation, and sociability with supervisors and coworkers," but he holds out hope that "the habits of everyday work and the noncognitive skills on which they are based can be developed in adulthood by the daily rehearsal of the routines of working life" (2008). Accordingly, Western proposes a massive, mandatory work program backed by threats of incarceration for noncompliance.

The existing, smaller-scale jobs programs developed by the Center for Employment Opportunities, and on which Western bases his proposal, already work closely with parole, in some cases as a mandatory placement (Broadus et al. 2016). This reliance on coercive criminal legal supervision, and its characterization as an antidote for the personal failings of formerly incarcerated people, reproduces a broader pattern in which reentry policy brackets off critical engagement with the policing and penal practices that produce the problems reentry attempts to solve (López 2014).

To be sure, Western's specific version of "community service employment" anticipates payment at the minimum wage and integration with supportive housing. Nonetheless, it is easy to see how his rehabilitative rationale could be deployed in favor of "community service" or "work experience" programs like those developed to enforce welfare work requirements and criminal legal debt obligations, programs designed to operate outside employment laws. In the reentry context, this could be facilitated by the prospect of linking up with the well-established punitive/rehabilitative analysis of prison labor discussed above and also deployed in the Oklahoma poultry-processing scheme.[18]

The critical juncture is when, persuaded that formerly incarcerated people often may not be able to find jobs that meet conventional labor standards, policy makers decide to make substandard work the solution. An explicit example of this arose recently in progressive Los Angeles as part of the nationwide Fight for $15 movement. The new City ordinance raising the minimum wage also contained a carve-out for transitional employment programs aimed at formerly incarcerated people, allowing them to pay substantially sub-minimum wages.[19] That exception was vigorously promoted by the prominent Homeboy Industries reentry employment program. The rationale, of course, was that any job is better than no job (Reyes 2015), and better than jail.

CONCLUSION

Highlighting carceral labor beyond the prison can enrich analysis of prison labor, market labor, and the broader racialized political economy of today's interconnected carceral/welfare state (Hatton 2018a). It confounds the divide between carceral and market labor and, in doing so, identifies mechanisms of downward pressure on labor standards that at once originate in the carceral state yet cannot readily be managed by the classic strategy of sequestration.

A long scholarly tradition dating back to Rusche & Kirchheimer (1939) has recognized the potential for carceral labor to be used to discipline free labor. Within this framework, the carceral state acts on labor markets at most indirectly, by creating alternate systems of production and by influencing the size of the market labor force through incarceration rates (Melossi 2003). Historically, the dominant political response from organized labor has been to insulate the market from prisoner-produced goods. This strategy relies upon the sharp differentiation and separation between incarcerated people and free workers. Indeed, it relies upon casting incarcerated people as dangerous and undeserving, a practice that "served to build and buttress the moral (and eventually, legal) wall that, down through the twentieth century, and for many years after the death of hard labor penology, separated the unfree convict from the free citizen" (McLennan 2008, 470).

Carceral labor beyond the prison—and integrated into conventional labor markets—challenges the separation that is essential to protecting "free" labor by suppressing carceral labor. Moreover, if free labor cannot readily be distinguished from carceral labor beyond the prison, the door opens to a chain of linkages crossing back into incarceration itself. This may occur via the continuities of parole, work release, and prison; the integration of pre- and post-release reentry strategies; or the linkage between "alternatives to incarceration" and incarceration itself.

In this fashion, we might glimpse the potential for new politics of solidarity amid the grim new technologies of labor control and extraction. Historically, there have been fleeting efforts to respond to the threat from prison labor by linking working conditions and labor rights inside and outside prison walls. In the 1910s, the American Federation of Labor explored a partnership with New York's Sing Sing prison that would have extended union membership to incarcerated workers (McLennan 2008). Recent prison strikes have been organized cooperatively through incarceration-focused organizations like the Free Alabama Movement and the contemporary incarnation of the Industrial Workers of the World (Bonsu 2017). Compared to conventional prison labor, carceral labor beyond the prison features a much larger potential scale, greater integration into "free" workplaces, and reduced applicability of "less eligibility" concepts; these workers either have not been convicted at all or are designated as reentering. These factors may make robust forms of solidarity more viable than has proven the case for prison labor, and also more necessary. The obvious analogy here is to the US labor movement's pivot—halting and contested though it has been—from a sustained effort at excluding immigrant workers from labor market competition toward incorporating them into labor standards and labor organizations (Gordon 2006).

Such a turn toward solidarity across different criminal legal system statuses—incarcerated, supervised, threatened, unthreatened—surely faces steep challenges, as has solidarity across immigration status. In both cases, racial cleavages are of paramount importance and particularly amenable to fusion with deserving/undeserving distinctions grounded in stigmas of illegality or criminality. The alternative path following such cleavages would involve construction of a new sequestration strategy, one that tracks and fortifies a boundary between "free labor" and carcerally supervised labor outside prison walls.

Such a new sequestration strategy would likely follow the pattern familiar not only from prison labor but from immigrant labor and welfare work programs, too. First, there would be separation through degradation: creating substandard forms of work institutionally demarcated as different from the conventional labor market and therefore stripped of protections. Such exclusion would be justified both as serving nominally noneconomic goals (rehabilitation, etc.) and as affirming participants' degraded status that deprives them of recognition as workers. Herein lies the reassertion of less eligibility. Second, there would be separation through noncompetition: concentration of carceral labor in forms of production either imagined to lie outside "the economy" (like the governmental and nonprofit sectors) or where the substitution at issue affects only other degraded or relatively powerless workers (e.g., substituting carceral labor for unauthorized immigrant labor). Unsurprisingly, we see the stirrings of such phenomena in carceral labor denoted as not employment but rather "community service" or "rehabilitation," as well as in labor standards exceptions like Los Angeles' subminimum reentry wage.

This potential—for the application of carceral power to create new forms of work that lie below the nominal "floor" of labor standards—has broader theoretical implications as well. First, it suggests a weakness in theories that relate carceral institutions to labor market dynamics but that treat labor market conditions as analytically prior to their carceral implications. For instance, as is true for many "warehousing" accounts of the contemporary US carceral state, Simon dismisses the relevance of parole work requirements where parolees face obdurate unemployment and labor market exclusion (1993). But such unemployment is itself contingent on the existence of binding labor market floors. People who (for example) cannot get a job at a minimum wage of $10 end up unemployed, even if an employer would hire them for $5 an hour. The unemployment outcome is a function both of limits on employers' ability to violate the minimum wage and of would-be workers having better things to do with their time. Degraded forms of carceral labor affect both of those constraints: potentially allowing employers to pay $5 rather than $10 an hour (by creating minimum wage exemptions) *and* pressuring workers to accept $5 (by making incarceration the alternative to work). Similarly, Rusche and Kirchheimer dismissed the viability of ordering criminal defendants to work off debt rather than incarcerating them because they assumed that "the administration would be obliged to procure a wage which would be sufficient to maintain him and his family and still permit the payment of the fine" (1939, 176); various forms of unpaid or unprotected community service upend this assumption. In these ways, the carceral state acts upon the range of labor market conditions and outcomes that themselves structure carceral institutions.

This point—that carceral labor beyond the prison helps constitute rather than merely respond to labor market conditions generally—also challenges influential frameworks for analyzing labor markets. Writing about the eighteenth and nineteenth centuries, Christopher Tomlins rejected the notion of a transition from legal compulsion to "free labor" "disciplined by the constraints of need" and grounded in "economic inequalities," where "[f]actory discipline was modern discipline—the discipline of the clock, not the dock" (1995, 59). Instead, Tomlins highlighted master-servant relationships grounded in the household and underwriting ongoing criminalization of labor indiscipline among the emergent category of employees. I suggest something analogous today, but grounded in contemporary institutions of mass incarceration, albeit linked to Tomlins's household account via the strand of child support enforcement.

When labor markets are denaturalized and analyzed as legally constituted institutions, that legal constitution generally is understood to operate through the law of economic allocation; this includes the building blocks of property and contract as then modified to greater or lesser extents by the welfare state techniques of tax-and-transfer redistribution or labor regulation. Criminal law plays no role, except in upholding property rights through criminalization of theft and trespass. In contrast, this chapter suggests how criminal punishment and prohibition alike operate within labor markets. They directly regulate work behavior but also go deeper. They contribute to work's legal constitution *as labor market participation* or, instead, as an extension of nominally "noneconomic" practices of punishment, rehabilitation, and so on. I previously analyzed this role with respect to carceral labor *inside* the prison (Zatz 2008), and here it extends beyond the prison.

At stake in carceral labor beyond the prison, then, is not only the *relationship* between criminal justice and the labor market but their constitution as distinct fields. That distinction, in turn, is fundamental to the articulation of law-abidingness to productive work. That linkage operates in racialized opposition to criminality and idleness and thereby provides an enduring cornerstone for racial capitalism.

ACKNOWLEDGMENTS

The author gratefully acknowledges feedback on prior drafts from Erin Hatton, Kelly Lytle Hernández, and participants in the UCLA Criminal Justice Faculty Workshop. Research for this chapter was supported in part by the Open Society Foundations. The opinions expressed herein are the author's own and do not necessarily express the views of the Open Society Foundations.

NOTES

1. 18 U.S.C. § 1584, originating in P.L. 80-772, 80 Cong. Ch. 645, 62 Stat. 683, 733 (June 25, 1948).

2. That explanation elides the stratified structure of the post–New Deal welfare state (Mettler 1998), which could have left room for continued carceral coercion of workers of color, as did welfare work regimes themselves (Roberts 1996). That welfare state also excluded newly institutionalized migrant guestworker programs, which allowed employers to leverage threats of racialized state violence in the form of deportation rather than criminal punishment (Glenn 2002).

3. Based on a Westlaw search last updated January 31, 2020.

4. P.L. 80-772, 80 Cong. Ch. 645, June 25, 1948, 62 Stat. 683, 785–86.

5. Although Sumners-Amherst introduced the provisions that survive today, the current statute often is referred to as Ashurst-Sumners (Office of Justice Programs 1999; *Hale v. Arizona* 1993; Thompson 2011), notwithstanding that the 1935 provisions largely were superseded by Sumners-Amherst. I use the latter to refer to today's statute.

6. 72 Cong. Ch. 443, July 7, 1932, 47 Stat. 609, 643.

7. 75 Cong. Rec. 2696, 2743, Jan. 26, 1932.

8. P.L. 85-767, Aug. 27, 1958; 72 Stat. 885, 896; Comptroller letter B-145000, Oct. 2, 1961, 41 Comp. Gen. 213.

9. See, e.g., 49 Cong. Ch. 213, Feb. 23, 1887, 24 Stat. 411, now codified at 18 U.S.C. § 436) (federal contracts); Pub. L 58-191, Ch. 1759 (1904), 33 Stat. 435; now codified at 39 U.S.C. § 2201 as modernized by Pub. L. 86-682 (1960) (U.S. post office); Executive Order 325A, May 18, 1905; Exec. Order No. 2960 (Sept. 14, 1918), reprinted in Nat'l Comm. on Prisons & Prison Labor, Prison Leaflets No. 44, The Use of Prison Labor on U.S. Government Work, at 9 (1918); 32 Comp. Gen. 32, 33 (July 21, 1952).

10. Comptroller letter B-145000, October 2, 1961, 41 Comp. Gen. 213.

11. Pub. L. 97-424, § 148, January 6, 1983, 96 Stat 2097.

12. 58 Fed. Reg. 38,973, 38,974, July 21, 1993; US Federal Highway Administration, Memorandum Re: Procurement of Signing Materials, May 8, 1985, https://www.fhwa.dot.gov/pgc/results.cfm?id=2802.

13. Justice System Improvement Act of 1979, Pub. L. No. 96-157, § 827(a), 93 Stat. 1215 (1979) (codified at 18 U.S.C. § 1761(c)).

14. Omnibus Consolidated Rescissions and Appropriations Act of 1996, Pub. L. No. 104-134, § 101(b) (tit. I, § 136), 110 Stat. 1321 (1996) (codified at 18 U.S.C. § 1761(b)).

15. New Orleans Education League of the Construction industry, *Staffing Solutions for the Residential Construction Industry* (n.d.)

16. In each case, the work at issue probably would *not* have run afoul of Sumners-Amherst either, but not due to the parole exception. Instead, the work in question was performed for an exempted governmental or nonprofit entity or involved only exempted intrastate economic activity.

17. 39 FR 779, Exec. Order No. 11755, 1973 WL 173193 (Pres.).

18. A federal district court recently rejected such arguments, however (Fochtman v. DARP, Inc., No. 5:18-cv-5047, 2019 WL 4740510 (W.D. Ark. Sept. 7, 2019).

19. Los Angeles, Cal., Ordinance 184320 (June 1, 2016), *codified as* Los Angeles Minimum Wage Ordinance, Ch. XVIII MUN. CODE art.7 (2016).

REFERENCES

Cases

Bailey v. Alabama, 219 U.S. 219 (1911)
Barnett v. Young Men's Christian Ass'n, Inc., No. 98-3625, 1999 WL 110547 (8th Cir. Mar. 4, 1999)
Batton v. Com. ex rel. Noble, 369 S.W.3d 722 (Ky. 2012)
Bennett v. Frank, 395 F.3d 409 (7th Cir. 2005)
Burleson v. State of California, 83 F.3d 311 (9th Cir. 1996)
Doyle v. City of New York, 91 F.Supp.3d 480 (S.D.N.Y. 2015)
Fenster v. Leary, 229 N.E.2d 426 (N.Y. 1967)
George v. SC Data Center, Inc., 884 F. Supp. 329 (W.D. Wis. 1995)
Hale v. Arizona, 993 F.2d 1387 (9th Cir. 1993)
In re Barber, 223 Cal. Rptr. 3d 197 (Cal. Ct. App. 2017)
Kentucky Whip & Collar Co. v. Illinois Central Railroad Co., 299 U.S. 334 (1937)
McMaster v. Minnesota, 30 F.3d 976 (8th Cir. 1994)
Moss v. Superior Court, 950 P.2d 59 (Cal. 1998)
Papachristou v. City of Jacksonville, 405 U.S. 156 (1971)
Pollock v. Williams, 322 U.S. 4 (1944)
Reimonenq v. Foti, 72 F.3d 472 (5th Cir. 1996)
State v. Lavelle, 255 A.2d 223 (N.J. 1969)
United States v. Reynolds, 235 U.S. 133 (1914)
Vanskike v. Peters, 974 F.2d 806 (7th Cir. 1992)
Walker v. City of Elba, Ala, 874 F. Supp. 361 (M.D. Ala. 1994)
Watson v. Graves, 909 F.2d 1549 (5th Cir. 1990)
Whitfield v. Ohio, 297 U.S. 431 (1936)

Major Statutes

Ashurst-Sumners Act of 1935, July 24, 1935, ch. 412, 49 Stat. 494

Hawes-Cooper Act of 1929, Jan. 19, 1929, ch. 79, 45 Stat. 1084
Sumners-Amherst Act of 1940, Oct. 14, 1940, ch. 872, 54 Stat. 1134, now
codified at 18 U.S.C. § 1761–62
Walsh-Healey Act of 1936, June 30, 1936, ch. 881, 49 Stat. 2036, now codified at
41 U.S.C. § 6502(3)

Books and Articles

Alexander, M. 2012. *The New Jim Crow: Mass Incarceration in the Age of Colorblindness*. New York: The New Press.
American Civil Liberties Union. 2010. *In for a Penny: The Rise of America's New Debtors' Prisons*. New York: American Civil Liberties Union.
Augustine, D. 2019. "Working Around the Law: Navigating Legal Barriers to Employment During Reentry." *Law & Social Inquiry* 44 (3): 726–51.
Austin, J., and B. Krisberg. 1982. "The Unmet Promise of Alternatives to Incarceration." *Crime & Delinquency* 28 (3): 374–409.
Bannon, A., M. Nagrecha, and R. Diller. 2010. *Criminal Justice Debt: A Barrier to Reentry*. New York: Brennan Center for Justice.
Beckett, K., and N. Murakawa. 2012. "Mapping the Shadow Carceral State: Toward an Institutionally Capacious Approach to Punishment." *Theoretical Criminology* 16 (2), May: 221–44.
Bingham, S., M. Castaldi, E. Della-Piana, M. Desautels, A. Dozier, K. Harootun, M. Herald, et al. 2016. *Stopped, Fined, Arrested: Racial Bias in Policing and Traffic Courts in California*. San Francisco: BOTRC. https://ebclc.org/backontheroad/problem/.
Birckhead, T. R. 2015. "The New Peonage." *Washington and Lee Law Review* 72 (4): 1595–678.
Blackmon, D. A. 2008. *Slavery by Another Name: The Re-Enslavement of Black Americans from the Civil War to World War II*. New York: Anchor Books.
Bonsu, J. 2017. "A Strike against the New Jim Crow." *Dissent* 64 (1): 64–68.
Broadus, J., S. Muller-Ravett, A. Sherman, and C. Redcross. 2016. *A Successful Prisoner Reentry Program Expands: Lessons from the Replication of the Center for Employment Opportunities*. New York: MDRC.
Bumiller, K. 2013. "Incarceration, Welfare State and Labour Market Nexus: The Increasing Significance of Gender in the Prison System." In *Women Exiting Prison: Critical Essays on Gender, Post-Release Support and Survival*, edited by B. Carlton and M. Segrave, 13. New York: Routledge.
Bushway, S. D., M. A. Stoll, and D. Weiman. 2007. *Barriers to Reentry? The Labor Market for Released Prisoners in Post-Industrial America*. New York: Russell Sage Foundation.
Camp, C. G., ed. 2003. *The 2002 Corrections Yearbook: Adult Corrections*. Hagerstown, MD: Criminal Justice Institute, Inc.

Cancian, M., R. H. Haveman, D. R. Meyer, and B. Wolfe. 2002. "Before and After TANF: The Economic Well-Being of Women Leaving Welfare." *Social Service Review* 76 (4): 603–41.

Childs, D. 2015. *Slaves of the State: Black Incarceration from the Chain Gang to the Penitentiary.* Minneapolis: University of Minnesota Press.

Colgan, B. A. 2014. "Reviving the Excessive Fines Clause." *California Law Review* 102: 277.

———. 2017. "Graduating Economic Sanctions According to Ability to Pay." *Iowa Law Review* 103: 53–112.

Crittenden, C. A., B. A. Koons-Witt, and R. J. Kaminski. 2018. "Being Assigned Work in Prison: Do Gender and Race Matter?" *Feminist Criminology* 13 (4): 359–81.

Daniel, P. 1972. *The Shadow of Slavery: Peonage in the South, 1901–1969.* Chicago: University of Illinois Press.

Davis, A. Y. 2000. "From the Convict Lease System to the Super-Max Prison." In *States of Confinement: Policing, Detention, and Prisons,* edited by J. James, 60–74. New York: St. Martin's Press.

Dawson, M. C. 2016. "Hidden in Plain Sight: A Note on Legitimation Crises and the Racial Order." *Critical Historical Studies* 3 (1): 143–61.

Dawson, M. C., and M. M. Francis. 2016. "Black Politics and the Neoliberal Racial Order." *Public Culture* 28 (1 [78]): 23–62.

Diller, M. 1998. "Working without a Job: The Social Messages of the New Workfare." *Stanford Law and Policy Review* 9: 19.

Doherty, F. 2015. "Obey All Laws and Be Good: Probation and the Meaning of Recidivism." *Georgetown Law Journal* 104 (2): 291–354.

Drake, E. 2007. "Does Participation in Washington's Work Release Facilities Reduce Recidivism?" No. 07-11-1201. Washington State Institute for Public Policy. http://www.wsipp.wa.gov/ReportFile/998.

Du Bois, W. E. B. 1935. *Black Reconstruction: An Essay toward a History of the Part Which Black Folk Played in the Attempt to Reconstruct Democracy in America, 1860–1880.* New York: Harcourt, Brace and Co.

Duwe, G. 2015. "An Outcome Evaluation of a Prison Work Release Program: Estimating Its Effects on Recidivism, Employment, and Cost Avoidance." *Criminal Justice Policy Review* 26 (6): 531–54.

Fang, C. 2017. "The California Inmates Fighting the Wine Country Wildfires." The Marshall Project. October 23. https://www.themarshallproject.org/2017/10/23/the-california-inmates-fighting-the-wine-country-wildfires.

Federal Highway Administration. 1996. "Applicability of Convict Labor Prohibition Transportation Enhancement Projects." HRC-08.

Frymer, P. 2008. *Black and Blue: African Americans, the Labor Movement, and the Decline of the Democratic Party.* Princeton, NJ: Princeton University Press.

Gilmore, R. W. 2007. *Golden Gulag: Prisons, Surplus, Crisis, and Opposition in Globalizing California*. Berkeley: University of California Press.

Glenn, E. N. 2002. *Unequal Freedom: How Race and Gender Shaped American Citizenship and Labor*. Cambridge, MA: Harvard University Press.

Goldberg, C. A. 2007. *Citizens and Paupers: Relief, Rights, and Race from the Freedmen's Bureau to Workfare*. Chicago: University of Chicago Press.

Goluboff, R. L. 2007. *The Lost Promise of Civil Rights*. Cambridge, MA: Harvard University Press.

———. 2016. *Vagrant Nation: Police Power, Constitutional Change, and the Making of the 1960s*. New York: Oxford University Press.

Gordon, J. 2006. "Transnational Labor Citizenship." *Southern California Law Review* 80: 503.

Gurusami, S. 2017. "Working for Redemption: Formerly Incarcerated Black Women and Punishment in the Labor Market." *Gender & Society* 31 (4), August: 433–56.

Hale, R. L. 1923. "Coercion and Distribution in a Supposedly Non-Coercive State." *Political Science Quarterly* 38 (3): 470–94.

Haley, S. 2016. *No Mercy Here: Gender, Punishment, and the Making of Jim Crow Modernity*. Chapel Hill: University of North Carolina Press.

Harcourt, B. E. 2011. *The Illusion of Free Markets: Punishment and the Myth of Natural Order*. Cambridge, MA: Harvard University Press.

Harris, A. 2016. *A Pound of Flesh: Monetary Sanctions as Punishment for the Poor*. New York: Russell Sage Foundation.

Harris, A. J., and S. Walter. 2017. "All Work. No Pay: They Thought They Were Going to Rehab. They Ended Up in Chicken Plants." *Reveal*, Oct. 4.

Harris, S. D. 2000. "Conceptions of Fairness in the Fair Labor Standards Act." *Hofstra Labor & Employment Law Journal* 18 (1): 19–166.

Hartman, S. V. 1997. *Scenes of Subjection: Terror, Slavery, and Self-Making in Nineteenth-Century America*. New York: Oxford University Press.

Hatton, E. 2015. "Work beyond the Bounds: A Boundary Analysis of the Fragmentation of Work." *Work, Employment and Society* 29 (6), December: 1007–18.

———. 2017. "Mechanisms of Invisibility: Rethinking the Concept of Invisible Work." *Work, Employment and Society* 31 (2): 336–51.

———. 2018a. "When Work Is Punishment: Penal Subjectivities in Punitive Labor Regimes." *Punishment & Society* 20 (2), April: 174–91.

———. 2018b. "'Either You Do It or You're Going to the Box': Coerced Labor in Contemporary America." *Critical Sociology*, April.

Helmick, A. 2017. "Hundreds of the Firefighters Battling Sonoma Fires—Inmates." KQED, October. 13.

Herrera, L., T. Koonse, M. Sonsteng-Person, and N. D. Zatz. 2019. *Work, Pay, or Go to Jail: Court-Ordered Community Service in Los Angeles*. UCLA Labor Center.

Jeffery, R., and S. Woolpert. 1975. "Work Furlough as an Alternative to Incarceration: An Assessment of Its Effects on Recidivism and Social Cost." *Journal of Criminal Law and Criminology* 65 (3): 405–15.

Joseph, M. 2014. *Debt to Society: Accounting for Life under Capitalism.* Minneapolis, MN: University of Minnesota Press.

Jung, H. 2014. "Do Prison Work-Release Programs Improve Subsequent Labor Market Outcomes? Evidence from the Adult Transition Centers in Illinois." *Journal of Offender Rehabilitation* 53 (5): 384–402.

Kaeble, D., and Lauren Glaze. 2016. *Correctional Populations in the United States, 2015.* NCJ 250374. Washington, DC: Bureau of Justice Statistics. https://www.bjs.gov/content/pub/pdf/cpus15.pdf

Kelley, R. D. G. 1990. *Hammer and Hoe: Alabama Communists during the Great Depression.* 25th anniversary edition. Chapel Hill: University of North Carolina Press.

Lichtenstein, A. 1996. *Twice the Work of Free Labor: The Political Economy of Convict Labor in the New South.* New York: Verso.

López, G. P. 2014. "How Mainstream Reformers Design Ambitious Reentry Programs Doomed to Fail and Destined to Reinforce Targeted Mass Incarceration and Social Control." *Hastings Race and Poverty Law Journal* 11: 1–110.

Lynch, M. 2012. "Theorizing the Role of the 'War on Drugs' in US Punishment." *Theoretical Criminology* 16 (2): 175–99.

Lytle Hernández, K. 2014. "Hobos in Heaven: Race, Incarceration, and the Rise of Los Angeles, 1880–1910." *Pacific Historical Review* 83 (3): 410–47.

———. 2017. *City of Inmates: Conquest, Rebellion, and the Rise of Human Caging in Los Angeles, 1771–1965.* Chapel Hill: University of North Carolina Press.

Martin, S. S., C. A. Butzin, C. A. Saum, and J. A. Inciardi. 1999. "Three-Year Outcomes of Therapeutic Community Treatment for Drug-Involved Offenders in Delaware: From Prison to Work Release to Aftercare." *The Prison Journal* 79 (3): 294–320.

McBride, K. D. 2007. *Punishment and Political Order.* Ann Arbor: University of Michigan Press.

McClanahan, W. S., S. B. Rossman, M. Polin, S. K. Pepper, and E. Lipman. 2013. *The Choice Is Yours: Early Implementation of a Diversion Program for Felony Offenders.* Washington, DC: Urban Institute, Justice Policy Center. https://www.urban.org/research/publication/choice-yours-early-implementation-diversion-program-felony-offenders.

McLennan, R. M. 2008. *The Crisis of Imprisonment: Protest, Politics, and the Making of the American Penal State, 1776–1941.* New York: Cambridge University Press.

McLeod, A. M. 2012. "Decarceration Courts: Possibilities and Perils of a Shifting Criminal Law." *Georgetown Law Journal* 100: 1587–674.

Mead, L. M. 1992. *The New Politics of Poverty: The Nonworking Poor in America*. New York: Basic Books.

———. 2007. "Toward a Mandatory Work Policy for Men." *The Future of Children* 17 (2): 43–72.

———. 2011. *Expanding Work Programs for Poor Men*. Washington, DC: AEI Press.

Melossi, D. 2003. Introduction. In *Punishment and Social Structure*, by G. Rusche, and O. Kirchheimer. New Brunswick, NJ: Transaction Publishers.

Mettler, S. 1998. *Dividing Citizens: Gender and Federalism in New Deal Social Policy*. Ithaca, NY: Cornell University Press.

Miller, J. 2017. "Both Red and Blue States Rely on Prison Labor." *The American Prospect*, October 17.

Murch, D. 2016. "Paying for Punishment: The New Debtors' Prison." *Boston Review*, 1 August.

Myers, M. A., and J. L. Massey. 1991. "Race, Labor, and Punishment in Postbellum Georgia." *Social Problems* 38 (2): 267–86.

Natapoff, A. 2015. "Misdemeanor Decriminalization." *Vanderbilt Law Review* 68 (4): 1055.

Nolan, J. 2002. "Therapeutic Adjudication." *Society* 39 (2): 29–38.

Office of Child Support Enforcement. 2014. "Flexibility, Efficiency, and Modernization in Child Support Enforcement Programs." US Department of Health and Human Services. 79 *Federal Register* 68548.

Palmer, P. 1995. "Outside the Law: Agricultural and Domestic Workers Under the FLSA." *Journal of Policy History* 7 (4): 416–40.

Petersilia, J., ed. 1997. *Community Corrections: Probation, Parole, and Intermediate Sanctions*. Readings in Crime and Punishment. New York: Oxford University Press.

———. 2003. *When Prisoners Come Home: Parole and Prisoner Reentry*. New York: Oxford University Press.

Pettit, B., and C. Lyons. 2007. "Status and the Stigma of Incarceration: The Labor Market Effects of Incarceration by Race, Class, and Criminal Involvement." In *Barriers to Reentry? The Labor Market for Released Prisoners in Post-Industrial America*, edited by S. D. Bushway, D. F. Weiman, and M. A. Stoll, 203–26. New York: Russell Sage Foundation.

Phelps, M. S. 2016. "Mass Probation: Toward a More Robust Theory of State Variation in Punishment." *Punishment & Society*, May.

Polanyi, K. 2001. *The Great Transformation: The Political and Economic Origins of Our Time*. Boston: Beacon Press.

Pope, J. G. 2020. "Mass Incarceration, Convict Leasing, and the Original Meanings of the Thirteenth Amendment's Punishment Clause." *New York University Law Review* 94.

Prison Industry Enhancement Certification Program. 2019. "Certification & Cost Accounting Center Listing: Statistics for the Quarter Ending

December 31, 2019." National Correctional Industries Association. https://435bd23a-f4be-41cf-aa06-68751a4fd6ce.usrfiles.com/ugd/435bd2_32bc2006882b43af919b81b575a9de79.pdf.

Office of Justice Programs. 1999. "Prison Industry Enhancement Certification Program Guideline." US Department of Justice. *Federal Register* 64, no. 66. https://www.govinfo.gov/content/pkg/FR-1998-07-07/pdf/98-17757.pdf

Reyes, E. A. 2015. "L.A. Nonprofits Aiding Hard-to-Employ May Get Temporary Wage Hike Exemption." *Los Angeles Times*, June 23.

Rhine, E. E., J. Petersilia, and K. R. Reitz. 2017. "The Future of Parole Release." In *Reinventing American Criminal Justice*, 279–338. Chicago: University of Chicago Press.

Rivers, J. L., and L. Anderson. 2009. "Back on Track: A Problem-Solving Reentry Court." Bureau of Justice Assistance Fact Sheet FS 000316. https://bja.ojp.gov/sites/g/files/xyckuh186/files/Publications/BackonTrackFS.pdf

Roberts, D. E. 1996. "Welfare and the Problem of Black Citizenship." *Yale Law Journal* 105 (6): 1563–602.

Robinson, C. J. 2000. *Black Marxism: The Making of the Black Radical Tradition*. London: Zed Press.

Roediger, D. R. 1999. *The Wages of Whiteness: Race and the Making of the American Working Class*. New York: Verso.

Routh, D., and Z. Hamilton. 2015. "Work Release as a Transition: Positioning Success Via the Halfway House." *Journal of Offender Rehabilitation* 54 (4): 239–55.

Rusche, G., and O. Kirchheimer. 1939. *Punishment and Social Structure*. New Brunswick, NJ: Transaction Publishers.

Schroeder, D., and N. Doughty. 2009. *Texas Non-Custodial Parent Choices: Program Impact Analysis*. Austin: Ray Marshall Center for the Study of Human Resources, University of Texas.

Seim, J., and D. J. Harding. 2020. "Parolefare: Post-Prison Supervision and Low Wage Work." *RSF: Russell Sage Foundation Journal of the Social Sciences* 6 (1): 173–95.

Simon, J. 1993. *Poor Discipline: Parole and the Social Control of the Underclass, 1890–1990*. Chicago: University of Chicago Press.

———. 2007. *Governing through Crime: How the War on Crime Transformed American Democracy and Created a Culture of Fear*. New York: Oxford University Press.

Soss, J., R. C. Fording, and S. Schram. 2011. *Disciplining the Poor: Neoliberal Paternalism and the Persistent Power of Race*. Chicago: University of Chicago Press.

Southern Poverty Law Center. 2017. "Alabama Town Agrees in Settlement to Stop Operating Debtors' Prison." Southern Poverty Law Center, March 14.

https://www.splcenter.org/news/2017/03/14/alabama-town-agrees
-settlement-stop-operating-debtors%E2%80%99-prison.

Stanley, A. D. 1998. *From Bondage to Contract: Wage Labor, Marriage, and the Market in the Age of Slave Emancipation*. New York: Cambridge University Press.

Steinberg, R., and D. Feige. 2015. "The Problem with NYC's Bail Reform." The Marshall Project, July 9. https://www.themarshallproject.org/2015/07/09 /the-problem-with-nyc-s-bail-reform.

Stephan, J. J. 2008. *Census of State and Federal Correctional Facilities, 2005*. NCJ 222182. National Prisoner Statistics Program. Washington, DC: Bureau of Justice Statistics.

Stuart, F. 2011. "Race, Space, and the Regulation of Surplus Labor: Policing African Americans in Los Angeles's Skid Row." *Souls: A Critical Journal of Black Politics, Culture, and Society* 13 (2): 197–212.

Sykes, G. M. 1971. *The Society of Captives: A Study of a Maximum Security Prison*. Princeton, NJ: Princeton University Press.

Taliaferro, W., D. Pham, and A. Cielinski. 2016. *From Incarceration to Reentry: A Look at Trends, Gaps, and Opportunities in Correctional Education and Training*. Washington, DC: Center for Law and Social Policy.

Thompson, H. A. 2011. "Rethinking Working-Class Struggle through the Lens of the Carceral State: Toward a Labor History of Inmates and Guards." *Labor: Studies in Working Class History of the Americas* 8 (3): 15–45.

Tomlins, C. 1995. "Subordination, Authority, Law: Subjects in Labor History." *International Labor & Working-Class History* 47: 56–90.

Travis, J. 2005. *But They All Come Back: Facing the Challenges of Prisoner Reentry*. Washington, DC: Urban Institute Press.

Travis, L. F., and J. Stacey. 2010. "A Half Century of Parole Rules: Conditions of Parole in the United States, 2008." *Journal of Criminal Justice* 38 (4), July: 604–8.

Turner, J. A., and T. Main. 2001. "Work Experience under Welfare Reform." In *The New World of Welfare*, edited by Blank, R. M., and R. Haskins, 291–310. Washington, D.C.: Brookings Institution Press.

Turner, S., and J. Petersilia. 1996. "Work Release in Washington: Effects on Recidivism and Corrections Costs." *The Prison Journal* 76 (2): 138–64.

Uggen, C. 2000. "Work as a Turning Point in the Life Course of Criminals: A Duration Model of Age, Employment, and Recidivism." *American Sociological Review* 65 (4): 529–46.

Wacquant, L. 2009. *Punishing the Poor: The Neoliberal Government of Social Insecurity*. Durham, NC: Duke University Press.

Waldinger, R., and M. I. Lichter. 2003. *How the Other Half Works: Immigration and the Social Organization of Labor*. Berkeley: University of California Press.

Waldo, G. P., T. G. Chiricos, and L. E. Dobrin. 1973. "Community Contact and Inmate Attitudes an Experimental Assessment of Work Release." *Criminology* 11 (3): 345–82.

Weisburd, D., T. Einat, and M. Kowalski. 2008. "The Miracle of the Cells: An Experimental Study of Interventions to Increase Payment of Court-Ordered Financial Obligations." *Criminology & Public Policy* 7 (1), February: 9–36.

Weiss, R. P. 2001. "'Repatriating' Low-Wage Work: The Political Economy of Prison Labor Reprivatization in the Postindustrial United States." *Criminology* 39 (2): 253–92.

Western, B. 2008. "From Prison to Work: A Proposal for a National Prisoner Reentry Program," Brookings Institution, December.

Western, B., and K. Beckett. 1999. "How Unregulated Is the U.S. Labor Market? The Penal System as a Labor Market Institution." *American Journal of Sociology* 104 (4): 1030–60.

White, A. A. 2004. "A Different Kind of Labor Law: Vagrancy Law and the Regulation of Harvest Labor, 1913–1924." *University of Colorado Law Review* 75: 667–744.

Williams, L. A. 1999. "Unemployment Insurance and Low Wage Work." In *Hard Labor: Women and Work in the Post-Welfare Era*, edited by J. F. Handler and L. White. Armonk, NY: M.E. Sharpe.

Wolfe, A., and M. Liu. 2020. "Want out of Jail? First You Have to Take a Fast-Food Job." *Mississippi Today*, January 9.

Zatz, N. D. 2006. "What Welfare Requires from Work." *U.C.L.A. Law Review* 54 (2): 373–464.

———. 2008. "Working at the Boundaries of Markets: Prison Labor and the Economic Dimension of Employment Relationships." *Vanderbilt Law Review* 61 (3): 857–958.

———. 2012. "Poverty Unmodified? Critical Reflections on the Deserving/Undeserving Distinction." *UCLA Law Review* 50: 550.

———. 2016. "A New Peonage? Pay, Work, or Go to Jail in Contemporary Child Support Enforcement and Beyond." *Seattle Law Review* 39 (3): 927–55.

———. 2020. "Get to Work or Go to Jail: State Violence and the Racialized Production of Precarious Work." *Law & Social Inquiry* 45 (2): 304–38.

Zatz, N. D., T. Koonse, T. Zhen, L. Herrera, H. Lu, S. Shafer, and B. Valenta. 2016. *Get to Work or Go to Jail: Workplace Rights Under Threat*. UCLA Labor Center. https://irle.ucla.edu/wp-content/uploads/2016/03/Get-To-Work-or-Go-To-Jail-Workplace-Rights-Under-Threat.pdf.

Zatz, N. D., and M. A. Stoll. 2020. "Working to Avoid Incarceration: Jail Threat and Labor Market Outcomes for Noncustodial Fathers Facing Child Support Enforcement." *RSF: The Russell Sage Foundation Journal of the Social Sciences* 6 (1): 55–81.

5 Held in Abeyance

LABOR THERAPY AND SURROGATE
LIVELIHOODS IN PUERTO RICAN
THERAPEUTIC COMMUNITIES

Caroline M. Parker

Enrique was twenty-one years old when a judge offered him a choice between four years in prison or an eighteen-month stint in residential drug treatment. It was 1969 and he was a trumpet player for *El Medio Dia*, a popular daily show in Puerto Rico. On the day of his sentencing, Enrique joined what was then the first generation of men to be diverted in the late 1960s from the Puerto Rican state penitentiary to the Home for the Re-education of Addicts, a promising new drug rehabilitation program known locally by its acronym, Hogar CREA.[1]

Founded in 1968 by a former heroin user, this mutual-aid-based residential drug treatment chain grew rapidly in the ensuing decades. Today, Hogar CREA is the single largest provider of residential treatment for drug addiction in Puerto Rico, where it accounts for 52 of the island's estimated 132 private nonprofit residential programs (IPR 2015). Like many of Puerto Rico's therapeutic communities, as they are sometimes called, Hogar CREA is a self-help organization staffed by peers who self-identify as *re-educados ex-adictos* ("re-educated ex-addicts"). Resources here are scarce. Like most of Puerto Rico's therapeutic communities, Hogar CREA's primary tools for treating addiction are limited to "labor therapy"—a heavy daily schedule of chores and manual labor, peer-led encounter groups in which residents criticize each others' moral and behavioral failings, and group prayer.

By the time I met Enrique in late 2016 he was seventy-four years old and had spent over forty years of his adult life, sometimes several years consecutively, residing in various tight-knit communities across Puerto Rico. During the years he spent as a resident, his days had been regimented through a busy schedule of domestic chores such as cleaning and cooking, offsite sales work, such as selling trash bags and bottles of water to passing cars, and various kinds of manual labor. This had mostly consisted of moving furniture, landscaping private property, and undertaking home improvements for local citizens who, for a very low fee, would hire out the services of residents from their town's local drug treatment program, with payments going straight to management to support the organization.

As mutual-aid networks that generally require very little in the way of capital investment, therapeutic communities have proven highly versatile and have varied widely across the sixty-five countries to which they are estimated to have spread since their emergence in Los Angeles in 1958.[2] During the 1960s and 1970s, therapeutic communities were a leading treatment for addiction in mainland United States, where the National Institute for Mental Health (NIMH) provided funding to dozens of centers (White 1998). Many mainland therapeutic communities closed down in the 1970s and 1980s, however, for a variety of political and economic reasons. One was governmental pressure to reform their methods, which were increasingly viewed as exploitative and amateurish (White and Miller 2007). Another was state pressure to professionalize, which substantially raised operating costs, prompting many to either close down or to relocate to prisons (Deitch and Drago 2010; White 1998). Most of those that managed to remain in operation were compelled to significantly reduce lengths of residency from between one and two years to three to six months. Today, therapeutic communities shoulder a much smaller fraction of the treatment burden on the mainland relative to outpatient treatments and short-term residential detox (Deitch and Drago 2010).

In Puerto Rico, in contrast, therapeutic communities have continued to thrive since their establishment in the 1960s, mostly in the nonprofit sector, and today they constitute the dominant form of treatment for addiction. Despite their ubiquity, these are highly contentious facilities. Drug treatment activists have decried their methods as "unscientific" and "exploitative" (OSF 2016; IPR 2015), taking issue with their use of unpaid labor as a method to treat addiction. Once standard practice in mainland therapeutic communities, labor therapy gradually became less popular as tasks of construction, decorating, and cooking came to be increasingly performed by hired hands (Deitch and Drago 2010). In contrast, unpaid work continues to be a central therapy in the programmatic design of many of Puerto Rico's therapeutic communities. Backed by recent government and private-sector contracts, residents of Puerto Rican therapeutic communities are increasingly sent to weed waterways for the Department of Water and Sewage, to pick up garbage from town squares and public parks, or, in 2016 when data collection for this project began, to remove thousands of tires from residential areas as part of the commonwealth state's response to the Zika epidemic (McNeil 2016).

This chapter explores how and why therapeutic communities and labor therapies continue to flourish as the leading treatment for addiction in Puerto Rico. In some ways, the fact that therapeutic movements can thrive, wane, and assume particular formations in particular places is a diffusionist tale that could be retold in any number of contexts and might not be so interesting anthropologically. Yet the fact that therapeutic movements, practices, and arrangements are constantly evolving and transforming into different things speaks to a broader dynamic—of the variable and often "extra-therapeutic" concerns that drive therapeutic movements. So, while existing accounts have provided valuable historical knowledge on the origins and trajectories of particular therapeutic communities (Clark 2017; Janzen 2005; Sugarman 1974; Densen-Gerber 1973), these works do not necessarily help us to understand the larger structures, contexts, and processes in which therapeutic movements unfold. Most importantly for the present inquiry, they are insufficiently attentive to the work of therapeutic communities as surrogate jobs. So as to better understand the historical growth and persistence of therapeutic labor as a treatment for drug addiction in Puerto Rico, this chapter examines therapeutic communities as "abeyance mechanisms."

"Abeyance" (usually understood as suspension) is an idea originally developed by Ephraim Mizruchi (1983) in his often overlooked sociological study of the historically variable ways that societies have responded to the recurring problem of "surplus"—that is, the mismatch between a society's "status vacancies" (social roles) and its potential claimants (1983: 1–24). Abeyance provided Mizruchi with a construct through which he was able to analyze the emergence of a variety of alternative economies, including compulsory apprenticeships and federal work programs in the nineteenth- and twentieth-century United States, which provided income or training to the otherwise unemployed. He also analyzed more encompassing abeyance mechanisms, including monasteries and breakaway religious orders in medieval Europe, which provided not just surrogate work, but also housing and even fully fledged social roles. What these varied institutions had in common, Mizruchi argued, was their capacity to provide the otherwise redundant with the functional equivalents of livelihood and home, while sequestering them, noncompetitively, "in abeyance" outside the formal labor market (Mizruchi 1983, 1–24).

Abeyance provides a useful construct for understanding how and why therapeutic communities and labor therapies have continued to flourish as the leading treatment for addiction in Puerto Rico. Challenging the argument that therapeutic communities are the simple result of the state failing to provide alternative treatments, this chapter argues that one important reason they persist is because of the role they play in allocating surrogate livelihoods to a group of people, mostly men, who would otherwise be excluded from formal labor, civic life, and home. Therapeutic communities' versatility is also relevant. As Puerto Rico underwent its own carceral turn in the 1970s, first triggered by the Nixon administration's declaration of a "war on drugs," therapeutic communities took on additional roles in absorbing drug offenders in a context of prison overcrowding. One important reason for therapeutic communities' endurance in Puerto Rico, then, relates to their malleability as abeyance mechanisms. Having initially emerged as low-cost addiction therapies in a context of medical scarcity, they came to thrive as institutions of informal enterprise and containment.

The data for this chapter were collected during thirteen months of ethnographic and archival fieldwork in Puerto Rico between 2016 and 2017. This chapter draws specifically on the archival research and on ethnographic interviews conducted with government officials and with therapeutic community leaders, residents, and steering-committee members. The chapter is organized as follows. First, it traces the carceral origins of Puerto Rico's therapeutic community movement, linking their emergence to early twentieth-century federal counter-narcotics projects, and paying particular attention to an influential strand of characterological theory that dominated understandings of addiction in North American psychiatry in the early and mid-twentieth century. Next, it examines the uptake of labor therapies by ex-addict entrepreneurs who, in a context of mass unemployment and state neglect, developed and routinized an economically viable treatment method and alternative livelihood. The chapter ends with an examination of the current status of labor therapies in Puerto Rico and a discussion of the implications for social scientific understandings of therapeutic and carceral labor.

CARCERAL ORIGINS OF THERAPEUTIC COMMUNITIES

As colonial theorists have long known, Puerto Rico's status as an "unincorporated territory" (since 1901) and "commonwealth" (since 1952) place it within an ambiguous field of sovereignty that has been a hallmark of American imperialism since at least the nineteenth century (Stoler, McGranahan, and Perdue 2007). As a colonial territory of the United States, Puerto Rico has been subject to federal counter-narcotics efforts since the early twentieth century. Up until 1958, narcotics control was administered by the US federal government, with offenders (drug users and dealers) tried in federal courts, and those found guilty sent to federal hospitals, one of which was the Public Health Service Hospital at Lexington, Kentucky, and the other in Fort Worth in Texas. That all changed, however, with the passing of Narcotics Law No. 48 in 1958, when Puerto Rico assumed jurisdiction over narcotics control. Because this legal change took place in the absence of any enabling legislation or resources for the establishment of new services, however, judges quickly found themselves with little choice but to confine people in the state penitentiary, whose lodgings rapidly superseded capacity (Planas, Lopez, and Alvarez 1965).

In the face an emerging crisis of prison overcrowding, the Center for the Investigation of Addiction (Spanish acronym CISLA) was established in July 1961 as a division of Puerto Rico's Mental Health Program. Its remit was to conduct research into the nature of addiction and to develop treatments. In 1961, CISLA's first director, Efren Ramirez, then still a psychiatry resident at the University of Puerto Rico, took over an abandoned outbuilding on the grounds of the State Psychiatric Hospital in Río Piedras, where he began an experiment to develop methods to treat addiction.

In the early 1960s, addiction was widely understood across North American psychiatry to be a problem of psychopathology. Psychiatrist Lawrence Kolb had been particularly influential; in the 1920s, he had popularized the idea that addiction resulted from inherent character flaws and defects of personality (Acker 2002; Kolb 1925). While serving as director at CISLA, Ramirez drew upon Kolb's work and also on ideas from psychoanalysis to argue that the addict's "pathological personality" was caused by early childhood experiences. Through a series of publications and lectures in the 1960s (Ramirez 1966a, 1966b, 1968a, 1968b), he advanced a theory of addiction as a personality disorder caused by a developmental failure during childhood, which resulted in the development of pathological personality. Addicts were not "psychotic," he argued, in that they were "legally and psychiatrically responsible for their behavior," and able "to distinguish between right and wrong." Yet, he argued, "they have adopted a system of values and an outlook on life that make their behavior contrary to what most citizens consider normal" (Ramirez 1966b). Thus, addicts were "sociopathic" in the sense that their "distorted personalities have oriented them away from the attitudes and activities pursued by the normal productive citizen" (Ramirez 1966b).

While serving as CISLA's director, Dr. Ramirez set out to develop a method to rectify psychopathic personality development. His vision of a therapeutic community involved a team of professionals and nonprofessional "ex-addicts" who acted as a bridge between professionals and patients. CISLA's basic structure was threefold. It consisted first of induction, an outreach phase that "utilizes ex-addicts to establish contact with active addicts on the streets, to attempt to motivate them so that they will enroll themselves" (Ramirez 1966a, 118). Next was intensive treatment, a "personality restructuring process" carried out through full-time residency (Ramirez 1966b). Finally, during reentry the addict underwent the "re-socialization training process" on an outpatient basis. During this phase, addicts were expected to recruit other addicts into the program in order to "to pay back their debt to society" (Macro Systems 1972, 26).

During its first three years, CISLA treated an estimated 1,083 residents (CISLA 1964) and claimed to have a relapse rate of just 5.6 percent (Jaffe 1966, 125). In 1964 there were eighty-six lectures across Puerto Rico about the CISLA method. CISLA graduates, who referred to themselves as *La Nueva Raza* ("the new breed"), had their own weekly Sunday radio program called 'The Voice of the New Breed' (Jaffe 1966). Soon CISLA was making international news, if not always with the hoped-for seriousness of coverage. "Junkie Cure Junkie" was the headline at *The Guardian*, a popular British newspaper (Fiddick 1967). In 1966, Ramirez was recruited by New York City's mayor, John Lindsay, who visited Puerto Rico and was greatly impressed by CISLA. Accompanied by three CISLA-trained ex-addicts, Ramirez left for New York in 1966, where Mayor Lindsey appointed him commissioner of the Addiction Services Agency. Soon a hyperactive period of government-facilitated addiction treatment began in New York City. Preexisting therapeutic communities, of which there were a handful, mostly modeled on Synanon (Deitch and Drago 2010), found their stability strengthened by a variety of city and federal grants, having previously scraped by through donations from charities or through pooling the welfare checks of residents. In addition, several new outreach clinics and residential therapeutic communities, modeled on both CISLA and Synanon, sprung up across the city's five boroughs, facilitated by city and federal funding (Densen-Gerber 1973; Sugarman 1974). Similar communities soon appeared in Miami, Philadelphia, Los Angeles, and Chicago (Deitch and Drago 2010). In a survey sponsored by NIMH in 1969, forty programs in mainland United States described themselves as therapeutic communities (Sugarman 1974, vii).

THE UPTAKE OF LABOR THERAPIES BY EX-ADDICT ENTREPRENEURS

The status of Puerto Rico's therapeutic communities, however, was quite different. Though widely considered to have shown promise, CISLA was closed down in 1966, when its commonwealth funding terminated after just five years of operation (Ríos 1983). Throughout CISLA's existence, the funds it had enjoyed courtesy of the mental health department had been disseminated only reluctantly. As an unknown and untested treatment method, CISLA had few champions within the health department. In fact, several members of the health department voted against renewing its annual budget, including the secretary of health, who had testified against CISLA at a funding meeting in 1962. The closure of CISLA is often attributed by former staff members to the loss of its first director, Efren Ramirez, who was not only highly energetic in his efforts to extract public funds, but was also extremely well connected in government, owing to the fact that his wife, Carmen Ramirez, was the daughter of Governor Luis Muñoz Marín.

So, as the 1960s drew to a close, the commonwealth government's response to a drug epidemic of unknown magnitude was limited to just a handful of small and chronically underfunded agencies (Macro Systems 1972).[3] The Permanent Commission for the Control of Narcomania, established in 1968, consisted of just nine members who were charged with evaluating all of the existing methods for combatting drug addiction. In San Juan, there were a handful of government-run intake units and outpatient clinics, while the only public institution providing addiction treatment outside the capital was the Addiction Rehabilitation Center in Ponce, also modeled on CISLA (Macro Systems 1972, 36–41).

Relief of sorts came two years after CISLA's closure with the resuscitation of Puerto Rico's therapeutic community movement, this time led by ex-addicts themselves with little in the way of professional input. Faced with a service vacuum, Juan José García Ríos ("Chejuán") founded the Home for the Re-education of Addicts (Hogar CREA) in 1968, with the assistance of three other CISLA graduates. A "star patient" at CISLA, affectionately nicknamed El Semántico by fellow patients for both his intellect and argumentativeness—as prisoner at Oso Blanco and subsequently as patient at CISLA Chejuán—had stood out among guards and staff members as a natural leader and "outstanding member of the group." As recalled by one of his CISLA therapists: "He was sharp, a fast learner. He had charisma and a following. I noticed that many addicts listened to what he said." Though his adolescence and early twenties had been marked by heroin addiction and periods of incarceration, Chejuán was atypical of CISLA's clientele: he had been raised in a middle-class household, he was the son of a successful businessman, and he had been educated in business administration (Velez 1986).

Politically savvy and well connected with Puerto Rico's elite, upon founding the first Hogar CREA in 1968, Chejuán immediately set about raising support from industry, commerce, and banks (Velez 1986). Within a few months, he and his associates had acquired not just financial donations, but also vehicles, furniture, land, and their first building in Trujillo Alto. To drum up community support, CREA would send representatives into the towns to give talks to interested citizens. Over the next decade, crowds would flock to public gatherings, press conferences, and public speeches, where Chejuán would exhort citizens to get actively involved in tackling the drug problem, now offering a concrete means of doing so: financially self-sustaining residential therapeutic communities, managed by local citizens through steering committees (*El Mundo* 1972b; Babb 1969).

Ignored by the state and shouldering a burden few knew how to manage, affected families pressed their communities to welcome Hogar CREA with open arms (*El Mundo* 1970b). Within a few years CREA achieved broad civic participation across the community, not just from parents and families, but also from pastors, priests, police, teachers, social workers, sororities, and a host of civic groups, from the Lion's Club to the Wives Club of the College of Engineers (*El Mundo* 1970b).

Reflecting the direct influence of his CISLA mentor, Dr. Ramirez, Chejuán conceived Hogar CREA's goal to be one of correcting for a childhood "stunting" of character development. Through "re-education," residents were taught to return to a childhood state to retroactively cultivate moral character. This entailed movement through successive therapeutic stages, each corresponding to phases of the life course (e.g., "newborn," "crawling," and "walking"). Until at least the 2000s, male residents were required to wear shorts; trousers and watches were privileges reserved for residents who had proven their maturity by reaching the final "adult" stage. For their part, "newborn" women were expected to wear dresses and take afternoon baths with fictive mother figures. Misbehavior was disciplined through a variety of punishments, ranging from the benign (unpleasant cleaning chores), to the more extreme (group humiliation). As one former resident recalled: "It was their way of letting you know . . . you are still a child, and you have to wear what we tell you."

CREA's fund-raising tactics combined political savvy with street theater. Chejuán once brought a group of teenage addicts, some as young as twelve, to a private meeting with members of the Legislative Assembly, where they persuaded legislators to commit over half a million dollars in funding (Cappa 1972). Equally impassioned were CREA's graduates, who commonly gave testimony to the press about how the organization had turned their lives around (*El Mundo* 1969). At a press conference at CREA headquarters about a year after it was founded, the baby-faced Carlos Pinto, aged twenty-two, smartly turned out in a shirt and tie with hair neatly combed to one side, spoke of his desire to save others like him: "I've got involved in the program because it is effective. I'm sure I'll never go back, not just because of what this would mean for me, but because I have an interest in saving others from this vice and destruction" (Cabrera 1969). Throughout the 1960s and 1970s, Hogar CREA was widely commended by the press and by politicians (Cabrera 1969; *El Mundo* 1969, 1970a, 1970c), who praised its capacity to produce "conscientious and responsible citizens . . . capable of getting along with life in accordance with the established norms of the community" (Babb 1969).

This therapeutic community reformation was not some simple result of an unmet need for drug treatment; it was also partly animated by a surrounding problem of mass unemployment. During the 1940s and 1950s, a series of state-led modernization projects, first initiated under the US-appointed Governor Rexford Tugwell in the 1940s but later extended under the popularly elected Governor Luis Muñoz Marín, had brought about rapid industrialization (Lapp 1995). As the sugarcane mills and home needle industries withered, Puerto Rico's largely rural population flocked to the towns in search of work in the rapidly expanding factories. By the mid-1960s, consumer goods such as garments, textiles, and electrical commodities had become Puerto Rico's biggest industries (Wells 1971). "Operation Bootstrap," as it became known (Manos a la Obra, in Spanish), rested on a dual strategy: direct state investment in industry, modeled on the US New Deal Programs of the 1930s, combined with enticing American investment through tax deductions and other financial incentives (Lapp 1995, 18485). Key was the Industrial Incentives Act of 1947 (amended in 1948), which granted private companies a ten-year exemption from a host of taxes and trade fees.

As several scholars have shown (Dietz 1986; Lapp 1995; Safa 1995, 2011), Operation Bootstrap ultimately failed to deliver anything approaching full employment. Owing to the vast tax exemptions awarded to American companies, the wealth generated by Puerto Rican manufacturing fed straight back to American investors, rather than remaining in Puerto Rico (Dietz 1986). While Puerto Ricans experienced a onetime leap in per capita income, from $121 per year in 1940 to $900 per year in 1965 (Hansen 2018: 78), the size of its labor force did not grow. In fact, total employment decreased from 603,000 in 1951 to 543,000 in 1960 (Planning Board of Puerto Rico 1964), and the labor force participation rate dropped from 55.5 percent in 1950 to 45.4 percent in 1965 (Planning Board of Puerto Rico 1984). By the end of the 1960s, unemployment remained stubbornly high, especially among men (Dietz 1986), and tens of thousands were leaving the island each year in search of work on the mainland, something that was actively encouraged by the Muñoz Marín administration (Lapp 1995).

It was in this context of widespread joblessness that Hogar CREA assumed the recognizable form of an abeyance mechanism (1983): in addition to providing treatment, it adopted an additional role in creating and allocating alternative "work" opportunities to men who were otherwise superfluous. Its microenterprises included a bread company, a car repairs shop, a car wash, and a furniture moving company. In addition, CREA dispatched its residents to walk the streets, clad in brightly colored CREA T-shirts, where members would spend hours each day selling goods, mostly cakes, bottles of water, and garbage bags to passing cars and members of the public.

From the 1970s onward, CREA entered into a variety of labor contracts and informal agreements with various mayors and city governments. For a very low fee, local governments could hire CREA residents to perform manual work for the municipality, such as cleaning the streets and mowing the lawns. Its thrift and industriousness impressed local governments and mayors, who appreciated having a cheap labor pool of "respectful" and "well-behaved" addicts to pick up garbage, clear scrap yards, weed town plazas, and landscape government property. As one long-standing CREA affiliate who helped set up several CREA branches in the Dominican Republic in the 1980s, recalled: "The mayors were sometimes very supportive ... because it was an asset to have an Hogar CREA, especially at the beginning. Hogar CREA was very respected. Because they were well behaved, they were courteous, if you were moving or if you were doing something like painting your house, for a very low fee they could be called upon to help."

These income-generating activities—which CREA would later term *terapia de ventas y representación* ("work and sales therapy")—came to constitute defining elements of CREA's economic apparatus and therapeutic approach, which became increasingly intertwined. Some ex-residents recall these activities as useful work experience: "It was an education. I'd sold drugs before, but now I was mowing lawns, cutting down trees, selling something actually useful for the hogar." Others recount feeling exploited: "I didn't agree that the patient was selling in the street all the time. I didn't like . . . being out in the sun all day." Regardless, these income-generating activities came to constitute defining elements of CREA's programmatic design.

CREA graduates, who often had limited alternative employment options, often jumped at the chance to stay on as volunteers after their treatment finished, where they were generally paid not formal wages but rather in shelter, sustenance, and sometimes a stipend. With a characteristic passion, many credit these opportunities with saving their lives.

Throughout the 1970s and 1980s, CREA absorbed hundreds of graduates into ex-addict caregiving positions (DSCA 1986). Many describe the decision to volunteer as "obvious" choices. One program director, who entered CREA in the 1990s and stayed for twenty years, recalled: "It was an easy decision. I'd just graduated, and my mindset had changed in the extreme. The fact that I could really give myself to something, have a purpose, and it would benefit others too." CREA graduates were not the only people to recognize the benefits of this arrangement. "It was a great option for a lot of people," recalled a government official. "At the graduation ceremonies there'd be all these addicts there. The families could see them there in good clothes, looking smart . . . as re-educated ex-addicts. Now they had a purpose."

In 1972, the commonwealth government contracted a private consultancy firm to assess existing drug treatment capacity. The consultants estimated that CREA was providing 42 percent of the island's rehabilitation capacity (Macro Systems 1972, 76), and noted that within just three years,

CREA had expanded from three residents living in one single hogar to a decentralized federation of twenty-two separately managed and financially independent centers (Macro Systems 1972, 88). Subsequent studies document that between 1968 and 1975 CREA served eleven thousand patients (Lebrón 1976). By 1986, it had sixty-five centers in Puerto Rico, and had also established satellite programs in the Dominican Republic, Colombia, Venezuela, Costa Rica, and in Pennsylvania in the United States (Velez 1986). Struck by CREA's rapid expansion, the consultants described Chejuán and the senior leadership as "'franchisors' of a locally owned treatment brand" (Macro Systems 1972, 89). Alert to CREA's ability to provide labor opportunities and professional recognition to a group of people who would otherwise be easily excluded from the formal economy, the evaluators concluded, somewhat prophetically: "should CREA be successful in its efforts to raise money for staff support, it will have the basis for the most realistic career ladder for ex-addicts in the commonwealth of Puerto Rico" (Macro Systems 1972, 89–90).

Other ex-addicts were quick to cotton on. Soon, several new Puerto Rican therapeutic communities were founded, mostly modeled on CREA, including Hogar Nueva Vida in 1973, followed by Hogar Nuevo Pacto in 1982. This rapid propagation of therapeutic communities, with their swelling pool of unwaged and under-waged laborers was a reflection not just of state neglect or straightforward unmet need for treatment. Not solely or even primarily propelled by concerns with illness and healing, much of the community support that gave early impetus to this movement derived instead from a concern with giving unemployed men a "purpose." What began as a treatment venture had quickly morphed into an abeyance mechanism, one who's chief affordance at this time was informal enterprise: that is, supplying alternative work, a sense of purpose, and civic recognition to a group of men otherwise easily scorned and excluded. Thus, this therapeutic regime was at once therapeutic, redemptive, and remunerative.

THE DEPARTMENT FOR SERVICES AGAINST ADDICTION

Were it not for the events of the 1970s, the rise of therapeutic communities might be reasonably interpreted as a creative response to the state's failure to provide alternative services. Indeed, state neglect is a commonly invoked local explanation (Cabán 2016), one that resonates with anthropological descriptions of self-help therapies in Latin America (O'Neill 2015; Garcia 2015; Biehl 2013). Though helpful for understanding therapeutic communities' emergence, state neglect is a poor explanation for understanding their persistence. The 1970s in fact saw the most comprehensive effort to expand addiction treatment in US narcotics history, with Puerto Rico actually making a *more* concerted effort than mainland United States to bring addiction treatment under the domain of government. So why did these alternatives to therapeutic community care fail to gain traction in Puerto Rico between 1973 and 1993?

Hogar CREA's first decade coincided with a mass overhaul of addiction treatment across the United States. President Richard Nixon, who had been elected in 1968 in a presidential campaign that promised to crack down on crime and drugs in the inner city and to bring treatment to addicted Vietnam veterans, became the first US president to declare a "war on drugs" in 1971 (Courtwright 1992). During the 1970s, through a host of administrative and legislative actions, addiction treatment was expanded and brought under the domain of Washington. The federal budget for drug treatment, research, and control rose nearly tenfold, from $81.4 million in 1969 to $760 million in 1974 (Goldberg 1980). Several new federal institutions were created to provide and to oversee addiction treatment, including the National Institute on Alcohol Abuse and Alcoholism (NIAAA) in 1971, and The National Institute of Drug Abuse (NIDA) in 1973. Federally funded addiction treatment programs, which had numbered 135 in 1971, spread across 54 mainland cities, numbered 394 by 1973, in 214 cities. Patients enrolled in federal treatment rose from twenty thousand in October 1971 to over sixty thousand in 1972 (Goldberg 1980).

Federal and commonwealth funds to support centralization were also made available in Puerto Rico, where the Department for Services against Addiction (Spanish acronym, DSCA) was established in 1973. Modeled on NIDA, DSCA's structure consisted of centralized intake units where people were diagnosed and then referred out to various treatment services. Taking its lead from ongoing drug treatment initiatives in US cities, in particular the pioneering work of Jerome Jaffe, who had established methadone maintenance in Chicago, DSCA elected to circumvent what was then a highly contentious debate about the ethics of methadone maintenance and committed itself to providing all of the major existing treatment methods. These included methadone maintenance, outpatient ("drug-free") counseling, and abstinence-based residential care (DSCA 1983a). In addition to treatment services, DSCA also provided emergency detox and had a host of educational programs, prevention initiatives, evaluation units, clinical and toxicology laboratories, justice divisions, and various research and training centers (DSCA 1983a).

By the late 1980s, DSCA was providing approximately five thousand people with outpatient counseling, four thousand with abstinence-based residential treatment, and twenty-four hundred with methadone maintenance (DSCA 1990, 4). In terms of overall treatment capacity, DSCA was the single biggest provider on the island by the late 1970s (DSCA 1977). In 1977, among the 7,292 people registered in any form of treatment, 46.9 percent were cared for through DSCA. The second biggest provider was Hogar CREA, which accounted for 44 percent of those enrolled in treatment; an additional 5.5 percent were treated through state correction and 2.6 percent through other community or private programs (DSCA 1977).

The centralization of addiction treatment in Puerto Rico differed in important ways from that on the mainland. In the first place, it was actually far more comprehensive. On the mainland, addiction treatment came to be organized according to a contract-based model, whereby federal agencies such as NIDA would award contracts to third parties such as individual states and private organizations to provide addiction treatment (Besteman 1992). In Puerto Rico, in contrast, the newly inaugurated DSCA assumed a much more central role as a public provider of addiction treatment. This may be attributed to the presence, at the time, of a regionalized public health care system, which had provided health care free of charge across the island since the 1950s (Mulligan 2014). Accustomed to socialized health care, the newly inaugurated DSCA was envisaged, above all else, as a service provider, with the vast majority of its budget dedicated to DSCA-operated services, rather than to private programs (DSCA 1986).[4] Unlike NIDA, DSCA-operated programs were highly centralized, administered according to standardized procedures, and staffed by employees who wore standardized uniforms and who drove government vehicles.

Such comprehensive centralization was hardly welcomed by therapeutic community leaders. In the run-up to DSCA's creation, senior leaders from Hogar CREA and CISLA petitioned Governor Hernández Colon to introduce a US-style subcontracting system in which DSCA's role would be to distribute funds to private providers rather than to provide services itself (Ramirez and Ríos 1985). When this did not happen, Hogar CREA's relationship with DSCA became highly acrimonious. In June of 1978, CREA actually obstructed DSCA's efforts to conduct a census by refusing to share its records (Rodriguez 1978). Despite this animosity, Hogar CREA would go on to have a profound influence on the state response to addiction throughout DSCA's twenty-year existence (1973–1993).

Although DSCA was conceived by its architects as a showcase of Puerto Rico's modernity on the international stage and as an emblem of medical advancement (Estado Libre Asociado de Puerto Rico 1973), almost immediately the agency encountered a significant staffing problem. In the early 1970s, professionals with expertise in the area of addiction were in short supply; fewer still were willing to assume frontline positions in service delivery. Within this professional vacuum, DSCA elected to employ, en masse, hundreds of ex-addict paraprofessionals, most of whom were graduates of either Hogar CREA or CISLA (DSCA 1975a). This mass employment of ex-addicts by government actually required careful legislation to exempt them from the minimum credential requirements that at the time operated across all other government departments (Estado Libre Asociado de Puerto Rico 1973, 8–9).[5] While it was the caring professions (social workers, occupational therapists, psychologists) that constituted the majority of the workforce in DSCA-operated treatment programs, by 1974 DSCA's treatment services employed three times more para-professionals than physicians, and twice as many para-professionals as nurses (DSCA 1975a, 132).[6]

Reflecting the presence of CISLA and Hogar CREA graduates within its workforce, therapeutic community approaches were taken up by DSCA's residential programs in the 1970s and 1980s (DSCA 1983b, 73). As revealed in government protocols from the period, DSCA's residential programs sought to instill "socialization skills," to develop "adaptive behavior," and to help the resident to "gradually abandon old habits like obscene language, fighting, and lack of respect for others" DSCA 1983b,

73). Consistent with therapeutic community logic, the discharge criteria at DSCA's residential programs demanded not only that participants achieve abstinence, but also that they adopt "acceptable attitudes and values" and responsibly perform assigned duties and chores (DSCA 1983b, 73).

Though DSCA employed paraprofessionals, compared to Hogar CREA, it offered far fewer occupational positions. In September 1982, a time when DSCA was providing care to twice as many patients as all private programs combined, Hogar CREA boasted by far the larger workforce (685 staff members, compared to DSCA's 420, see DSCA 1986). This relatively bloated workforce was a reflection of the fact that 71 percent of CREA's staff were unpaid graduates (DSCA 1986, 30–31). This ability to absorb ex-addicts, remunerated not through formal wages but through food, board, and stipend, lent CREA a significant competitive advantage over DSCA's services, one that would prove crucial to the former's survival of the funding crisis that enveloped the government-run services decades later. An additional design feature that would later ensure CREA's sustainability was its entrepreneurial amalgamation of therapy with revenue generation. While "hard work was a core therapeutic value in DSCA's residential programs, government regulations prevented DSCA from using resident labor as a source of income. Work activities were therefore limited to in-house chores and peer-mentorship responsibilities, leaving programs entirely dependent on government investment.

Between 1973 and 1993, therapeutic communities coexisted alongside the commonwealth program. The persistence and extension of labor-based therapies, when a range of publicly funded alternative treatments was also available, obliges us to consider two additional historical developments: the challenges that engulfed DSCA's methadone program, but more importantly, the manner in which therapeutic communities were enlisted by various other actors to serve a variety of alternative political interests.

Bursting Therapeutic Banks

As a condition of its federal funding, DSCA had instituted methadone maintenance alongside abstinence-based residential treatment. But from its inception, DSCA's methadone program was the object of intense public controversy. Therapeutic community leaders, including not just those from Hogar CREA but also various Evangelical addiction ministries, publicly opposed methadone (*El Reportero* 1981; DSCA 1975b). Through press statements and community talks, their leaders campaigned against methadone, arguing that it kept people addicted indefinitely and treated only the visible symptoms of addiction (DSCA 1975b). In the towns, methadone became deeply unpopular and was widely interpreted as merely swapping one drug for another (Macro Systems 1972). Even the independence party campaigned against it, arguing that it was a weapon of colonial domination concocted by the United States with the intention of keeping Puerto Ricans addicted and docile (Lebrón 1976).

Practical challenges arose within the methadone clinics themselves, where staff were underpaid, and a lack of security led to high staff turnover (Lebrón 1976). Former employees recall that methadone was routinely under-prescribed to levels below the recommended dose, and that patients who relapsed were often excluded from treatment. The appearance of homeless encampments around methadone clinics prompted fierce community resistance (Lebrón 1976). Faced with rising community opposition, DSCA's methadone clinics were scaled back from 1976 onward. At their peak in 1976 there had been fifteen clinics serving 1,893 patients (Lebrón 1976, 72); by 1997, just four methadone clinics provided care to 1,078 patients (SAMHSA 1997).

While DSCA struggled to maintain its methadone program, therapeutic communities not only grew in number (Macro Systems 1972; DSCA 1990), but extended their institutional charter, taking on various extra-therapeutic roles and cultivating new political allies. At the community level, they assumed many of the risks and costs of managing drug violence, which by the mid-1980s was wreaking havoc across Puerto Rico's towns (Navarro 1995). Throughout the 1980s, newspaper stories of armed robberies, gun violence, and frequently homicide abounded (El Vocero 1984b). In one instance, a "death squad" of six shooters armed with AK-47s broke in to a CREA center in Trujillo Alto, killing two residents and injuring three (*El Vocero* 1984b). At another hogar, a director and two residents were taken hostage when a group of intruders, armed with machine guns, broke in to steal $3,500, having been tipped off by a current CREA resident about a recent car sale (*El Vocero* 1984a). Though such attacks prompted outcry about the inadequacy of the existing security (*El Vocero* 1984b), they also indirectly attest to the limited capabilities of existing social structures to contain the violence of the drug economy. Families, who were sometimes caught in the crossfire of drug-related violence, appreciated the protection from violence that came with having their relative out of the house.

An additional and related reason for Hogar CREA's endurance was the role it adopted as a safety valve for the Department of Correction. Exchanging one abeyance mechanism for another, Mizruchi (1983) might remark, CREA absorbed hundreds of prison inmates each year from the mid-1970s onward, as did several other therapeutic communities (Department of Correction and Rehabilitation 1994). Prison overcrowding, which had been an enduring problem in Puerto Rico since at least the 1950s (Planas, Lopez, and Alvarez 1965), had reached crisis point in the late 1970s when inmates filed a class-action lawsuit against the Puerto Rican government, which subsequently was forced to pay $250 million in federal fines (*Seattle Times* 2014). Following outbreaks of infectious diseases including tuberculosis and mange, several of Puerto Rico's prisons were under orders from federal judges to make improvements (Wright 1982). Faced with a budget deficit, chronic overcrowding, and mounting federal fines, corrections found a ready way out in therapeutic communities, which presented both an expedient safety valve and a cost-shifting maneuver (the modest per diem that corrections awarded for court-ordered residents was significantly lower than the equivalent cost of incarceration). As the institutional ties between therapeutic communities and the criminal justice system grew strong through the development of contracts and similar arrangements, and as a growing portion of therapeutic community residents began to enroll under court order (and credible threat of incarceration), therapeutic labor and carceral labor (Zatz, this volume) became increasingly intertwined.

Now squarely integrated into carceral state projects, and financially bolstered by a variety of criminal justice contracts, CREA was also courted by various local elites including mayors, police chiefs, and senators. Politicians found Hogar CREA's canvassing troops particularly useful. In 1988, CREA residents in Santurce distributed leaflets for Senator Marco Rigau; the same year, its residents went door to door seeking signatures to put Senator Rolando Silva on the ballot (Ross 1995b). Governor Hernández Colón himself, who served two terms (1973–1977 and 1985–1993), benefitted from Chejuán's vocal support during his election campaign, and subsequently dispatched his senators to visit CREA programs to gather information that would help draft legislation to support the organization (*El Mundo* 1970a).

Avoiding allegiance to any single political party, CREA gained support among both the Popular Democratic and the New Progressive parties, a feat delivered chiefly by way of the mayors, for whom CREA provided a handy pool of cheap labor for home improvements, construction work, and moving furniture (Gutiérrez 1996). CREA's extensive municipal coverage, popularity among the mayors, and widespread community support soon invited attention from the central government. The words of one public official highlight the extent to which CREA had succeeded in bursting its therapeutic banks: "What you have to understand about Puerto Rico is that come election time, the governors need the mayors. Without the mayors, the governors can't do anything. . . . Chejuán was able to establish very good relationships with most of the mayors. In Puerto Rico there are seventy-eight mayors, one for every municipality. That's how they maintained alliances on both sides. That's what was genius."

Cross-party support eased access to fresh funding. The commonwealth legislative assembly supplied the organization with a steady stream of donations throughout the 1970s and 1980s (Ross 1995a). Specifically, this was from an annual fund dedicated to "Private Organizations with Social Welfare Purposes," which was distributed among a variety of charitable organizations that offered shelter and other basic forms of social assistance (Legislative Assembly of Puerto Rico 1977, 487). From the 1970s onward, Hogar CREA scooped up the lion's share of this fund (Legislative Assembly of Puerto Rico 1977, 487; Ross 1995a). Structured within the tradition of charity rather than policy, this funding was awarded not in the form of a contract but as a donation. In practice, this meant few governmental requirements and little in the way of oversight, something that various officials objected to at the time (*El Mundo* 1972a). As one former government employee from the Department of Health recalled: "As a matter of fact, one of the things that DSCA kept complaining about when they had to distribute money to Hogar CREA was that this money came from the Legislature and they couldn't even ask: 'What are you going to use it for?' They couldn't send an accountant to look at CREA's books. . . . They just had to disburse the money and close their eyes."

In the late 1980s, Chejuán ratcheted up CREA's community mobilization, initiating what became hugely popular annual "crusades of faith and hope," orchestrated to expand community participation and to raise funds for the organization (*El Mundo* 1989). On campaign trails that snaked through each of the island's seventy-eight municipalities, Chejuán led public demonstrations that drew thousands of people, including interested citizens, civic groups, politicians, police chiefs, religious leaders, and trade union leaders (*El Mundo* 1989, 1990; Ross 1995b). By now, Chejuán was indisputably a public hero. The Puerto Rican Industrialists Association named him citizen of the year in 1974, as did the Puerto Rican Chamber of Commerce in 1976.

CREA's success in winning over the Puerto Rican political class is revealed by its attendance lists at graduation ceremonies, which in 1988 included Governor Hernández Colón, the president of the Chamber (José Ronaldo Jarabo) and the president of Association of the Mayors (Pedro Padilla), as well as a host of senators, judges, and businessmen and various Catholic and Evangelical religious leaders (*El Mundo* 1988).

Such broad political support should not be interpreted, however, simply as the result of the direct favors the organization conferred upon individual politicians. CREA was unquestionably an enormous boon for several distinct sectors of the Puerto Rican polity, serving simultaneously as a source of relief for overburdened families, a cost-cutting device for the corrections department, a cheap labor supply for mayors and municipal governments, and a campaign resource for political leaders. In this respect, the commonwealth addiction program was an underequipped competitor: its remit restricted to treatment, its methadone program widely reviled and, by virtue of the fact that it paid its staff formal wages, it was unable to perform the work of abeyance in absorbing "surplus" laborers.

Therapeutic communities, in contrast, allocated substitute work to hundreds of volunteer graduates across dozens of segregated communities. Seen thus, CREA's persistence and invigoration throughout the twenty-year period of the commonwealth addiction program is best explained not so much by the failure of the state to offer alternative treatments, as by the adaptability of therapeutic communities as abeyance mechanisms.

They were repeatedly and routinely co-opted by diverse interests to serve a variety of purposes. The trajectory of therapeutic communities in mainland United States during this same period offers a contrasting case.

"REFORMED" MAINLAND THERAPEUTIC COMMUNITIES

Two distinct regulatory histories are evident in the fate of therapeutic communities in Puerto Rico and the mainland. An unintended and overlooked consequence of the comprehensive centralization that took place in Puerto Rico was the regulatory freedom it actually afforded to organizations operating outside the commonwealth system. Unable to obtain DSCA contracts, therapeutic communities turned to the mayors, local government, the department of corrections, and the commonwealth legislative assembly, none of whom had, within their formal institutional remit, any responsibility for providing or overseeing health care. Inadvertently then, comprehensive centralization positioned Puerto Rico's therapeutic communities outside of the commonwealth regulatory systems governing health care, effectively immunizing them from the various pressures to reform that swept through mainland US therapeutic communities during the 1970s and 1980s.

On the mainland, the subcontracting model provided therapeutic communities with a steady stream of public contracts. In the 1960s and 1970s, this was done through the NIMH (Sugarman 1974). When federal programs were phased out by the Reagan administration in the 1980s, they obtained contracts from city and state governments (Besteman 1992, 78). But public contracts entailed heavy regulatory demands, many of which were broadly similar to those made on hospitals and other medical institutions.

Though complex historical reasons underlie the changes that were instituted across mainland therapeutic communities between the 1970 and 1990s (see White and Miller 2007), the regulatory reach of the mainland subcontracting model was crucial in facilitating such reforms as the abandonment of harsh punishments, the introduction of a forty-hour work week, and the employment of professionally trained staff including psychologists, social workers, cooks, cleaners and mechanics (Deitch and Drago 2010). Ballooning operating costs associated with mandated professionalization prompted many therapeutic communities to close down in the late 1970s and 1980s (White 1998: 318-325). To sustain financial viability, those that remained either relocated to prisons, or privatized and significantly reduced lengths of stay from one to two years to three to six months. "Such reformed therapeutic communities" as they are sometimes called, continue to be held in high esteem in the United States.[7] But today they shoulder a much smaller fraction of the treatment burden relative to out-patient treatments and short-term residential detox (Deitch and Drago 2010).

LA REFORMA

Immunized from government regulatory demands to professionalize, Puerto Rico's therapeutic communities continued to enjoy low operating costs and financial independence from government, something that proved crucial to their survival of a series of health care reforms known as La Reforma. Between 1993 and 2001, the public health care system that had operated in Puerto Rico since the 1950s was dismantled and a private managed care system installed (Mulligan 2014). In 1993 DSCA was closed down altogether and replaced by a new department that unified addiction and mental health services (ASSMCA), a change modeled on similar consolidations on the mainland. Through a series of administrative and legislative actions, the state's role shifted from provider of addiction treatment to that of administrator.

Under La Reforma, many government-operated residential programs were closed down and counseling services transferred to managed care companies (Hansen 2005). Methadone clinics, whose capacity had been in decline since the late 1970s, managed to remain in the public sector, but were soon treating far fewer patients (SAMHSA 1997; Lebrón 1976). The number of people attending government-operated programs of any kind dropped by 73 percent, from 33,975 in 1993 to 8,935 in 2003 (DSCA 1993; ASSMCA 2004). Residential programs were greatly depleted, with census dropping from 6,117 in 1993 to 450 in 2003 (DSCA 1993; ASSMCA 2004). By 2014, residential care was almost exclusively the preserve of private nonprofit organizations. In terms of bed capacity,

93 percent were provided by private nonprofits; nearly half (44 percent) just by Hogar CREA, 30 percent by faith-based organizations and 19 percent by other community-based entities. A small proportion (7percent) of residential care was provided by government, almost all in correctional facilities (IPR 2015). This dismantling of government-operated addiction services was welcomed by Hogar CREA's senior administration.[8] It elevated therapeutic community care as the leading providers of addiction treatment across the commonwealth of Puerto Rico.[9]

Aside from becoming the primary providers of residential care, private nonprofit organizations also saw their independence from government reinforced through legislation. Crucial was the 2000 Mental Health Act, which was a bill of rights that was supposed to establish minimum standards of care in mental health care facilities. As Helena Hansen (2018) has documented, during the lead-up to the Mental Health Act, there was considerable disagreement between treatment leaders and the Puerto Rican legislature as to how addiction ought to be dealt with. When legislators drafted one version of the law that would have required residential centers to employ clinically trained staff, Chejuán, along with several Evangelical drug treatment groups, denounced the proposed law. Evangelical leaders even threatened to mobilize Christian voters against the governor in the upcoming election. In an invited response to the Legislature, a coalition of community-based organizations, which included Hogar CREA, Teen Challenge, and the Assembly of God successfully lobbied to include an additional article to the law that exempted community-based organizations from the health care standards set out in the bill. This means that currently the apex of the commonwealth government's regulatory leverage over licensed therapeutic communities is restricted to compliance with basic safety standards (fire escapes, occupancy limits). As of 2019, ASSMCA's licensing procedure contains no criteria pertaining to therapeutic practice.[10]

CONCLUSION

A long-standing critic of Hogar CREA once observed that however uncertain their clinical success, "therapeutic communities provide a highly structured environment that keeps addicts off the street and largely out of trouble" (Ross 1995b:12). This chapter has tried to highlight precisely this abeyance function, along with its sheer adaptability, as key to the therapeutic community's success. Having initially emerged as a low-cost treatment at a time when there were few alternatives, within five years Hogar CREA had morphed into an island-wide federation of financially independent work colonies able to provide work, a sense of purpose, and civic recognition to a group of men otherwise easily excluded, all while meeting its financial needs primarily through entrepreneurial activities of its own design and industry. As this chapter has shown, throughout the second half of the twentieth century Puerto Rico's therapeutic communities have been successively recruited to serve a variety of alterative interests. For the overwhelmed corrections department, they have provided a highly convenient safety valve and cost-shifting device. For municipal governments, mayors, and individual politicians, they have provided a cheap workforce. Their endurance, therefore, reflects not only their capacity to act as surrogates for multiple faltering systems (including employment, corrections, family), but also their protean capacity for appropriation—that is, their tendency to be co-opted by other actors for alternative utilities.

Conceiving of therapeutic communities as abeyance mechanisms suggests that whatever criticism they may draw from treatment activists as "exploitative" or "unscientific" (IPR 2015; OSF 2016), they might well persist, owing to their utility-infielder role in what Hopper and Baumohl call "the dirty work of system maintenance" (1994, 543). In Puerto Rico, they continue to flourish in a highly hospitable local habitat where mass unemployment, prison overcrowding, and drug violence assure, for now, their continued demand.

What broader conclusions can be drawn from the rise of therapeutic communities as a method to treat addiction in Puerto Rico? For one, this analysis adds nuance to understandings of abeyance, which in its initial "structuralist" formulation was conceived as magical adjustments to the problem of surplus guided by the hidden intelligence of "organizational inter-dependency" (Mizruchi 1983, 20). Detailed historical consideration of *how* therapeutic communities have variously been conscripted and deployed, however, reveals abeyance as a messy and contested process that in the present account has involved individual initiative, political deal making, and state cost shifting, with all of these efforts unfurling amid a historically contingent collection of local opportunities, constraints, and pressures.

Second, this chapter provides further evidence of the wide variety of labor that is undertaken under the purview of the carceral state. As Zatz (this volume) convincingly shows, a great deal of criminally regulated work now takes place in the civic economy, rather than "behind bars." This chapter has highlighted therapeutic communities for addiction as an additional site where carceral labor is undertaken.

Third, this chapter calls into question the argument that therapeutic communities are the simple result of the state failing to invest in alternative treatments. The commonwealth addiction program, as instituted through the Department of Services against Addiction (DSCA) between 1973 and 1993, in fact constituted one of the most comprehensive efforts (in design, not scale) to provide centralized publicly funded addiction treatment in US narcotics history. Yet, in the end, therapeutic communities were never seriously challenged by the commonwealth's widely unpopular methadone maintenance program. Instead, their character-building approaches were imitated and reproduced by the commonwealth's own residential centers. In contrast to other Latin American accounts of self-help (Garcia 2015; O'Neill 2015) or zones of abandonment (Biehl 2013)—residual dumps left behind by an uninvolved and retreating state—Puerto Rico's therapeutic communities have arguably been both supported and manipulated by various state actors (municipal governments, mayors, senators, and governors) for reasons that are multiple, distinct, and shifting. Evidencing the now familiar observation that a single unified "state" has never existed (Sharma and Gupta 2009), therapeutic communties continue to find champions within a complex state infrastructure composed of legislative assembly donations, corrections contracts, informal labor agreements, and legal-regulatory mechanisms. Unlike the commonwealth's Department for Services against Addiction, their imbrication into a complex and deeply reticulated collection of political projects favorably positioned them to weather the neoliberal turn.

A number of caveats, however, are in order. Despite therapeutic communities' continued prevalence, biomedical treatment modalities such as medically assisted treatment with buprenorphine are now growing in

Puerto Rico. Having consistently declined from the late 1970s to late 1990s (DSCA 1977; SAMHSA 1997), the treatment capacity of government-run methadone programs has picked up in the last decade (ASSMCA 2016). Since La Reforma, there has also been the emergence of a variety of biomedical for-profit clinics. Though still relatively small in capacity (SAMHSA 2013), for-profit clinics now offer a range of alternative therapies, ranging from evidence-based treatments (e.g., motivational interviewing), to laser therapies that are widely criticized by clinicians as scientifically unfounded. In departure from its predecessor (DSCA), the current administrative body responsible for overseeing addiction treatment (ASSMCA) has pointedly aligned itself with the DSM-IV model of addiction as one disease—substance use disorder—that ranges from low to high severity (DoH PR 2008). Similarly, the Puerto Rican Office for Drug Control has set out, in its strategic plan, a "public health" response to the drug problem that emphasizes that addiction is a chronic relapsing disease, not a sign of moral weakness (OCD PR 2002). Whatever their aspirations and doctrinal commitments, however, public health officials in Puerto Rico continue to operate in an environment shaped by historically entrenched political, institutional, and regulatory mechanisms that are highly conducive to the persistence of labor therapies.

The Puerto Rican therapeutic community story should also serve as a reminder, therefore, that in our efforts to comprehend the management of any illness or disorder, we must also be attuned to the wide variety of interests and concerns that shape and animate therapeutic regimes. These extend far beyond "therapeutic" matters of sickness and healing. As this chapter has shown, Puerto Rico's therapeutic communities historically owe their form, practice, and survival to a complex collection of locally defined needs, pressures, and opportunities. Mass unemployment, prison overcrowding, comprehensive centralization, and political patronage, to name but a few of the historical processes discussed in this chapter, are each salient dimensions of the historical context in which therapeutic communities and labor therapies have thrived.

As Puerto Rico's public services and infrastructure continue to crumble under a variety of economic and environmental crises, therapeutic communities may well take on additional roles in disaster relief. This should come as no surprise. As we have seen, this exchange of one abeyance mechanism for another has been an enduring, if not defining, character-istic of Puerto Rico's therapeutic community movement. In the aftermath of hurricanes Irma and Maria, further scholarly engagement with Puerto Rico's therapeutic communities is much needed.

NOTES

1. *Hogar* literally means "home" or "hearth," and the acronym CREA stands for Center for the Re-education of Addicts.

2. The first therapeutic community for addiction in the United States was Synanon, established in 1958 in Los Angeles (see Clark 2017).

3. One of the earliest studies, implemented by CISLA, estimated that there were ten thousand addicts in 1964 (CISLA 1964). This figure should be treated with caution, however, since the study simply asked current residents to estimate how many addicts they knew personally.

4. In 1985 the agency's total annual budget was $16,113,483. Of this, 88 percent was dedicated to the services and operational costs of the agency itself, with just 8.8 percent spent on community-based or private programs (DSCA 1986).

5. This was achieved through an amendment to Law 60 of 1973 (the law that created DSCA), which restricted minimum education requirements to the department's clerical and administrative staff.

6. In 1974 the ratio of staff to patients in DSCA-operated residential treatment facilities was: 1/8 for paraprofessionals, 1/34 for doctors and 1/3 for non-clinical professionals. Across its treatment modalities (including residential, outpatient, and methadone), the ratio of staff to patients was: 1/13 for paraprofessionals, 1/42 for doctors, 1/26 for nurses, 1/5 for non-clinical professionals (DSCA 1975a).

7. Phoenix House, which is probably the largest single provider with over 120 programs across the United States, is listed in Substance Abuse and Mental Health Services Administration's (SAMHSA) National Registry of Evidence-Based Programs and Practices.

8. In an invited submission to the Legislature in the run-up to DSCA's closure, it had denounced the agency as a "monstrosity" and declared private organizations as cheaper, more agile, and therefore best equipped to deal with the epidemic (Ríos 1993).

9. In 2000, among all registered facilities providing drug treatment in Puerto Rico, 83.2 percent described themselves as residential while 16.8 percent described themselves as outpatient.

10. Under article 13.02 of the 2000 Mental Health Act, which remains in operation at time of this writing despite several amendments to the law, community

organizations "will continue providing their community services according to their historic, traditional and customary practices" (Department of Health Puerto Rico 2000).

REFERENCES

Acker, Caroline Jean. 2002. *Creating the American Junkie: Addiction Research in the Classic Era of Narcotic Control*. Baltimore: Johns Hopkins University Press.

Administración de Servicios de Salud Mental y Contra la Adicción (ASSMCA). 2004. "Puerto Rico Substance Abuse Needs Assessment Program: 2002 Provider Survey Final Report. Hato Rey, PR: Mental Health and Anti Addiction Services Administration; 2004."

———. 2016. "Need Assessment Study of Mental Health and Substance Use Disorders and Service Utilization among Adult Population of Puerto Rico." Final Report, December 2016.

Babb, Margarita. 1969. "Piden ciudadania ayude combatir los Drogas" [Citizens asked to help combat drugs]. *El Mundo*, March 13.

Besteman, Karlst J. 1992. "Federal Leadership in Building the National Drug Treatment System." *Treating Drug Problems* 2: 63–88.

Biehl, João. 2013. *Vita: Life in a Zone of Social Abandonment*. Berkeley: University of California Press.

Cabán, Cynthia López. 2016. "No creo que tengamos una política de drogas en Puerto Rico." *El Nuevo Dia*. October 18. http://www.elnuevodia.com /cuentame/cuentame/nota/nocreoquetengamosunapoliticadedrogasen puertorico-2252829/.

Cabrera, Alba. 1969. "CREA, programa efectivo en re-educacion de adictos" [CREA, effective program in the re-education of addicts]. *El Mundo*. January 25.

Cappa, Luis. 1972. "Censuran conducta Efrain Santiago, Comisiones Senado aprueban $200 mil para CREA" [Behavior of Efrain Santiago criticized, Senate Committee approve $200 thousand for CREA]. *El Mundo*, February 4.

Centro de Investigaciones Sobre la Adicción (CISLA). 1964. "Centro de Investigaciones Sobre La Adicción (CISLA) [Center of Research on Addiction]. *Boletin Informativo* 1 (1).

Clark, Claire. 2017. *Recovery Revolution: The Battle Over Addiction Treatment in the United States*. Columbia University Press.

Courtwright, David T. 1995. "A Century of American Narcotic Policy." *Treating Drug Problems* 2: 1–62.

Deitch, David, and Liliane Drago. 2010. "The Therapeutic Community for Drug Abuse Treatment: A Journey yet Unfolding in the Recovery Movement." In *Addiction Medicine*, 905–23. New York: Springer.

Densen-Gerber, Judianne. 1973. *We Mainline Dreams: The Odyssey House Story*. New York: Doubleday.

Department of Correction and Rehabilitation. 1994. "Intermediate Sanctions Plan." Departamento de Corrección y Rehabilitación. Biblioteca Legislativa de Puerto Rico.

Department of Health Puerto Rico (DoH PR). 2008. "Ley No. 408—Ley de Salud Mental de Puerto Rico (Act No. 408—Puerto Rico Mental Health Act)." 2008.

Departamento de Servicios Contra la Adicción (DSCA). 1975a. "Descripción de la estructura administrativa y programática" [Description of administrative and programatic structure]. Estado Libre Asociado de Puerto Rico. Biblioteca Legislativa de Puerto Rico.

———. 1975b. "Drug Abuse Prevention Plan for Puerto Rico. Department of Services against Addiction. Annual Performance Report 1974–75." Estado Libre Asociado de Puerto Rico.

———. 1977. "Drug Abuse Prevention Plan for Puerto Rico." Program Planning Division.

———. 1983a. "Descripción de la estructura administrativa y programática" [Description of administrative and programatic structure]. Estado Libre Asociado de Puerto Rico.

———. 1983b. "Informe anual 1981–1983" [Annual report 1981–1983]. Estado Libre Asociado de Puerto Rico. Biblioteca Legislativa de Puerto Rico.

———. 1986. "Memorial explicativo para el prepuesto de gastos de funcionamiento y de mejoras permanentes año fiscal 1985–1986." Estado Libre Asociado de Puerto Rico.

———. 1990. "Memorial explicativo para el prepuesto de gastos de funcionamiento y de mejoras permanentes año fiscal 1989–1990." Estado Libre Asociado de Puerto Rico.

Dietz, James L. 1986. *Economic History of Puerto Rico: Institutional Change and Capitalist Development*. Princeton, NJ: Princeton University Press.

El Mundo. 1969. "Rehabilitando al adicto" [Rehabilitating the addict]. November 4.

———. 1970a. "Senador Colon alaba labor centro rehabilitacion adictos" [Senator Colon praises work of addict rehabilitation center]. April 8.

———. 1970b. "Organizan comite pro Hogar CREA" [Committee Pro Hogar CREA organized]. February 16.

———. 1970c. "Es un exito casa CREA juncos" [It's a success CREA house juncos]. May 2.

———. 1972a. "Logran enmienda resolucion asignara $200 Mil a CREA" [Amendment achieved resolution will assign $200 thousand to CREA]. February 3.

———. 1972b. "Director Hogares CREA dice hay mas de 50 mil adictos a drogas en isla" [Director of Hogares CREA says there are more than 50 thousand drug addicts across island]. October 18.

———. 1988. "Creando hombres nuevos" [Creating new men]. April 8.

———. 1989. "Cruzada de fe y esperanza" [Crusade of faith and hope]. May 26.

El Reportero. 1981. "Teen Challenge Contra Metadona." http://pciponline.org/.

El Vocero. 1984a. "Encausan asaltantes CREA: 59 cargos graves" [CREA Assailants Prosecuted, 59 grave charges]. August 6.

———. 1984b. "Móvil tumbar dominio rivales: Asesinatos en CREA" [Death squad defeats rivals: Assasinations at CREA]. May 18.

Estado Libre Asociado de Puerto Rico. 1973. "Diario de sesiones del proyecto del senado 495 de 1973," April 6. Biblioteca Legislativa de Puerto Rico.

Fiddick, Peter. 1967. "Junkie Cure Junkie." Manchester Guardian Weekly, February 16.

Garcia, Angela. 2015. "Serenity: Violence, Inequality, and Recovery on the Edge of Mexico City." Medical Anthropology Quarterly 29 (4): 455–72.

Goldberg, Peter. 1980. "The Federal Government's Response to Illicit Drugs, 1969–1978." The Drug Abuse Council. http://www.druglibrary.org/schaffer/library/studies/fada/fada1.htm.

Gutiérrez, Pedro. 1996. "Calderón Praises Hogar CREA Record." San Juan Star, February 1.

Hansen, Helena. 2005. "Isla Evangelista—a Story of Church and State: Puerto Rico's Faith-Based Initiatives in Drug Treatment." Culture, Medicine and Psychiatry 29 (4): 433–56.

———. 2018. Addicted to Christ: Remaking Men in Puerto Rican Pentecostal Drug Ministries. Oakland: University of California Press.

Hopper, Kim, and Jim Baumohl. 1994. "Held in Abeyance: Rethinking Homelessness and Advocacy." American Behavioral Scientist 37 (4): 522–52.

Intercambio Puerto Rico (IPR). 2015. "Humiliation and Abuse in Drug Treatment Centers in Puerto Rico." https://es.scribd.com/doc/265551445/Humillaciones-y-Abusos-en-Centros-de-Tratamiento-Para-Uso-de-Drogas-PR.

Jaffe, S. 1966. Narcotics—An American Plan. New York: PS Eriksson.

Janzen, Rod. 2005. "The Rise and Fall of Synanon: A California Utopia." Nova Religio 9 (1): 116–17.

Kolb, Lawrence. 1925. "Types and Characteristics of Drug Addicts." Mental Hygiene 9: 300–313.

Lapp, Michael. 1995. "The Rise and Fall of Puerto Rico as a Social Laboratory, 1945–1965." Social Science History 19 (2): 169–99.

Lebrón, Edna Martinez. 1976. "Los centros de metadona en el área metro-politana" [Methadone centers in the metropolitan area]. Universidad de Puerto Rico.

Legislative Assembly of Puerto Rico. 1977. Acts and Resolutions of Puerto Rico. 1st Regular Session. 1st and 2nd Special Sessions. Eighth Legislature. Hato Rey, Puerto Rico.

Macro Systems. 1972. "Drug Treatment and Prevention Programs in the Commonwealth of Puerto Rico." Prepared for the Senate of the Common-wealth of Puerto Rico. San Juan, Puerto Rico. Archivo Histórico Universitario.

McNeil, Donald G. 2016. "Puerto Rico Braces for Its Own Zika Epidemic." *New York Times*, March 19. http://www.nytimes.com/2016/03/20/health/zika -virus-puerto-rico.html.

Mizruchi, Ephraim Harold. 1983. *Regulating Society: Marginality and Social Control in Historical Perspective*. New York: Free Press.

Mulligan, Jessica M. 2014. *Unmanageable Care: An Ethnography of Health Care Privatization in Puerto Rico*. New York: New York University Press.

Navarro, Mireya. 1995. "Puerto Rico Reeling under Scourge of Drugs and Rising Gang Violence." *New York Times*, July 23. http://www.nytimes.com /1995/07/23/us/puerto-rico-reeling-under-scourge-of-drugs-and-rising -gang-violence.html.

Office for Drug Control Puerto Rico (OCD PR). 2002. "Strategic Plan for Drug Control for the Free Associated State of Puerto Rico." Free Associated State of Puerto Rico.

O'Neill, Kevin Lewis. 2015. *Secure the Soul*. Oakland: University of California Press.

Open Society Foundation (OSF). 2016. "No Health, No Help: Abuse as Drug Rehabilitation in Latin America and The Caribbean." https://www.open societyfoundations.org/events/no-health-no-help-abuses-drug-rehabilitation -centers-latin-american-caribbean.

Planas, Lydia Pena de, Myriam Rodriguez de Lopez, and Carmen Alvarez. 1965. "El tratamiento de adictos a drogas en Puerto Rico" [The treatment of drug addicts in Puerto Rico]. Universidad de Puerto Rico.

Planning Board of Puerto Rico (PBPR). 1964. "Economic Report to the Gover-nor, 1964." http://lcw.lehman.edu/lehman/depts/latinampuertorican /latinoweb/PuertoRico/Bootstrap.htm#_edn9.

———. 1984. "Historic Employment and Unemployment Rates by Labor Group in Puerto Rico, 1984." http://lcw.lehman.edu/lehman/depts/latinampuerto rican/latinoweb/PuertoRico/Bootstrap.htm.

Ramirez, Efren. 1966a. "Puerto Rican Blueprint." In *Narcotics: An American Plan*, edited by Saul Jeffee, 112–28. New York: PS Eriksson.

———. 1966b. "The Mental Health Program of the Commonwealth of Puerto Rico." *Rehabilitating the Narcotics Addict.* Washington, DC: Vocational Rehabilitation Administration, US Dept. of Health.

———. 1968a. "A New Program to Combat Drug Addiction in New York City." *British Journal of Addiction to Alcohol & Other Drugs* 63 (1–2): 89–103.

———. 1968b. "The Existential Approach to the Management of Character Disorders with Special Reference to Narcotic Drug Addiction." *Review of Existential Psychology & Psychiatry.* http://psycnet.apa.org/psycinfo/1968 -10792-001.

Ramirez, Efren, and Juan José García Ríos. 1985. "Letter from Efren Ramirez and Juan José García Ríos to Governor, Hon. Rafael Hernández Colón." March 19. Ocean Park Ambulatory Therapeutic Community.

Ríos, Juan José García. 1983. "Hogar CREA, INC. A Puerto Rican Alternative for the Treatment of Addiction." The International Council on Alcohol, Drugs & Traffic Safety. http://www.icadtsinternational.com/files/documents /1983_047.pdf.

Rodriguez, Wilda. 1978. "CREA le responde a Sila Nazario" [CREA responds to Sila Nazario]. *El Nuevo Dia,* June 15.

Ross, Karl. 1995a. "CREA Easily Takes Lion's Share of Legislative Cash Hand-outs." *San Juan Star,* September 26.

———. 1995b. "CREA Rehabilitation Claim of 87% Unsubstantiated." *San Juan Star,* September 26.

Safa, Helen I. 1995. *The Myth of the Male Breadwinner: Women and Industrialization in the Caribbean.* Boulder, CO: Westview Press.

———. 2011. "The Transformation of Puerto Rico: The Impact of Modernization Ideology." *Transforming Anthropology* 19 (1): 46–49.

Seattle Times. 2014. "Puerto Ricans Struggle over Once-Grisly Oso Blanco Prison." May 17.

Sharma, Aradhana, and Akhil Gupta. 2009. *The Anthropology of the State: A Reader.* John Wiley & Sons.

Stoler, Ann Laura, Carole McGranahan, and Peter C. Perdue. *Imperial Formations.* Santa Fe, NM: SAR Press, 2007.

Substance Abuse and Mental Health Services Administration (SAMHSA). 1997. "Uniform Facility Data Set (UFDS): 1997 Data on Substance Abuse Treatment Facilities." http://wwwdasis.samhsa.gov/dasis2/nssats/1997_ufds_rpt.pdf.

———. 2013. "National Survey of Substance Abuse Treatment Services (N-SSATS): 2013 Data on Substance Abuse Treatment Facilities." http:// www.samhsa.gov/data/sites/default/files/2013_N-SSATS/2013_N-SSATS _National_Survey_of_Substance_Abuse_Treatment_Services.pdf.

Sugarman, Barry. 1974. *Daytop Village: A Therapeutic Community.* New York: Holt Rinehart and Winston.

Velez, Edwin. 1986. "Estudio descriptivo sobre los Hogares CREA, Inc." [Descriptive study of Hogares CREA, Inc.]. Universidad de Puerto Rico.

Wells, Henry. 1971. *The Modernization of Puerto Rico. A Political Study of Changing Values and Institutions.* Cambridge, MA: Harvard University Press.

White, William L. 1998. *Slaying the Dragon: The History of Addiction Treatment and Recovery in America.* Bloomington, IL: Chestnut Health Systems/ Lighthouse Institute.

White, William L., and William R. Miller. 2007. "The Use of Confrontation in Addiction Treatment: History, Science and Time for Change." *Counselor* 8 (4): 12–30.

Wright, Michael. 1982. "Puerto Rican Prisons 'Ready to Explode' Despite Reform Effort." *New York Times*, November 19. http://www.nytimes.com/1982/11/19 /us/puerto-rican-prisons-ready-to-explode-despite-reform-effort.html.

6 "You Put Up with Anything"

ON THE VULNERABILITY AND EXPLOITABILITY
OF FORMERLY INCARCERATED WORKERS

Gretchen Purser

"My resume is all spotty. It's all over the place," explained Bryan, a forty-two-year-old biracial man with a history of employment in landscaping, broken up by multiple bouts in prison on drug-related charges. "And addressing that with a new employer, addressing the criminal record? That can be very stressful. . . . What I have come to find," Bryan continued, "is that the only places who don't care about your record, they treat you bad. You know, there's employers around that I've worked for and they look for people specifically like me that are formerly incarcerated. Because two things: they can pay you less and they don't have, you know, they can just treat you like rubbish. . . . They take advantage of people who need a job."

Like Bryan, Don—a forty-eight-year-old Black man who has spent fourteen years of his life behind bars—has found himself relegated to "things that everybody else don't wanna do" since his release from prison. "It seems that I'm walkin' around with this mark on my forehead," he explained. "I already have some scores against me. For one, I'm poor, in a bracket of economics. And, bein' a ex-con, they don't look at me as nothing but a serpent, you know? So, what I have to pick up on is things that everybody else don't wanna do, and none of 'em really last too long." And the worst part, Don later added in a voice filled with rage, is that "they act like they're doing you such a big favor by lettin' you work there!"

. . . . .

The prison, scholars argue, operates as an increasingly important labor market institution, one that conceals unemployment in the short run by absorbing many who would otherwise be jobless, but exacerbates it in the long run, by increasing joblessness among inmates after release (Western and Beckett 1999). One result of the roughly seven hundred thousand inmates released from state and federal prisons each year has been the formation of, as Peck and Theodore (2008, 7) put it, a "criminalized class as a structurally salient, racialized labor market category."

There is a voluminous body of research documenting the paltry prospects of, and barriers faced by, former prisoners in the labor market. Most of this research is animated by the belief that employment is the lynchpin to economic stability, desistance from criminal activity, and, therefore, "successful" reentry (Sampson and Laub 1993; Uggen 1999; Visher and Travis 2003). Despite the work requirements that abound in prison (explored in earlier chapters in this volume), the experience of incarceration is widely recognized to diminish both human and social capital, dramatically lowering formerly incarcerated workers' already low chances in the labor market (Visher and Travis 2003). Moreover, an array of punitive and ineffective "post-incarceration policies" limit ex-offenders' access to jobs and to the educational opportunities that could help them navigate the labor market (Hall, Wooten, and Lundgren 2016; Oliver 2010). Finally, the routine use of largely unregulated criminal background checks in the employment application process has opened the floodgates to rampant discrimination against those bearing the "mark," or negative credential, of a criminal record (Emsellem and Mukamel 2008; Harris and Keller 2005; Pager 2003, 2007). Studies conducted with employers have shown that they are more averse to hiring applicants with criminal history records than any other disadvantaged group (Holzer 1996; Holzer, Raphael, and Stoll 2003). This aversion is particularly pronounced in the case of Black applicants with criminal history records; for white applicants, a criminal record decreased their chances of an employer call back by 50 percent, whereas for Black applicants, the criminal record decreased their chances of an employer call back by over 60 percent (Pager 2003, 2007). Indeed, Pager (2003) found that white applicants with a criminal history record were more likely to get a call back than were Black applicants without a record. Thus, "Blacks with criminal records are doubly branded, the penalty of their delinquent status amplified by their racial identity" (Martin 2013, 504). Bruce Western (2006, 109) concludes that "men tangled in the justice system" are trapped at the very tail end of the hiring queue and "become permanent labor market outsiders."

These well-documented barriers to employment have spawned considerable research on the employment-related "reentry" services available to the formerly incarcerated. Organizations in the prisoner reentry industry have increased by 240 percent between 1995 and 2010 (Mijs 2016; Miller 2014). Moreover, they are a striking example of the mounting convergence between carceral and welfare institutions and ideologies, a trend captured by reference to, and theorization of, the "penal welfare" state (Garland 2001; Hatton 2018). These programs tend to be significantly modeled off of welfare-to-work programs (Kaufman 2015; Mijs 2016; Thompkins 2010; Wacquant 2010). Indeed, Wacquant argues that reentry organizations, as a form of what he calls "prisonfare," "prosper on the penal side thanks to their organizational isomorphism with workfare on the social policy side."[1] These organizations channel clients on what Mijs (2016) calls a "road to reentry" that is premised upon a particular diagnosis of their problems and that prescribes a particular course of action. Given that the structural conditions in the labor market are largely outside of these organizations' spheres of influence, reentry programs overwhelmingly tend to focus on the "job-readiness" or "employability" of former inmates: their attitudes, character, soft skills, moral selves, and psychological dispositions (Caputo-Levine 2018; Halushka 2016; Miller 2014; Purser and Hennigan 2017). Halushka (2016), for instance, refers to reentry curriculum as "work wisdom," a "tough love approach to labor market reintegration" (87) aimed at getting clients to see that they can "overcome obstacles through hard work, tenacity, and a positive attitude" (85). Miller (2014, 315) concludes that "psychological processes and outcomes, rather than prisoners' economic ones have become the primary site of intervention in criminal justice and social policy." Prisoner reentry programming, in other words, is largely a "dispositional intervention," occurring "inside former prisoners' heads." Its aim is the moral redemption or rehabilitation of "clients." As a result, Wacquant (2010, 617) argues, these organizations tend to "put the onus of failed 'reintegration' on former convicts, thereby screening out the accelerating degradation of the condition of the American working class in the 'gloves-off economy' which increasingly consigns them to long-term subemployment and laborious poverty."

As the quotes above make clear, men like Bryan and Don have not been barred from employment so much as they have been channeled toward, and relegated to, the bottom segment of the labor market characterized by, as they describe it, opportunistic, even predatory, employers. Contrary to claims of a "labor market lockdown" (Peck and Theodore 2008) that animate so much of the existing research, most former prisoners rely on employment as a significant source of income after their release (Harding et al. 2014, 12). However, they tend to find themselves in extremely precarious, low-wage jobs—often via day labor and temporary staffing agencies (Elcioglu 2010; Purser 2012; Ray, Grammon and Rydberg 2016)—earning annual incomes that are 30 to 40 percent lower than the average of their non-incarcerated peers (Western 2006; see also Pettit and Lyons 2009). Bumiller (2015), for instance, found that employers who are willing to hire applicants with criminal records explicitly acknowledge the "undesirability" of the work. They admit to strategically turning to this "criminalized class" out of a rather desperate need to find "good workers to do bad jobs."

Still, surprisingly little is known about the actual experiences of the formerly incarcerated once on the job, navigating not the inequitable power dynamics of the labor market but those of the workplace. Thus Hallett (2012) calls for deeper theoretical and empirical engagement with the "subaltern context of prisoner reentry" and the "broader symbiotic relationship [that] exists between the social control of former prisoners through the social control exerted by markets" (Hallett 2012, 222–23). "Criminologists," he argues, "must work to extensively document the experiences of former prisoners as they negotiate the 'neoliberal penality' of employment markets, so that the 'invisible hand' which may render aspects of former prisoners' experiences also invisible may be brought to light" (222).

In this chapter I heed Hallett's call. Drawing on in-depth interviews with formerly incarcerated men in the city of Syracuse, New York, I highlight three distinct but overlapping challenges that they face on the job: status degradation ceremonies, the perpetual presumption of criminality, and the extra-economic pressure of parole supervision. In so doing, I make two contributions, or correctives, to the existing research on and programmatic response to reentry. On the one hand, I attend to the qualitative experience, as opposed to the quantitative deficiency, of jobs available to the "criminalized class" at the tail end of the hiring queue. On the other hand, I focus on the "exploitability" rather than the "employability" of formerly incarcerated workers. In so doing I show how the carceral state exacerbates vulnerability in the workplace, producing a highly exploitable labor force and depressing labor standards at the bottom of the labor market.

RESEARCH METHODS AND DATA

Between the fall of 2012 and the fall of 2014, I conducted in-depth, semi-structured interviews with sixty formerly incarcerated men residing in the city of Syracuse. A medium-sized Rust Belt city in upstate New York, Syracuse has the highest rate of concentrated poverty among both Blacks and Hispanics in the nation (Jargowsky 2015). Fully one-third of all residents and nearly half of all families with children under the age of eighteen live below the federal poverty level. Over the past half century, Syracuse has undergone the familiar saga of deindustrialization and depopulation, losing more than 34 percent of its population since its peak in 1950. The result is a city-wide vacancy rate of 11 percent and a labor market that is dominated by the low-wage jobs of the service economy. Today, Syracuse is a significant site of social service provision for the poor, including returning inmates.

All participants in this study had felony convictions for crimes that run the gamut from drug possession to robbery, arson, and homicide. Although they were not necessarily working at the time of the interviews, all interviewees had some work experience in the formal labor market since their release from prison. Roughly two-thirds (68%) of interviewees identified as Black, 28 percent identified as white, and 4 percent identified as Latino or Native American. Sixteen percent were under thirty years old, 26 percent were in their thirties, 36 percent were in their forties, and 20 percent were fifty years or older. At the time of our interviews, slightly more than half of respondents were under post-correctional supervision in the form of parole or federal probation.

Interviewees were recruited with the assistance of job counselors, one at a local homeless shelter and another at a local prisoner reentry program; both referred potential participants to me and posted recruitment flyers in their respective facilities. Recruitment was also conducted via snowball sampling, as participants referred me to others they knew in a similar predicament. A semi-structured interview protocol was used to facilitate conversations with former inmates about, primarily, their job-searching strategies, employment histories, and experiences in the workplace. Still, these conversations were open-ended enough to enable participants to share what was on their minds and to bring up unanticipated concerns. Many of the men revealed that they were yearning for conversation and eager to discuss the challenges they had faced prior to, during, and since their incarceration. These one-on-one, face-to-face interviews ranged from seventy-five minutes to nearly three hours in length and were conducted in a variety of locations, including local coffee shops, public libraries, and offices at the shelter, the reentry program, and the researcher's university. After each completed interview, participants were remunerated $20 in cash for their time. With participants' written consent, all interviews were digitally recorded, transcribed, and iteratively analyzed and coded for thematic content using Atlas.ti qualitative data analysis software.

"GO BACK TO JAIL": STATUS DEGRADATION CEREMONIES

Many of the men I interviewed talked about having experienced what Harold Garfinkel calls "status degradation ceremonies," or acts of public shaming and harassment on the job. Through such ceremonies, Garfinkel (1956, 420) argues, individuals are formally denounced and "made strange" through "communicative work directed to transforming an individual's total identity into an identity lower in the group's scheme of social types." The frequency with which interviewees described such experiences reveals that their criminal justice involvement has not served as a barrier to employment so much as it has served as a permanent badge of dishonor and a warrant for public belittling. Although these encounters with degradation were widespread among my respondents, they were especially pronounced, and often explicitly racialized, for Black men.

Terrence, for instance, is a fifty-five-year-old, Black man who served a fifteen-year prison sentence for a homicide conviction. Since his release on lifetime parole, Terrence has been hit with a string of technical violations that have kept him cycling in and out of prison, the most recent of which kept him behind bars for a full five years. As Terrence calmly explained:

> I was furious, I was angry, um . . . hopeless. I was devastated. I was a little nutty by the time I was released. 'Cause I had lost everything: I lost my wife, my children, my family had died. Ya know, relationships, bridges were broken. And I was homeless and had to go in the shelter. I had a hard time with that because it reminded me so much of a prison. And so, my thing was, okay, I'm gonna do what I always done. I'm gonna get a job. Ya know, one of the things I came out knowin' is that I had to be employed, because for me, not bein' employed is a setup [to re-incarceration].

Though Terrence was admittedly "willin' to do anything," his job search left him in a tailspin. As he matter-of-factly put it, "How do I go to a prospective employer and say, well, I was incarcerated for takin' somebody's life. I mean, how do you do that? You know what I mean?" Like so many individuals released from prison, Terrence eventually secured a job with a temporary staffing agency, one that specializes in blue-collar employment in the janitorial, construction, and "light industrial" sectors. Terrence recalled the day of his hire: "I said, well, listen, ma'am, I was just released. She said, I don't care about that. Let's get you workin'!" He was placed on a long-term assignment in a unionized manufacturing facility. Though immensely thankful for the job, Terrence's experience in the workplace quickly descended to one of routinized personal humiliation and racialized degradation, of being "made to stand as 'out of the ordinary'" (Garfinkel 1956, 422). As Terrence explained:

> That's what I did for two years and it was the most stressful two years of my life. I've never been in a more hostile environment. At the beginnin',

they didn't actually know that we had been incarcerated. But [the staffing agency] hired a lot of ex-inmates because they needed people willing to go into this hostile environment, do the work, and not be intimidated. So it was a bunch of us out there. I was one of the first ones out there. I worked for the maintenance department, cleaning the bathrooms. And [the other workers] would mess 'em up. They'd go in there and defecate on the wall and piss all over the floors. Deliberately! So I had to go right back in there and clean it again. That's what I dealt with every day for two years. . . . And there were all kinds of incidents of violence 'cause they didn't want us there. . . . It was always hostile. They would write on the walls "go back to jail" and call us apes, baboons, and monkeys. Anything to provoke you.

Later in our interview, Terrence commented on the psychological impact of this kind of perpetual public denunciation, as well as the fear—rooted in his constrained labor market opportunities and hence the very real possibility of joblessness—that drove him to put up with it for so long:

I knew I didn't have to put up with what I was puttin' up with, ya know, the hostility, the violence, the humiliation. And I ended up having to go and like talk to somebody about that because it was affectin' me, ya know. It was just this tightrope. I knew I could do better. But I was scared to quit because with my background, I didn't think I could get a job. So I held on for as long as I could. But it affected me every day. Some nights I slept only two, three hours a night. I had to start takin' medication.

Jim, a forty-nine-year-old white man, had similar, if less striking, experiences of status degradation in the workplace. He works over sixty hours a week at a family-owned restaurant in nearby Auburn, New York, "'cause they didn't ask about my record or nothin'." Even still, his boss and coworkers discovered that he had served time in prison, and since then he, like Terrence, has experienced routine and public belittling on the job. Once a respected participant in the workplace, the revelation of his criminal history has led to him being denounced as "outside" of the legitimate order. As he recalled:

I did time in Auburn Prison. And one of the COs [correctional officers] came in there—'cause I'm a dish washer, you know, I clean the place, I do all the dishes, this and that—he's like, "I know you, scum bag." Of course, I'm a scum bag 'cause I was prison. And then he went to the lady, you know, the owner of the place, talkin' to her. [Mimicking the voice of the female owner]

"Oh, you been in prison? You ain't told me." Well, you didn't ask! Since then, since the CO recognized me, they constantly put me down, callin' me a "dirty convict" and "our little inmate" and this and that.

In fact, he has nearly become inured to such daily degradation, which includes the routine denial of the lunch breaks to which he is legally entitled. As he explained, "I think they actually enjoy having someone around they can treat any kind of way. 'Cause they haven't fired me!"

Other men I interviewed met a quite different fate when their criminal records were revealed. Indeed, several described a distinct kind of status degradation ceremony that entailed being dramatically escorted off of a job site by police officers when higher-level corporate management caught wind of their criminal backgrounds and insisted that they be let go. For these workers, this "communicative work" not only transformed their identities, but also stripped them of their actual and symbolic membership in the workplace.

This is precisely what happened to Michael, a thirty-four-year-old Black man who had, after more than four months of consistent job searching, secured employment at a dollar store following his release from prison. As he explained:

I worked at, um, Family Dollar, which was crazy. I worked there for seven weeks and then they said Human Resource called us, the Family Dollar I was workin' at, after seven weeks of employment, and they said, "Oh we gotta let him go." And they actually had two police come and get me! Why would they hire me if my background was gonna be a problem? And why would they send police to escort me off the premises, humiliating me and shit in front of customers? Like I committed some kinda crime by working?

Two months after this occurrence, Michael could still feel the sting of that unanticipated and unnecessary humiliation. He went on to explain that the store's application had simply asked, "Have you ever been convicted of a felony in the last seven years?" Michael, whose conviction dated from ten years prior, explained: "So I said no. So I didn't lie or nothin' like that. So why, ya know? . . . I don't feel like I'm gettin' a fair shake. It's like, Family Dollar, how is you an equal opportunity employer? You hired me and I'd been workin' there for seven weeks, never caused no problems. But then you escort me off the premises like a criminal, tryin'na humiliate me and shit in front of customers? You're not an equal opportunity employer, 'cause I'm not equal. Ya know, fuck that."

For Terrence, Jim, and Michael, then, the acquisition of work neither removed the stigma of criminal justice involvement nor led to proof of their moral redemption. Indeed, and as I continue to explore in the next section, the workplace serves as a site where this stigma and moral devaluation are reproduced.

"I'M AN EASY TARGET": THE PRESUMPTION OF CRIMINALITY

As formerly incarcerated individuals, many of the men I interviewed explicitly lamented the fact that their dedication to work was not enough to counter the stigma of a criminal record or to erase the perpetual presumption of criminality that shades their day-to-day experience on the job. These men were hired only to discover that they would be treated with the kind of suspicion and subjected to a level of surveillance that they thought they had left behind upon their release from prison.

Ronnie, for instance, is a fifty-three-year-old, Black, formerly incarcerated veteran who works in maintenance at a local synagogue. Though the stigma of his criminal background has not prevented him from obtaining employment, it has narrowed the kinds of jobs he has been able to obtain and deeply colored his experiences on those jobs. Specifically, Ronnie talked about the heightened level of surveillance and scrutinization that he faces, and his being a convenient scapegoat for any wrongdoings in the workplace, he explained:

> I'm privy to a lot of cash, jewelry, and stuff like that. Going into offices and your purse is layin' there, you got your wallet over there. And I know at first, they was like, "Well, what is he gonna do? Let's see." 'Cause I'm not just from prison, but a Black man from prison. It [the criminal conviction] sticks with you. It's, "Ah, he did this, that's who he is." And nowadays people don't believe people can change. . . . So they'll be like, he's gonna do it, you know, like he's gonna rob this place, you know, if not now, then eventually. 'Cause he did it before. So yeah, I'm vulnerable in the sense that anything that they say, they would automatically like say, "Yeah, he did it, because he's

Black and he's been in prison." Because I've been a prisoner, I'm scrutinized more and I'm an easy target.

Despite his recognition of his doubly determined and inextricably linked vulnerability—"'cause I'm not just from prison, but a Black man from prison"—Ronnie maintained that he has "no problem tellin' anybody, you know, hey, you know, yeah, I've been locked up before." "And you'd be surprised," he assured me, echoing Bryan. "A lot of people on the kind of jobs I've had," Ronnie claimed, "they've been locked up before, too. So it's like almost a common thing: welcome to the club!"

A similar experience was shared by Daryl, a forty-nine-year-old Black man who two weeks prior to our interview had been laid off from his job working for a company contracted to provide mailroom services within a large office building. He enjoyed his job and had thought everything was going well. In recent months, he had even received a pay raise and was making $11.35/hour. But like Ronnie, he, too, struggled to navigate the presumption of criminality, and when something went inexplicably missing in the workplace, he found himself the sole target of suspicion and blame:

> So my job, I work in the mail room, get the FedEx packages and the mail and drop it on your desk. Well, they told me a cell phone was missin'. They told me there was a cell phone on the table. But only thing I did is come, throw a package on there, and then leave. . . . But they came and asked me about the cell phone. I said, I don't even know what you're talkin' about. He said, "Uh, well we got you on camera." I said, "You got me on camera doin' what? My job?" 'Cause I didn't touch no cell phone. I said, "Well since you got me on the thing, let me see." . . . It never showed me reachin', grabbin' nothin' off there. Nothin' goin' in my pocket or anything. So, I said, "I don't see where you see me grabbin' any cell phone." I said, "Where's the proof at?" He said, "Well, I don't need no proof." I said, "Well, if y'all wanna let me go, that's what y'all tryin'na do is get me outta here. I know I ain't got no grounds 'cause you already think I'm a criminal." You know, I mean. And that's basically what happened up there.

Particularly striking about Daryl's account is his sense that he "ain't got no grounds" to contest management's suspicion and blame, since they already think of him as a criminal.

"THEY THINK THEY GOT THE UPPER HAND
ON YOU": THE PRESSURES OF PAROLE

The final challenge raised by numerous interviewees concerned managing the coercive stipulations and extra-economic pressures of parole. For the more than half of my interviewees who were on parole or federal probation, the pressure to find and maintain gainful employment was particularly acute. As Zatz et al. (2016) report, on any given day, roughly nine thousand people nationwide are incarcerated for violating a probation or parole requirement to hold a job. Nevertheless, nearly all of my respondents reported that they received little help from their parole officer when it came to job searching, and many reported, perversely, that parole supervision itself made it difficult to hold down the jobs that they *did* manage to secure. As Pogrebin et al. (2015, 424) observe, these two roles—of being a worker and a parolee—are "not necessarily compatible."

Jeff, for instance, is a fifty-three-year-old white man with considerable experience in the trades. Upon his release from prison, he had a high degree of confidence in his ability to find work. And sure enough, within a month of his release, he was hired by a local masonry company. But given the stipulations of his parole, which restricted his freedom of movement, he was—in a striking blow to his confidence—soon fired. Dismayed and discouraged, he was, through no fault of his own, once again out of work. As he explained: "My PO was lettin' me go like to Rochester, Buffalo, you know, he didn't have a problem with that. But then, they had a job in Pennsylvania—'cause we was doin' the Rite Aids and Eckerds, uh—and my PO told me, he's like, 'You can't go. Can't cross state lines.' So, yeah, the guy [boss] told me, he's like, 'If you're not there, you don't have a job.' The guy was a straight prick. He had that whip out." Jeff found himself out of work given the intransigence of his employer and the incompatibility of his parole stipulations with the demands and expectations of the job.

For still others, the intrusions and inquisitions of parole officers made it difficult for them to blend in and to see themselves and be seen by others as valued members within, the workplace. In this sense, parole generated a "humiliating dynamic," directly contributing to the status degradation ceremonies and scapegoating explored in the previous sections (Pogrebin et al. 2015). Take, for example, the experience of Grant, a forty-six-year-old Black man. With a warm demeanor and excellent skills in self-presentation, Grant easily secured a job following his release from prison working in maintenance for a low-income, nonprofit housing developer. But as soon as he started the job, Grant discovered what he views as the nearly insurmountable challenges of working while on parole:

> They're [the parole officers] startin' to come to my job. And they're startin' to embarrass me. I'm gettin' tired of it, ya know? One day they came to my job and I'm sittin' there. We're sittin' there in the office, and they just like come in with their vests on, their guns on their side, with their badges out, and I'm like, what's goin' on? And they're like, "Oh, just comin' in to check on you, you know, blah, blah." I was like, "This is embarrassin'! We got other employees here that, you know, they see this?" They were like, "Oh, you don't tell us; we do what we wanna do." So now they're mad at me because I got mad at them. They've done this three times already. I'm gettin' tired of it. It's ridiculous.

Grant went on to explain the fallout from these random, but repeated, workplace visits and the ways in which they served to separate and distinguish him from the—in his words—"decent people" around whom he now worked:

> One of my coworkers said, like, "Why are police here?" And I said, 'Scuse me, so I'm on parole, this is my parole officer, and they're here to check on me, to make sure I'm workin', make sure I'm not lyin' and all of that. . . . I didn't feel I was gonna lose the job. . . . That wasn't it. It's just, 'cause it's embarrassing. 'Cause I'm meetin' decent people now, I know decent people at work, people that's never got caught doin' anything wrong in their life. And even though they know my background, still it's embarrassing, you know, to have them snoopin' around, bossin' you around, treatin' you like you nothin' but a criminal.

Richard, a fifty-seven-year-old Black man who did five separate bids in prison, described much the same experience as Grant. He had managed to secure a janitorial position at the DoubleTree Hotel, a job for which he was repeatedly recognized as "employee of the month." But he, too, soon encountered what he viewed as the embarrassing dynamics and "sabotaging" impact of parole: "But the parole officer was comin' to my job. Came to my job out there. And I said, 'Let me meet you outside at DoubleTree.' He said, 'I'm gonna do it how I want to do it because I need to see that you really work there.' I'm already bringing him the checks [pay stubs]! And at nighttime the only doors that are open are the front doors. I'm like, 'You don't need to be doin' this. It doesn't help me.'" Richard described the acrobatic labor it took to manage the capricious whims of his surveilling parole officer while doing his job of ensuring the safety and comfort of the guests in the hotel. He eventually had to talk to his coworkers about these visits, to ward off any suspicions of wrongdoing: "'Cause he [the parole officer] came out there all sneaky like. It looked like we were maybe rendezvousing for a drug transaction or something like that. But I wasn't lettin' him in the building. He wasn't gonna come in there making no announcement, making me, the hotel people, uncomfortable. Man, you shouldn't be doin' that! This is not—your job is to assist me, not to sabotage me."

But, for Richard, the primary effect of such intrusive parole supervision was that it made him reticent to bring up legitimate concerns on the job, including what he saw as unfair and racially discriminatory scheduling practices. The mere possibility of being violated due to job loss—and hence the threat of reincarceration—was enough to keep him quiet and complacent in the workplace. In this respect, the extra-economic pressure of parole—as one instance of the coercive power of the carceral state— heightened his deference to, and thus vulnerability in the hands of, his employer. As he explained:

'Cause if you lose that job, you could be violated. Especially if you're fired. They like, it's, "Do I wanna actually go back to prison for standin' up for my rights on this job?" Because that's where it can lead. You know, so a lotta people when they do lose their job, they end up not reportin' [to parole]. I'm not gonna take a chance that the man puttin' handcuffs on me, not today I ain't. I'm not. This is ridiculous. And you call 'em and they say, "No, get down here now." And now you really like, he's *really* gonna lock me up, so I *really* ain't gonna go. It's like a no-win situation. And once they do catch you, they'll say, "I wasn't gonna lock you up, but we're not gonna let you dictate when you can come down here, blah, blah, blah." And so, fear plays a factor.

As Richard explained, working under the coercive threat of the carceral state creates a "no win situation": you can stand up for your rights in the workplace and risk another bout of incarceration on a parole violation or you can dutifully submit to exploitative and degrading working conditions.

Indeed, other workers talked about raising such concerns in the workplace, only to see coworkers and bosses evoke their parole status in a deliberate effort to silence them into submission. In this regard, we see how employers use the threat and weight of the revolving door of the criminal justice system to stifle worker dissent and induce submission. Michael, for instance, is a thirty-five-year-old Black man who works for a day labor agency that provides the staff for, among other places, a recycling facility. "So, you know, in my position, bein' a convicted felon and stuff like that, you tend to just take whatever. You take freakin' whatever. You like, shit, *somebody* give me an opportunity." Although Michael seemed to be managing the stench, dangers, and drudgery of this notoriously dirty job, he was struggling with the way he was being treated by coworkers and supervisors alike, many of whom used his status as a parolee as a warrant for "taking the upper hand" by threatening and intimidating him:

> It's just they got some younger dude who keeps hounding me. 'Cause he knows that I'm on parole. Makin' threats and shit. If I complain about something, he be like, "I called my sheriff buddy and I'm gonna get you in trouble," and shit. Even the supervisor be like, "I'm callin' your fucking parole officer on you." I'm like, "What he got to do with anything? Why would you be threatenin' me with that?" Should be concerned about why I wanna walk out this motherfucker in the first place. Why I'm feelin' the way I'm feelin'. When you on parole, they think they got the upper hand on you or some shit. They like, "You lucky you even got a job here." I'm like, "So y'all think you can just treat me like shit 'cause you gave me a job?"

As much as Michael wanted to leave his job, he felt unable to do so. Pointing to the looming threat of prison, he explained that he "can't afford to be like ... oh, I'm'a quit 'cause then I always end up right back there. So, I can't. Even if they treat you like shit or whatever, you can't. So you just suck it up. You got to."

DISCUSSION: THE EXPLOITABILITY
OF THE FORMERLY INCARCERATED

In his account of post-Fordist social control, De Giorgi (2007: 261) argues that "work and exploitation—as common grounds for the construction of a shared sense of belonging—are thus replaced by fear and insecurity." Yet, as my findings suggest, work and exploitation have not been replaced by, but rather operate through, fear and insecurity. In the words of Richard above: "fear definitely plays a factor." Due to the intertwined fears of joblessness and reimprisonment, the formerly incarcerated experience a profound vulnerability to exploitation in the workplace, exhibited in my respondents' expressed willingness to "do just about anything," to "put up with anything," and to "just suck it up."

Several of my interviewees highlighted the fear that underpins this vulnerability, but they also pointed to subjective dispositions and, more specifically, the way the experience of incarceration "primes" them, to cite Hatton's introduction to this volume, to embrace low-wage, precarious work upon release. It does so by eroding one's sense of oneself as a rights-bearing citizen, as someone—to echo Daryl's quoted above—lacking the "grounds" to contest egregious forms of mistreatment. As Bryan, the forty-two-year-old biracial man quoted at the start of this chapter, astutely explained: "A guy from prison comes home not aware at all of his rights. He don't believe he has any rights. You know you have a right to go back to the prison if they wanna send you, but that's about pretty much all. . . . So when you come out, you put up with anything man. You put up with anything. And you have to put up with more when the person knows that you been locked up."

Don, the forty-eight-year-old Black man also quoted at the start of this chapter, explained it in these terms: "And that's the thing. If somebody, if you were told that you were unattractive, to a point where you, you felt that way, it's kinda hard to convince you that you're beautiful, right? We're dealin' with self-esteem here. So, when you're told that you have no rights, right, you often believe that. You lose yourself when you're told that you can't do something, or ya know, you're limited."

Whether they believe they have no rights, as Bryan and Don attest, or are simply too reticent and afraid to claim those rights, these men raised countless examples of "sucking it up," "putting up with anything," or "just going along." In his current job doing outreach for a social service agency, Terrence, for instance—whose story I shared earlier—admitted to routinely working "off the clock" in an effort to prove his worth. Though he is regularly required to work at least forty hours each week, he is only paid for thirty-two of those hours. Though he knows that this is wrong, and that his employer is required by law to pay him for the hours worked, he hasn't even considered contesting it. "I gotta do better," he explained. "Because I'm a third-class citizen. I'm a convicted felon. And I come from a community of color. I gotta outdo. And that, all that's not correct thinkin'. You know what I'm sayin'? But that's where I'm at."

Lewis, to cite yet another example, is a Black, thirty-six-year-old man who served a four-year sentence for drug possession. Following his release from prison, he exclusively sought jobs through temporary staffing agencies, "because I knew I had the felony on the record, so I would go to places that wouldn't check. Temp agencies, they don't check into you that hard." He eventually got hired on by a company directly, only to lose the job six months later when the company finally pursued a criminal background check: "I knew they were gonna do the check, 'cause they informed me they was about to it. So, I just didn't come back to work that following Monday. And it was like I didn't call or nothin', they didn't call or nothin'. 'Cause everybody understood why. It was like that was that." In fact, Lewis did nothing to contest the fact that he never received his final paycheck. As he explained, "I didn't press it, because I didn't wanna go through the embarrassment and have to face, you know, all that stuff, so I just went along, ya know. Even though I knew they owed it to me. Ya know, it was a good run while it lasted."

Finally, Anthony, a thirty-two-year-old Black man residing in the homeless shelter since his release one month prior, had just started a job as a line cook at Applebee's, where he was making $9 per hour. "Anything's better than nothin' right now, ya know?" He elaborated on his willingness to accept just about any terms and conditions of the job:

> It turns out, a lot of prior convicts or ex felony members are some of the hardest workers you can get. Like me, now that I got a job, I'm not gonna screw it up. 'Cause I can't just go get another job. . . . [Quitting] that's not an option for me. I have to deal with stuff, including stuff that no worker

should have to deal with. I can't—'cause it's not easy for me to walk into a place and say, "Hey, I'm a ex-con, I did ten years for a robbery; hire me!" It's, it's not easy at all. It's a blessin' to even get this job I have. So it may not be much, but it's somethin' I wanna hold on to, and I can't do anything to jeopardize that.

Thus, the criminal justice system exacerbates workers' vulnerability to, as Anthony put it, "stuff that no worker should have to deal with": the exploitative practices and dangerous, degraded, and degrading working conditions at the bottom of the labor market. Moreover, as Gomberg-Munoz (2012, 341) has argued, criminalization not only "render[s] certain workers . . . more vulnerable to oppressive labor practices." It also "justif[ies] such oppression with a rhetoric of moral inferiority."

CONCLUSION

Scholarly and policy attention has overwhelmingly focused on documenting and mitigating the labor market barriers faced by the formerly incarcerated. But left unaddressed are the actual workplace experiences of this growing, structurally salient population. Without knowing what workers encounter on the job, we have only a superficial understanding of their struggles, especially those pertaining to high turnover and low labor market participation. In this chapter, I have endeavored to broaden our understanding of the labor market and workplace consequences of mass incarceration, documenting how the combination of the stigma of incarceration and the coercive force of the carceral state shapes workers' experiences on the job, rendering them vulnerable to public belittling, scapegoating, and exploitation.

These findings have a twofold significance. First, they provide much-needed empirical support for the claim that mass incarceration should be recognized not simply as a "barrier to good jobs" but as an "enforcer of bad ones," contributing to the exacerbation of worker vulnerability and the depression of labor standards (Zatz 2016; see also Wacquant 2009). Second, they call into question the dominant practices of employment-related "reentry" programming, which tends to be structured as a dispositional intervention aimed at preparing participants for, and subordinating them to, the precarious, low-wage labor market. Rather than such "workforce development" initiatives, this paper underscores the serious need for "workforce empowerment" initiatives targeted at the formerly incarcerated, a population who so often experience employment as a "punitive curtailment of rights" (Hatton 2018:187) and who are thus particularly susceptible to degrading treatment and degraded conditions at work. Workers' rights advocates need to make a more concerted effort to reach out to and organize this vulnerable segment of the workforce.

ACKNOWLEDGMENTS

This research was conducted with the generous support of an Early Career Research Grant from the W.E. Upjohn Institute for Employment Research, a Spivack Community Action Research Initiative Grant from the American Sociological Association, and a faculty mini-grant from the Program for the Advancement of Research on Conflict and Collaboration from the Maxwell School of Syracuse University. I would like to thank Marsha Weissman and the anonymous reviewers for feedback on earlier versions of the chapter.

NOTE

1. Wacquant (2010, 616–17) continues: "Both offer meager and temporary support on condition that recipients submit to disciplinary monitoring pointing them to the substandard employment slots of the service economy. Both use the same case-based techniques of surveillance, moral stigma, the abridgement of privacy and graduated sanctions to 'correct' wayward behavior. Both produce not material improvement and social incorporation, but forced capitulation to extreme precarity and civic liminality as the normal horizon of life for their clientele."

REFERENCES

Bumiller, K. 2015. "Bad Jobs and Good Workers: The Hiring of Ex-prisoners in a Segmented Economy." *Theoretical Criminology* 19 (3): 336–54.

Caputo-Levine, D. 2018. "Learning to Be a 'Safe' Ex-con: Race, Symbolic Violence, and Prisoner Reentry." *Contemporary Justice Review* 21 (3): 233–53.

De Giorgi, A. 2007. "Toward a Political Economy of Post-Fordist Punishment." *Critical Criminology* 15 (3): 243–65.

Elcioglu, E. F. 2010. "Producing Precarity: The Temporary Staffing Agency in the Labor Market." *Qualitative Sociology* 33 (2): 117–36.

Emsellem, M., and D. A. Mukamel. 2008. "The New Challenge of Employment in the Era of Criminal Background Checks." In *The Gloves-Off Economy: Workplace Standards at the Bottom of America's Labor Market*, edited by A. Bernhardt, H. Boushey, L. Dresser, and C. Tilly (Eds.), 191–215. Ithaca, NY: ILR Press.

Garfinkel, H. 1956. "Conditions of Successful Degradation Ceremonies." *American Journal of Sociology* 61 (5): 420–24.

Garland, D. 2001. *The Culture of Control: Crime and Social Order in Contemporary Society*. Chicago: University of Chicago Press.

Gomberg-Muñoz, R. 2012. "Inequality in a 'Post-racial' Era: Race, Immigration, and Criminalization of Low-Wage Labor." *DuBois Review* 9 (2): 339–53.

Hall, T. L., N. R. Wooten, and L. L. Lundgren. 2016. "Postincarceration Policies and Prisoner Reentry: Implications for Policies and Programs Aimed at Reducing Recidivism and Poverty." *Journal of Poverty* 20 (1): 56–72.

Hallett, M. 2012. "Reentry to What? Theorizing Prisoner Reentry in the Jobless Future." *Critical Criminology* 20 (3): 213–28.

Halushka, J. 2016. "Work Wisdom: Teaching Former Prisoners How to Negotiate Interactions and Perform a Rehabilitated Self." *Ethnography* 17 (1): 72–91.

Harding, D., J. J. B. Wyse, C. Dobson, and J. D. Morenoff. 2014. "Making Ends Meet after Prison." *Journal of Policy Analysis and Management* 33 (2): 440–70.

Harris, P. M., and K. S. Keller. 2005. "Ex-offenders Need Not Apply: The Criminal Background Check in Hiring Decisions." *Journal of Contemporary Criminal Justice* 21 (1): 6–30.

Hatton, E. 2018. "When Work Is Punishment: Penal Subjectivities in Punitive Labor Regimes." *Punishment & Society* 20 (2): 174–91.

Holzer, H. J. 1996. *What Employers Want: Job Prospects for Less-Educated Workers*. New York: Russell Sage Foundation.

Holzer, H. J., S. Raphael, and M. A. Stoll. 2003. "Employment Barriers Facing Ex-Offenders." Urban Institute Reentry Roundtable. http://www.urban.org/sites/default/files/alfresco/publication-pdfs/410855-Employment-Barriers-Facing-Ex-Offenders.PDF. Accessed January 10, 2016.

Jargowsky, P. 2015. "The Architecture of Segregation: Civil Unrest, the Concentration of Poverty, and Public Policy." The Century Foundation. https://tcf.org/content/report/architecture-of-segregation/. Accessed October 10, 2015.

Kaufman, N. 2015. "Prisoner Incorporation: The Work of State and Non-governmental Organizations." *Theoretical Criminology* 19 (4): 534–53.

Martin, L. 2013. "Reentry within the Carceral: Foucault, Race and Prisoner Reentry." *Critical Criminology* 21 (4): 493–508.

Mijs, J. J. B. 2016. "The Missing Organizational Dimension of Prisoner Reentry: An Ethnography of the Road to Reentry at a Nonprofit Service Provider." *Sociological Forum* 31 (2): 291–309.

Miller, R. J. 2014. "Devolving the Carceral State: Race, Prisoner Reentry, and the Micro-politics of Urban Poverty Management." *Punishment & Society* 16 (3): 305–35.

Oliver, B. E. 2010. "My Sentence Is Over but Will My Punishment Ever End." *Dialectical Anthropology* 34 (4): 447–51.

Pager, D. 2003. "The Mark of a Criminal Record." *American Journal of Sociology* 108 (5): 937–75.

———. 2007. *Marked: Race, Crime, and Finding Work in an Era of Mass Incarceration*. Chicago: University of Chicago Press.

Peck, J., and N. Theodore. 2008. "Carceral Chicago: Making the Ex-Offender Employability Crisis." *International Journal of Urban and Regional Research* 32 (2): 251–81.

Pettit, B., and C. J. Lyons 2009. "Incarceration and the Legitimate Labor Market: Examining Age-Graded Effects on Employment and Wages." *Law and Society Review* 43 (4): 1–32.

Pogrebin, M. R., P. B. Stretesky, A. Walker, and T. Opsal. 2015. "Rejection, Humiliation, and Parole: A Study of Parolees' Perspectives." *Symbolic Interaction* 38 (3): 413–30.

Purser, G. 2012. "'Still Doin' Time': Clamoring for Work in the Day Labor Industry." *WorkingUSA: The Journal of Labor and Society* 15: 397–415.

Purser, G., and B. Hennigan. 2017. "Work as Unto the Lord: Enhancing Employability in an Evangelical Job Readiness Program." *Qualitative Sociology* 40 (1): 111–33.

Ray, B., E. Grommon, and J. Rydberg. 2016. "Anticipated Stigma and Defensive Individualism during Postincarceration Job Searching." *Sociological Inquiry* 86 (3): 348–71. doi:10.1111/soin.12124.

Sampson, R. J., and J. H. Laub. 1993. *Crime in the Making: Pathways and Turning Points through Life*. Cambridge, MA: Harvard University Press.

Thompkins, D. E. 2010. "The Expanding Prison Reentry Industry." *Dialectical Anthropology* 34 (4): 589–604.

Uggen, C. 1999. "Ex-offenders and the Conformist Alternative: A Job Quality Model of Work and Crime." *Social Problems* 46 (1): 127–51.

Visher, C. A., and J. Travis. 2003. "Transitions from Prison to Community: Understanding Individual Pathways." *Annual Review of Sociology* 29: 89–113.

Wacquant, L. 2009. *Punishing the Poor: The Neoliberal Government of Social Insecurity.* Durham, NC: Duke University Press.

———. 2010. Prisoner Re-entry as Myth and Ceremony. *Dialectical Anthropology* 34 (4): 605–20.

Western, B. 2006. *Punishment and Inequality in America.* New York: Russell Sage Foundation.

Western, B., and K. Beckett. 1999. "How Unregulated Is the U.S. Labor Market? The Penal System as a Labor Market Institution." *American Journal of Sociology* 104: 1030–60.

Zatz, N. 2016. "How Criminalizing Unemployment Creates Bad Jobs." *Talk-Poverty* (blog). https://talkpoverty.org/2016/04/28/how-criminalizing-unemployment-creates-bad-jobs/. Accessed August 10, 2016.

Zatz, N., T. Koonse, T. Zhen, L. Herrera, H. Lu, S. Shafer, and B. Valenta. 2016. "Get to Work or Go to Jail: Workplace Rights under Threat." Research Brief of the UCLA Institute for Research on Labor and Employment, UCLA Labor Center, and A New Way of Life Reentry Project. http://www.labor.ucla.edu/publication/get-to-work-or-go-to-jail/. Accessed May 1, 2016.

7 Working Reentry

GENDER, CARCERAL PRECARITY,
AND POST-INCARCERATION GEOGRAPHIES
IN MILWAUKEE, WISCONSIN

Anne Bonds

As stated at the start of this volume, the United States has the largest prison population in the world. Over 2.1 million people are in state and federal prisons or in local jails, with more than 6.6. million—one in every thirty-eight adults—under some form of correctional supervision, including probation and parole (Kaeble and Cowhig 2018). Though far eclipsed by patterns of male incarceration, the number of women incarcerated in prisons and in jails in the United States is at a historic high (Kajstura 2018), with populations growing over 800 percent in just forty years (Chesney-Lind and Pasko 2013).[1] Each year an astonishing eleven million people cycle through local jails (Wagner and Rabuy 2015) and nearly seven hundred thousand people leave prisons and return home. Limited access to resources following incarceration intensifies the challenge of reentry, and many experience difficulties finding housing and employment (Nixon et al. 2008; Bushway et al. 2007). These numbers paint a stark picture of the sheer magnitude and reach of mass criminalization in the United States, which includes the vast network of practices, policies, laws, and assumptions that undergird and sustain contemporary landscapes of carcerality and social control.[2] The carceral system extends into households and neighborhoods, stretching across numerous scales and jurisdictions, and is reworking family formations and gender identities (Roberts 2012; Simmons 2012) and the reproduction of community and everyday life.

In this chapter, I draw from research with formerly incarcerated women in Milwaukee, Wisconsin, to analyze the gendered and racialized implications of reentry and the ways in which gendered socially reproductive demands complicate what McKittrick (2011) has identified as "prison life," which she defines as "the everyday workings of incarceration as they are necessarily lived and experienced . . . a form of human life and struggle inside and outside of prisons" (956). Understanding more about women's circulation through the carceral system is critically important, not only because the number of incarcerated women is rapidly increasing, but also because women's incarceration is often obscured and overlooked, despite growing scholarly and popular attention to prison expansion. Too often, examinations of expanding carceral geographies eclipse women's entanglement within the vast carceral system and reinforce gendered dichotomies about state violence and the regulation of the poor (Bonds and Loyd 2017).[3]

My research with formerly incarcerated women in Milwaukee explores the ways in which women negotiate and experience the enduring effects of incarceration within the context of gendered racial capitalism. In this chapter, I first situate women's incarceration and reentry trends within the dynamics of mass criminalization. I then consider social reproduction and the precarious circumstances of carcerality in a neoliberal context. Following this discussion, I introduce Milwaukee trends and discuss how the women participating in my study have negotiated reentry and connect their experiences to neoliberal precarity, gendered assumptions of criminality, and the demands of socially reproductive labor. I conclude by arguing against the development of more gender-responsive programing in prisons that further entrench the carceral state.

WOMEN AND REENTRY IN THE ERA OF MASS CRIMINALIZATION

Though proportionally men make up the vast majority of those who are under correctional supervision, feminists reject "majority-rule" analyses of incarceration (Simmons 2012, 72) to examine the gendered implications of a prison system largely designed for and operated by men.[4] In fact, the number of women in prison is growing at a far faster rate than the number of men (Richie 2012; Roberts 2012; Kajstura 2018). In the significant prison-building years of 1995–2009 the number of imprisoned women grew by 87 percent (Chesney-Lind and Pasko 2013). Very troubling gender disparities characterize contemporary trends in incarceration. While the total number of people in state prisons has decreased since 2009 as a result of growing jail incarceration and reforms, shifting supervised populations from prisons to parole, and other forms of monitoring, this decline is only visible among men, and in some states, expanding populations of incarcerated women have offset any overall prison population decrease (Sawyer 2018). As of 2018, 1.2 million women were under some sort of correctional supervision (Kajstura 2018). These statistics make it abundantly clear that women are being criminalized at historically unprecedented levels. However, critiques of mass incarceration often overlook the dramatic growth in women's incarceration or emphasize women's experiences with incarceration vis-à-vis men's imprisonment. Critiques often emphasize how women are implicated by the prison system as it relates to male displacement from families and communities, rather than examining the ways in which women *themselves* are being confined and entangled within the violence of the carceral system.

The trajectory of growth in women's incarceration tracks with the overall growth of incarceration. The number of women incarcerated in state prisons has rapidly expanded over the past four decades, while the growth in federally incarcerated female populations has been much less dramatic. That is, the incarceration of women is primarily driven by local and state policies. One of the most significant dynamics distinguishing women's pattern of incarceration from men's is that a much larger proportion of women are incarcerated in jail (Sawyer 2018). Many women in jail have not been convicted (60%), but rather are being held as they await trial (Kajstura 2018). In many instances, women are unable to pay for bail. Women's marginalized position in labor markets and households means that they often have fewer resources to pay bail and other court fees. Those who have been convicted and are incarcerated in jail are generally serving sentences of under one year. Women's high rate of jail incarceration is particularly alarming, as jails offer fewer services than state institutions, leaving many women without critical health care or access to educational or employment training (Sawyer 2018). It is also important to note the geography of women's incarceration. State institutions, which are often remotely located, make family contact and visitation much more difficult. This distance compounds the difficulty of sustaining relationships and parenting for the 80 percent of incarcerated women with children under the age of eighteen (Scroggins and Malley 2010).

In spite of commonly held conceptions of the prison as spatially and socially confining criminal populations from society on a semipermanent basis, the prison is better understood as being just one site in a larger circulation within the carceral system (Peck and Theodore 2008 252). In fact, the average stay in prison is typically quite short, and 95 percent of those who are incarcerated will eventually be released back into society (Pager 2007). Given the number of people circulating through the system, surprisingly few provisions are in place to support those released from prison (Nixon et al. 2008; Pager 2007; Peck and Theodore 2008; Bushway et al. 2007; Clear 2007). As Peck and Theodore (2008) note, "'Going home' very often means returning to impoverished central-city neighborhoods, many of which are practically devoid of living-wage jobs" (251). These employment constraints are compounded by conditions that further criminalize former prisoners, including bans on particular forms of employment and housing resulting from a felony record.

This context leaves little room for post-incarceration success, and 40 percent will return to prison within three years, suggesting that "the revolving door of the prison has now become the source of its own growth" (Pager 2007, 2). This pattern is particularly marked for women. In many states, the number of women in prison because of parole violations (as opposed to new crimes) supersedes the number incarcerated for new convictions (Chesney-Lind and Pasko 2013). While most incarcerated women will be released from prison, less than half successfully navigate reentry. Nearly two-thirds of women convicted for property and drug offenses will be rearrested within three years of their release (Scroggins and Malley 2010). In the next section, I turn to a discussion of carceral precarity and social reproduction to consider the particularly gendered barriers formerly incarcerated women encounter as part of "prison life."

CARCERAL PRECARITY AND SOCIAL REPRODUCTION

As state capacities across scales are increasingly invested in sustaining the vast carceral system, it has also been necessary to make sharp reductions in state spending in areas like education, housing, employment, and social welfare (Gilmore 2007; Peck 2003). Drastically reduced social programs and investments in basic infrastructure and community development have displaced key functions of the state onto communities, households, and individuals and have facilitated the expansion of a burgeoning "shadow state" nonprofit and voluntary sector delivering services formerly provided by the state (Wolch 1990; Gilmore 2009). As scholars working in the field of feminist political economy have well established, processes of neoliberalization and devolution have reworked the scales of social reproduction, placing additional burdens on women's work in the household, the community, and in workplaces, where they often labor in highly uncertain, segmented occupations in ways that are deeply racialized and classed (Mitchell et al. 2004; Folbre 2002; Meehan and Strauss 2015).

This neoliberal reconfiguration of the state was legitimated through widely circulated discourses about the inefficiencies of "big-government" and culture-of-poverty narratives that identified moral depravity and individual failings rather than structural inequality as the source of poverty (Bonds 2015a; Peck 2003). As is well documented, these shifts were buttressed by highly racialized and gendered myths about "welfare queens" and "the underclass" (Mink 1998; Albelda and Whithorn 2002) that pathologized and criminalized poor people. Meanwhile vulnerable workers—particularly women and people of color—have increasingly relied on contingent, low-wage jobs, as neoliberal restructuring has engendered the rapid expansion of "flexible" employment systems and the proliferation of poorly paid service work (Mitchell et al. 2004; Folbre 2002). These processes have unfolded unevenly, producing highly unequal urban geographies mutually produced through the socio-spatial processes of racism, deindustrialization, disinvestment, and planned urban abandonment.

Racial, class, and gender disparities define the carceral system, and women who have experienced incarceration are seen to have violated social norms on multiple grounds in a racist and heteropatriarchal society.

Women's marginalization in prisons reflects that of other hegemonic social institutions—labor markets, families, community—within which dominant assumptions about gender limit women's access to power and resources (Richie 2012; Scroggins and Malley 2010). Incarcerated women have transgressed both the law *and* norms of proper femininity, and this status will mark and punish them far beyond time spent on the "inside" (Moran 2014; Allspach 2010). Assumptions about violated norms of femininity are particularly marked in the treatment of mothers who are or have been incarcerated (Roberts 2012). Gendered social relations assign to women greater standards of family responsibility and care, and mothers who breach these societal values by becoming incarcerated are considered culpable in a way that incarcerated fathers are not. Intersecting systems of race, class, and gender expose women to higher rates of poverty and insecurity and multiple forms of gendered and racialized violence (Richie 2012; Roberts 2012; Crenshaw 2012). Indeed, the vast majority of women who have experienced incarceration have been in prison for crimes connected to their economic and social marginalization.

Rather than being peripheral to capitalism, the "prison fix" resolves capitalist contradictions and insecurities, disappearing large portions of the poor, under-, and unemployed and, in the post-prison context, ensuring the availability of a pliable and dependent working population. As LeBaron and Roberts (2010) argue, incarceration "instantiate[s] and secure[s] the market in ways that reproduce class-based, gendered, and racialized" insecurities and inequalities (26). Linking carcerality to state regulation of capital and social movements, Julia Sudbury (2005) maintains that the global expansion of carceral institutions can be traced, in part, to efforts to suppress resistance to processes of neoliberalization and to criminalize activities that create alternatives to market dependence.

As a way to synthesize the precariousness of prison life within gendered racialized neoliberal capitalism, I develop the notion of *carceral precarity*. My use of the term *precarity* draws from Waite's (2009) notion of "life worlds characterized by uncertainty and insecurity" (426). This notion brings together conceptualizations of precariousness in work in highly flexibilized, low-wage labor markets and precariousness as a condition of life in a time of increasing economic and social insecurity (Meehan and Strauss 2015). I use the term *carceral precarity* to refer to an embodied form of "capitalist and carceral unfreedom" (LeBaron and Roberts 2010, 19) characterized by the contingency and uncertainty of post-incarceration social relations and labor markets. Carceral precarity is a specific iteration of processes of neoliberalization, securitization, and social reproduction, taking shape across a range of geographic scales: the violence of the prison is embodied through trauma and psychological harm; households are reworked both by incarceration, which separates families, and by the neoliberal devolution of social reproduction. In addition, communities and neighborhoods that have already borne the brunt of earlier rounds of capitalist restructuring experience further disinvestment, reinforcing highly uneven urban geographies.

The condition of carceral precarity is both spatial and temporal, characterized by intense movement and fixity. On one hand, incarceration is defined by forced movement and circulation through the system (Turner 2013), reflecting the coercive power of the state. This includes various transfers from across corrections institutions—from the state prison to county jails to private, out-of-state facilities, back home, and then perhaps back to prison again—as well as the regimented movements of daily life that take place within the prison. Outside of the prison, these forced mobilities include frequent travel (in some cases daily) between parole offices, job sites and labor centers, day care, and other governmental agencies of surveillance. These compulsory post-prison mobilities are required for meeting various benchmarks mandated by the state, those required for parole, for example, or to regain custody of children.

However, carceral precarity also involves fixity, including various forms of confinement, isolation, invisibility, and the structural immobilities created by incarceration (e.g., labor market immobility). These various fixities surfaced in several of my interviews where women expressed, upon returning home, a halting and in some cases debilitating fear of the city, the neighborhoods, and households that had previously been called home. These delimiting anxieties were described in a variety of ways: as fears and traumas stemming from incarceration and the highly regimented daily schedule that makes unscheduled time terribly uncertain; as anxieties about returning to unsafe home spaces where violence and harm are a very likely possibility; and as a constant apprehension about being surveilled and slipping up in some way that might require a revisitation of the horrors of incarceration. Carceral precarity is thus contoured by obligatory movement and containment—forced mobilities and fixity.

Carceral precarity is also temporal, incorporating (among other things) the duration and requirements of incarceration and parole, the enduring mark of a criminal record and the social and economic insecurity engendered by incarceration, and the immediacy of daily survival and social reproduction—as stated clearly by one of my interviewees, the pervasive feeling of "what do I need to do right now to survive." Practices of incarceration literally confine as people "pay their debts" to society, but formerly incarcerated people carry with them the debt of the prison beyond the walls of the prison (LeBaron and Roberts 2010). These debts take many forms and stretch across time: familial and financial liabilities incurred while in prison, restitution, parole payments, employment requirements, the ongoing liability of a criminal record.

As Mitchell et al. (2004) argue, "social reproduction is about how we live" (1). Yet understanding "how we live outside of work"—how we survive and are sustained—has not received sufficient attention in analyses focusing only on formal work and labor markets. I extend their critique to understandings of reentry and prison life, following McKittrick's (2011) definition. The growing body of literature on barriers to reentry overwhelmingly emphasizes the labor market implications of mass criminalization, though it largely excludes the experiences of women and the gendered demands of social reproduction (e.g., Bushway et al. 2007). Social reproduction is "life's work," characterized as the "messy, fleshy components of material life: shopping, cooking and cleaning, daily paperwork, social networking, minding the family store during or after hours, participating in religious or civil organizations, caring for children and the elderly (which also includes mediation with educational, medical, and religious institutions)" (11). These activities have been feminized and associated with the private sphere, historically constructed as the responsibility of women and other marginalized groups. Developing a full understanding of women's negotiation of prison life, therefore, requires attention not only to employment in the formal sphere, but also to the labor of "life's work" as they struggle through the reentry process. It is within this context that I examine the experiences of formerly incarcerated women in Milwaukee, Wisconsin.

"PUNISHED FOR LIFE": WOMEN'S POST-INCARCERATION GEOGRAPHIES IN MILWAUKEE, WISCONSIN

Milwaukee, Wisconsin, has a distinct racial and urban geography that contours reentry and discourses about mass criminalization. The city is consistently ranked according to its "worsts:" It is considered the most racially segregated city in the nation (Denvir 2011), the worst place to raise a Black child (Downs 2016), and the fourth-poorest metro area in the country (Kennedy 2015). Studies place joblessness for African American men above 50 percent (Levine 2014) and find that Wisconsin has the highest Black male incarceration rate in nation (Pawasarat and Quinn 2013). Neighborhoods of color, produced over decades through racist federal, state, and local policies (Bonds 2018), experience routine surveillance and heightened police contact (Loyd and Bonds 2018) and residents from these areas of the city comprise a significant portion of the state's incarcerated population (Pawasarat and Quinn 2013).

Over 41,000 people are currently incarcerated in Wisconsin, with 23,685 in state prisons (WDOC 2019), 13,000 in local jails (Vera Institute 2018), and 65,383 on probation or parole (WDOC 2019). Of those incarcerated in state prisons in Wisconsin 1,334 are women (Vera Institute 2018). Wisconsin's prison population grew dramatically in the late 1990s alongside the implementation of "truth-in-sentencing" measures and other "tough-on-crime" legislation, resulting in a prison building boom in the early 2000s (Bonds 2015b). As with state trends in male imprisonment, women's rate of incarceration grew sharply in the late 1990s. While the number of men incarcerated in Wisconsin has remained fairly consistent over the past twenty years, the number of women incarcerated peaked in 2007, declined slightly in 2010, and has been in a rise since 2013 (The Vera Institute 2018). A notable proportion of those incarcerated in Wisconsin are from Milwaukee County, and the city of Milwaukee: in 2008, 42,046 adults from Milwaukee County were incarcerated, recently released, or on probation or parole (Pawasarat 2009). Much of this population is concentrated in near-northside neighborhoods, an area ravaged by urban renewal, white flight, deindustrialization, and ongoing urban disinvestment (Loyd and Bonds 2018).

To understand more about women's reentry and the sorts of services available to them in the absence of state supports, I interviewed social service providers in organizations offering reentry services to women as well as women who have experienced incarceration in Milwaukee.[5] All of the participants in the study spent time at Taycheeda, the women's correctional institution, located in Fond du Lac, Wisconsin, sixty-seven miles north of Milwaukee. While Taycheeda is the primary facility where the women in my study completed their sentences, all had been moved to other facilities at some point in their incarceration, some to county facilities and others out of state to facilities as far away as Oklahoma and West Virginia. These carceral geographies characterize both the scope of the system and the movement and mobility that define the contemporary carceral experience (Turner 2013; Peck and Theodore 2008; Pager 2007). All of the women that I spoke with noted that this distance and movement compounded the difficulty of their incarceration.

For many of the women I interviewed, release dates brought competing emotions of elation, fear, and apprehension. Freedom was both exciting and full of uncertainties after years of confinement. The women in my study all expressed a sense of isolation, invisibility, and abandonment following incarceration. They note that this sense of abandonment was compounded by the relative lack of reentry services—both from the state and from nonprofit agencies—geared specifically for women. Indeed, most of the women that I spoke with had had no contact with organized, nonprofit services for assistance in their reentry experience. Those that did reach out to nonprofit reentry organizations noted dissatisfaction. As Kamila noted, "When I came home from prison, I tried to get help from [a reentry program] and some these agencies that are still in business and they didn't really help me. They put me in front of a computer and said search for jobs. And so I found my own way." When asked specifically about why the reentry organizations were not helpful, Kamila said, "[They] have never experienced it [incarceration]. Have never—do not know what it feels like. I mean, some of the people who work there do, but they don't know what it feels like to come out . . . and not have a home to go to. They don't know what it feels like to not have food to eat, to struggle and, you know, live on the street."

In line with findings in the literature, the women I interviewed clearly saw their marginalization from having been incarcerated to be compounded by their gender and assumptions of femininity. In particular, several argued that their experience with prison was seen as the ultimate transgression of femininity, particularly for mothers. Given the high number of incarcerated mothers, this underscores the generational implications of women's growing incarceration (Scroggins and Malley 2010). But this figure also points to the significant number of women negotiating reentry while endeavoring to care for children or regain custody of children while contending with social norms about crime, value, and appropriate femininity. These beliefs shape the way that women are viewed in a range of arenas. As Michelle fiercely explained,

> Because [as] a woman, you're viewed as . . . you were a mother, you know. You're a piece of shit. You had an obligation and a duty to your kids, and you chose drugs over them. You chose stealing, or you chose committing crimes over being a mother to your kids. Or, "You have been back seventeen times and you have family. . . . You've deteriorated your mother's health, or you've broken your family." Women who commit crimes are viewed as pathetic and weak and "how could you?" And we point to finger at them and it's accusatory. And so, when they [women] now come and say, "You know what, I would like to try something different and I want this job; will you give me a chance?" we look at them and say no. "Why didn't you try to do this before you committed all these crimes? You don't deserve a chance." We're going to continue to punish them. Society continues to punish women who do wrong because we can't comprehend how a woman who's supposed to be a nurturer and a caretaker and a caregiver and you know all of these things could do something that could be so harmful to other people. With men, it's expected, almost, or it's understandable. You know, but with women we can't comprehend it, and so we're going to continue to punish them whether it's, you know, consciously or otherwise.

Michelle's sharp synopsis strongly resonates with feminist theories about women, crime, and incarceration. Feminist criminologists have traced the ways in which, historically, women committing crimes have been viewed as particularly "morally depraved" and engaged in activities that directly contradict their "moral organization" (Chesney-Lind and Pasko 2013, 127). And yet, as Chesney-Lind and Pasko point out, these assumptions have always been highly racialized. For women of color, who have long been constructed as dangerous or immoral, dominant narratives have always placed them outside of moral boundaries. Feminists have also documented the ways in which violence against women is entangled within the dynamics of mass incarceration (Richie 2012; Chesney-Lind and Pasko 2013; Scroggins and Malley 2010). Sexual violence, physical abuse, and familial obligations critically shape women's imprisonment and their reentry. These flow through stories of the women participating in my study.

Indeed, there are multiple ways in which gendered assumptions shaped women's incarceration and reentry experience. A clear theme emerging from my interviews is the almost complete lack of job skills or educational training offered to prepare women for employment following incarceration. While few would argue that the programs available to incarcerated men are adequate either, the lack of programs for women is especially pronounced (Sawyer 2018). Assumptions about gender and employment clearly shape the very limited programs available to women. For example, interviewees reported participation in programs focused on clerical training and work in beauty salons. By contrast, long-standing programs in men's facilities involve training in the industrial trades and in activities that open up the possibility of higher paid employment following incarceration, despite the mark of a criminal record. Michelle argued that these trends reflect the fact that "society hasn't caught up to the reality that women do go to prison and that they do need training just as much as men." She went on to explain that "Men have like a million different things at their disposal. They have BSI [Badger State Industries], they have, you know, different woodworking classes and, you know . . . I don't know what they call it anymore, but it's like correspondence courses. They get the correspondence courses, they get different schooling, they get all this different reentry programming and boot camp if they qualify for it. And just cognitive training, and I mean they get all of these opportunities that are afforded to them. Women have next to nothing." Moreover, among the women that I spoke with, there is a strong sense that the training options available to women do little to help them outside of prison. As Kamila explained, "The men have more training in the prison. . . . You know, they can do welding and all this other stuff. And the women don't . . . they just have . . . they're just now getting a beauty salon inside Taycheeda. . . . I took the office assistant program. When I came with my certificate everyone was like, 'So, you got a certificate. So what?'"

Sadly, and not surprisingly given the preponderance of practices that continue to criminalize those who have been incarcerated, all of the women in my study emphasized the hardship of finding employment when they returned home from prison. We discussed the challenges of finding employment in terms of experience, skills, and the need for references. Gina, for example, explained the constant burden of having to explain her criminal record:

> I looked for other employment, but once they found out I was a felon . . . . One lady, she called me back and she said, "Oh I'd like to set you up for an interview," and she said, "You sure you're a felon?" And I said, "I'm very sure . . ." [She said,] "You sure this ain't a misdemeanor?" And I wanted to say, "Yeah it's just a misdemeanor," but they would've found out anyway. She said, "Well they frown on those felons you know," so. And that was a hotel joint. So, you know, a lot of times you . . . the door just closes . . . it's like you never stop doing time 'cause you're still being punished, you know, for one mistake. I'm still being punished for one mistake.

Gina went on to talk about her long-term employment in low-wage service work that offered no benefits and her fears about getting older in the context of carceral precarity:

> The job I'm on now I've been at for at least ten years. But it's fast food. I'm tired of fast food, you know, that's for the kids. It doesn't have anything to offer me, you know, as far as no benefits. Now if I get sick or something, you know, I'm out of money. I had to file bankruptcy because I had a big hospital bill and I couldn't afford it. So there's no health, nothing. They don't have any retirement plan. I don't want to grow old and have to live paycheck to paycheck. I want to be able to do something, you know. No 401k or nothing. So I'm in the process of trying to find something, you know, that's better, because fast food, like I said, it was good while it lasted, but I'm up in my fifties now, you know.

By contrast, Kamila, who had a college background, felt as though fast food wasn't even an option for her as a consequence of her record of incarceration. "When I came home, I had three years of college education, [and] McDonald's wouldn't hire me. I went to [a university] freshman, sophomore, and junior year and then I messed up my senior year and nobody would hire me. I used to tell [them], when the officers used to talk crazy [to me] in prison, and I was like, 'I have more education than you do,' but nobody would hire me. I've never worked at a McDonald's. They would not give me the opportunity."

The need for employment is essential, both as a means for survival, but also to fulfill the obligations of parole. Moreover, for those women who've lost their children, they can't begin the process of gaining custody until they've fulfilled their parole requirements. And yet, a record of incarceration makes gaining access to stable employment difficult, compounding the difficulties of reuniting with children and rebuilding disrupted relationships. As noted previously, women enter prison with fewer resources as a result of the gendered pay gaps and assumptions about employment, and they leave prison with fewer training programs and employment skills (Scroggins and Malley 2010; Sawyer 2018). Incarceration disrupts regular employment and the accrual of human and social capital and women's unequal status in society further amplifies their post-incarceration marginalization and precariousness.

Yet, for many participating in my study, the most immediate needs when returning from prison were even more basic: shelter and food. Women with records of incarceration are particularly challenged in housing markets because of both their financial and legal histories. One social service provider I interviewed described this process—limited housing options that require women to return to highly stressful family dynamics—as "immediately setting women up for failure." While several of the women I spoke to were able to call upon friends or family in this time, some were not. Kamila, who was homeless for a period after returning from prison, explained her fundamental needs in this way: "You have to find somewhere to rest, somewhere safe, not just anywhere, but somewhere safe. Because I need to be able to lay my head down and be like, okay, and get some rest." Staying with family during this time created strife for many respondents. Sharmaine, for instance, stayed for a brief time with her sister, but when tensions arose from her presence, she was forced to move out and seek alternative housing just a few weeks after returning home. Marie maintained that she was only able to get a reliable housing situation after incarceration because she found a landlord that was "willing to take a chance on her." For some women, returning to their former residences also put their recovery and reentry in jeopardy. Gina recounted what it meant for her to return to home to an environment of drugs, noting, "But I came home . . . and everybody's on drugs and all. But I stayed strong and I didn't go back to it and I thank God for that."

And yet, for many women, finding someone willing to take that chance may be slim. When asked what women do under these circumstances, Kamila, who operates an informal support group that she personally funds, clarified that post-incarceration survival very often means calling upon prison experiences and relying on extralegal activities:

> Women who are incarcerated learn to survive and they do whatever they have to do to survive. So that means, if I don't have food in my house, I know how to get food. I know how to make food. You learn how to make a meal out of anything in prison. So they take those resources that they have, and they come out here and they survive. If I have to write a check, I'm surviving. So I'm going to deal with it right now, 'cause I need the money right now and if I have to bounce a check, write fraudulent checks . . . they go to the blood bank, and they go and give [sell] blood.

The liminal networks essential to women's post-incarceration survival described in interviews include a range of strategies from living in cars to couch surfing and prostitution. However, the survival strategies described, to a significant degree, have not included participation in formalized supports offered by nonprofit agencies. This absence of participation stems both from a lack of knowledge about the programs available and a sense that the services available are impersonal, not administered by individuals who have experienced incarceration, and are geared primarily toward men. Many, when asked what would be most useful in assisting them in reentry, discussed the need not only for housing and employment support, but also for programs to connect them back to their children, noting that rebuilding family was significant work. As Gina explained, "[I'd like to see] probably some programs to do with your children, you know. Because I felt so guilty. I've been out of their lives so long. You know, a program to, you know, bind you back with your children. Where you can talk and they can express themselves, you know. Because like people say, you can't make up for the time you lost with them. You know I'd love to, but I can't. That's just years I lost, you know."

In the absence of these sorts of programs, several women in my study have forged their own community to support social reproduction, drawing from and building on networks established while incarcerated. This informal network functions by word of mouth and via Facebook. The Facebook page advertises jobs and the needs of women experiencing reentry, and it provides inspiration and community by connecting women who are negotiating reentry with one another. Kamila, who administers the page, explains how it functions: "They can go on Facebook and say, 'Oh I got a job' and 'somebody pray for me 'cause I'm going on this job and I'm a felon and blah, blah, blah.' And we'll be like, 'Oh we praying for you.' They say 'OK, can I use you as a reference?' 'Yeah, you can use me as a reference,' and this and that. And then they get the job and they like, 'Oh this is so awesome. My kids are gonna be able to eat,' and 'I feel good' and this and that."

In many ways, incarceration creates a condition of permanent precarity, a context in which the most vulnerable and marginalized are persistently criminal and experience the profound foreclosure of even the most basic opportunities. Configured through racial and gender hierarchies, carceral precarity is spatialized through processes that literally confine and by neoliberal rationalities that work within and beyond color lines to demarcate and sustain uneven geographies. Carceral precarity is a racialized, gendered, and classed condition of life in the era of mass criminalization, but it is also profoundly material: Interviewees reported the deaths of two women prisoners who had died within the year, each within two years of her release. Within this context, women negotiating post-incarceration in Milwaukee resist being considered "statistics," as one interviewee put it, and have created networks of mutual care in order to support "life's work" and to negotiate the vulnerabilities of prison life.

CONCLUSION: WORKING REENTRY

The empirical results of my research support existing studies documenting women's unmet requirements as they return home from prison, including the need for health care, housing and transportation, education, employment and training, and childcare and parental support (see Scroggins and Malley 2010). In fact, the rise in women's incarceration has generated growing interest in developing "gender-responsive programming" within the carceral system (Lawston and Meiners 2014). This kind of carceral feminism understands women's marginalization in prisons and in reentry as a problem of reform, while leaving the existing ideological and material structures of carcerality intact. That is, rather than questioning how prisons have emerged as the catchall solutions to societal problems (Gilmore 2007), they instead prompt us to consider how the practice of caging humans can be more equitable across the lines of gender. Scholarship in the vein of "women and incarceration" has informed the creation of more gender-responsive programs that often strengthen and expand prison systems in ways that are particularly devastating to low-income communities of color (Lawston and Meiners 2014; Richie 2012). To be clear, in making this critique, I'm not suggesting that we don't account for gender. I also agree that expanding services and support for the incarcerated and for those leaving prisons is a critical necessity. But we must carefully consider how reforms, including liberal reforms premised on gender justice, work to fortify and extend the reach of the carceral state. With this in mind, discussions about the needs of women following incarceration should focus both on the expansion of material and social supports *and* the structural and ideological commitments that have given rise to the largest prison system in the world. When faced with the complexities of better supporting women without reinforcing mass criminalization, we should ask, as Lawston and Meiners (2014, 5) say, "Do these reforms, and the arguments and rhetoric deployed to mobilize support for them, expand, legitimate, or scaffold a carceral logic?"

As I've discussed in this chapter, the challenges women encounter in the reentry process are contoured not just by their incarceration, but also by their racialized and gendered marginalization in society. Attention to social reproduction as a key aspect of carceral precarity broadens our focus beyond formal employment and the labor market to further consider "life's work": the labor, social relations, and practices that sustain households, communities, and human life, more generally (Mitchell et al. 2004). This work includes not just the care of families and the daily requirements of everyday life, but also the creation of community networks. The women in my study, all mothers or caregivers, discussed the various ways in which caregiving was unsettled and displaced via incarceration, even as they highlighted their own challenges of daily survival. They have created networks of mutual aid that were critical to the reproduction of life and community for others navigating reentry. Disrupting dichotomous understandings of labor (productive or reproductive) to instead consider the multiple forms of labor—care work, daily survival, community building—reveals how reproductive work is deeply embodied and entangled with other forms of labor. Recognizing socially reproductive demands is thus critically important for developing better understandings of the gendered and racialized dimensions of reentry and for accounting for the multiple forms of labor necessary for survival in the context of carceral precarity.

In closing, it's important to return to McKittrick's (2011) powerful critique of research on "prison life." Specifically, she argues that research on prison expansion—as it connects to racism, the legacy of slavery, and urbicide, a term she uses to describe the killing of cities and dispossession of urban populations—often unwittingly reifies the production of spatialized racial hierarchies. Through their focus on blight, poverty, criminalization, and capital accumulation, she argues that these conceptualizations reproduce racial violence—even while seeking to challenge it—by again positioning particularly racialized bodies and spaces as already dead or dying. She encourages scholars to embrace complexity and relationality, to move beyond simplistic binaries that reproduce notions of Black places as singularly dispossessed and to instead view marginalized communities as sites of activism, community building, resistance, and care and mutual aid. Discussions of prisons must, therefore, be relational to consider not only how carceral precarity conditions premature death (Gilmore 2007), but also the ways in which it has always fostered communities of resourcefulness and resistance.

NOTES

1. My use of the terms *women* and *men* is not meant to reproduce static, binary categories of gender or to suggest that these categories are singular. Instead, I understand these categories as socially, politically, and economically produced and fractured by difference. Individuals are incarcerated and categorized according to binary gender frames, which is reflected in this chapter.

2. I use the term *mass criminalization* rather than *mass incarceration* to expand the focus beyond prison populations to also include wider logics and systems of carcerality and securitization. The term *mass criminalization* includes a broad and often taken-for-granted nexus of policies, institutions, and discourses

that includes, for example, "tough on crime" legislation and the expansive (and expanding) criminalization of behaviors and geographies, contemporary techniques of policing and surveillance, and the naturalization of incarceration as the solution to societal problems.

3. As Loyd and I have argued, gender-bifurcated analyses of the state regulation of the racialized poor have tended to focus on the carceral state as managing men and the welfare state as governing the lives of women (see, for example, Desmond 2016). Such a framing masks both the inseparability of the welfare state and the carceral state and the ways in which both systems extend into the daily lives of both men and women.

4. It is important to note, as I discuss later in the chapter, that many feminists—especially abolitionist and Black feminists—reject forms of carceral feminism that argue for more inclusive prisons that are better suited for the incarceration of particularly gendered bodies (Lawston and Miners 2014).

5. This chapter is based on in-depth, open-ended interviews with five social service organizations and ten formerly incarcerated women, which took place between 2013 and 2014. The interviews focused on the themes of incarceration, gender, and reentry. All interviewees have been assigned pseudonyms in order to protect their identities.

REFERENCES

Albelda, R., and A. Whithorn. 2002. *Lost Ground: Welfare Reform, Poverty, and Beyond.* Cambridge, MA: South End Press.

Allspach, A. 2010. "Landscapes of (Neo-)liberal Control: The Transcarceral Spaces of Federally Sentenced Women in Canada. *Gender, Place and Culture* 17 (6): 705–23.

Bonds, A. 2015a. "Geographies of Poverty." In *The International Encyclopedia of the Social and Behavioral Sciences,* edited by J. D. Wright, 18:722–27, 2nd ed. Oxford: Elsevier.

———. 2015b. "From Private to Public: Examining the Political Economy of Wisconsin's Private Prison Experiment." In *The Historical Geography of Jails and Prisons,* edited by K. Morin and D. Moran, 205–18. New York: Routledge.

———. 2018. "Progress Report on Race and Ethnicity I: Property, Race, and the Carceral State." *Progress in Human Geography,* 43 (3): 574–83.

Bonds, A., and J. M. Loyd. 2017. "Wacquant's Theory of Neoliberal Urban Carcerality and the Marginalization of Difference." Presentation at the Association of the American Geographers Annual Meeting, Boston, MA, April 5–8, 2017.

Bushway, S., M. A. Stoll, and D. F. Weiman. 2007. *Barriers to Reentry? The Labor Market for Released Prisoners in Post-industrial America*. New York: The Russell Sage Foundation.

Chesney-Lind, M., and L. Pasko. 2013. *The Female Offender: Girls, Women, and Crime*. 3rd ed. Los Angeles: Sage Publications.

Clear, T. R. 2007. *Imprisoning Communities: How Mass Incarceration Makes Disadvantaged Neighborhoods Worse*. Oxford: Oxford University Press.

Crenshaw, K. 2012. "From Private Violence to Mass Incarceration: Thinking Intersectionally about Women, Race, and Social Control." *UCLA Law Review* 1418: 1420–71.

Denvir, D. 2011. "The 10 most segregated urban areas in America." *Salon*, http://www.salon.com/2011/03/29/most_segregated_cities/. Accessed November 2016.

Desmond, M. 2016. *Evicted: Poverty and Profit in the American City*. New York: Crown Publishing.

Downs, K. 2016. 'Why Is Milwaukee So Bad for Black People?' *PBS Newshour*, http://www.pbs.org/newshour/rundown/why-is-milwaukee-so-bad-for-black-people/. Accessed October 28, 2016.

Folbre, N. 2002. *The Invisible Heart: Economics and Family Values*. New York: The New Press.

Gilmore, R. W. 2007. *Golden Gulag: Prisons, Surplus, Crisis, and Opposition in Globalizing California*. Berkeley: University of California Press.

———. 2009. "In the Shadow of the Shadow State." In *The Revolution Will Not Be Funded: Beyond the Non-Profit Industrial Complex*, edited by INCITE! Women of Color Against Violence, 41–52. Boston: South End Press.

Kaeble, D., and M. Cowhig. 2018. *Correctional Populations in the United States, 2016*. Washington DC: The Bureau of Justice Statistics. https://www.bjs.gov/content/pub/pdf/cpus16.pdf. Accessed April 26, 2019.

Kajstura, A. 2018. "States of Women's Incarceration: The Global Context." The Prison Policy Institute." https://www.prisonpolicy.org/global/women/2018.html Accessed April 26, 2019.

Kennedy, B. 2015. "America's 11 Poorest Cities." *CBS Moneywatch*. http://www.cbsnews.com/media/americas-11-poorest-cities/11/. Accessed March 23, 2015.

Lawston, J. A., and E. R. Meiners. 2014. "Ending Our Expertise: Feminists, Scholarship, and Prison Abolition." *Feminist Formations* 26 (2): 1–25.

LeBaron, G., and A. Roberts. 2010. "Toward a Feminist Political Economy of Capitalism and Carcerality." *Signs: Journal of Women in Culture and Society* 36 (1): 19–44.

Levine, M. 2014. "Zipcode 53206: A Statistical Snapshot of Inner City Distress in Milwaukee: 2000-2012," Center for Economic Development Data Brief,

University of Wisconsin-Milwaukee. https://www4.uwm.edu/ced/publications
/53206_revised.pdf. Accessed October 28, 2016.

Loyd, J., and A. Bonds. 2018. Where Do Black Lives Matter? Race, Stigma, and
Place in Milwaukee, Wisconsin. *Sociological Review* 66 (4): 898–918.

McKittrick, K. 2011. "On Plantations, Prisons, and a Black Sense of Place."
Social & Cultural Geography 12 (8): 947–63.

Meehan, K., and K. Strauss. 2015. *Precarious Worlds: Contested Geographies of
Social Reproduction*. Athens: The University of Georgia Press.

Mink, G. 1998. *Welfare's End*. Ithaca, NY: Cornell University Press.

Mitchell, K., S. A. Marston, and C. Katz. 2004. *Life's Work: Geographies of
Social Reproduction*. Oxford: Blackwell.

Moran, D. 2014. Leaving Behind the Total Institution? Teeth, Transcarceral
Spaces, and (Re)inscription of the Formerly Incarcerated Body. *Social &
Cultural Geography* 21 (1): 35–51.

Nixon, V., P. Ticento Clough, D. Staples, Y. Johnson Peterkin, P. Zimmerman,
C. Voight, and S. Pica. 2008. "Life Capacity beyond Re-entry: A Critical
Examination of Racism and Prisoner Re-entry Reform in the U.S." *Race/
Ethnicity: Multidisciplinary Perspectives*, 2 (1): 21–43.

Pager, D. 2007. Two Strikes and You're Out: The Intensification of Racial and
Criminal Stigma. In *Barriers to Reentry? The Labor Market for Released
Prisoners in Post-industrial America*, edited by S. Bushway, M. A. Stoll, and
D. F. Weiman, 151–73. New York: The Russell Sage Foundation.

Pawasarat, J. 2009. "Ex-offender Populations in Milwaukee." Employment and
Training Institute, University of Milwaukee. http://www4.uwm.edu/eti
/2007/Prison.htm. Accessed December 12, 2010.

Pawasarat, J., and L. Quinn. 2013. "Wisconsin's Mass Incarceration of African
American Males: Workforce Challenges for 2013." Employment and Training
Institute, University of Milwaukee. http://www4.uwm.edu/eti/2013/Black
Imprisonment.pdf. Accessed October 28, 2016.

Peck, J. 2003. "Geography and Public Policy: Mapping the Penal State." *Progress
in Human Geography* 27 (2): 222–32.

Peck, J., and N. Theodore. 2008. Carceral Chicago: Making the Ex-offender
Employability Crisis. *International Journal of Urban and Regional Research*
32 (2): 251–81.

Richie, B. 2012. *Arrested Justice: Black Women, Violence, and America's Prison
Nation*. New York: New York University Press.

Roberts, D. E. 2012. "Prison, Foster Care, and the Systemic Punishment of
Black Mothers." *UCLA Law Review* 1474: 1476–500.

Sawyer, W. 2018. "The Gender Divide: Tracking Women's State Prison Growth."
Prison Policy Initiative, January 9. https://www.prisonpolicy.org/reports
/women_overtime.html. Accessed December 23, 2020.

Scroggins, J. R., and S. Malley. 2010. "Reentry and the (Unmet) Needs of Women." *Journal of Offender Rehabilitation* 49 (2): 146–63.

Simmons, M. 2012. "Voices on the Outside: Mass Incarceration and the Women Left Behind." *International Journal of Interdisciplinary Social Sciences* 6 (4): 71–83.

Sudbury, J., ed. 2005. *Global Lockdown: Race, Gender, and the Prison Industrial Complex*. New York: Routledge.

Turner, J. 2013. "Re-'homing' the Ex-offender: Constructing a 'Prisoner Dyspora.'" *Area* 45 (4): 485–92.

Vera Institute of Justice. 2018. "Incarceration Trends by State." http://trends .vera.org/incarceration-rates?data=pretrial&geography=states. Accessed September 24, 2018.

Wagner, P., and B. Rabuy. 2015. "Mass Incarceration: The Whole Pie 2015." Prison Policy Initiative, March 24. https://www.prisonpolicy.org/reports/pie2020 .html?c=pie&gclid=CjwKCAiArbv_BRA8EiwAYGs23HEq0G3SCUDkCxnwf PkWbRposBrn4Qr68ioQXlPXQYLNpzrdWosmzhoCrXcQAvD_BwE. Accessed April 26, 2019.

Waite, L. 2009. "A Place and Space for the Critical Geography of Precarity?" *Geography Compass* 3 (1): 412–33.

Wisconsin Department of Corrections (WDOC). 2019. "Weekly Population Report." https://doc.wi.gov/DataResearch/WeeklyPopulationReports /04262019.pdf. Accessed April 30, 2019.

Wolch, J. 1990. *The Shadow State: Government and Voluntary Sector in Transition*. New York: Foundation Center.

Conclusion

Philip Goodman

In March 2020, the World Health Organization declared that the novel coronavirus, COVID-19, had become a worldwide pandemic (Ducharme 2020). By the end of May of that same year, more than a third of a million people had died worldwide due to the virus, with more than six million confirmed global cases (Reuters 2020). Despite these numbers being a small fraction of the annual preventable deaths caused by inequality through the interrelated killers of poverty, hunger, diarrhea, malaria, and so on, COVID-19 dominated life in most countries in the early months of 2020. This was, perhaps, because victims included the comparatively wealthy and privileged in many industrialized nations. Politicians, scientists, public health officials, and others—keen to encourage people to stay inside their homes and to physically interact with as few people as possible—frequently repeated the mantra that COVID-19 "does not discriminate" (e.g., Carbert 2020).

In the United States and Canada, during the late spring and early summer months of 2020, a smaller group of critical scholars, activists, and their allies began to argue precisely the opposite: while it's a truism that COVID-19, as a non-person, does not care about someone's racial category and lived experience, the aggregate impact of the virus is indisputably

more devasting for some groups versus others, in part because of racialized inequality, and in part because of racism by state actors and institutions (Flanagan 2020; Bain, Dryden, and Walcott 2020; Valiante 2020).
At a demographic level, this includes racialized individuals and their communities, as well as people who live in close quarters with many others,
especially older people living in care facilities and those incarcerated in
penal and immigration detention facilities (Li and Lewis 2020; Span
2020). One overarching agenda of this critical cadre was therefore to shed
light on how COVID-19 exacerbated existing inequalities, vulnerabilities,
and injustices, while creating anew the same.

Specific to people who are incarcerated, Human Rights Watch released
a statement on May 27 summarizing the grim conditions in prisons, jails,
and detention facilities worldwide made worse by COVID-19; the authors
advocated for more releases from these places. "Governments are releas-
ing from jails and prisons far too few people. . . . The virus is spread-
ing rapidly through jails and prisons, putting detainees, staff, and their
families at unacceptable risk" (Human Rights Watch 2020). Even mainstream and conservative news outlets in the United States and Canada
episodically paid some attention to the great(er) risk of infection for the
incarcerated, perhaps this is because those infected during incarceration
can spread the virus upon release (e.g., Thompson 2020; Flagg 2020).
Since we know that prisons and other forms of incarceration, even in the
absence of a pandemic crisis, can make some people physically and men-
tally unwell during and/or after incarceration (e.g., Schnittker and John
2007; Kupers 1999; Mills and Kendall 2018), one can be certain that the
situation in 2020 for prisoners and others involved in the criminal justice
apparatus has been dire indeed.

Save for this conclusion chapter, which I drafted mid-pandemic while
living and working in my home in Canada, each of the chapters of this
volume were written before COVID-19 began to infect large numbers of
people. Nevertheless, the current situation speaks to several key themes
of this book. Consider, for instance, the media coverage of the intersection of COVID-19 and criminal justice: it almost exclusively addresses
prisons and jails (and those who live and work inside) as the problem and
the risk to society more generally. The result is too much silence regarding other forms of criminal justice sanction, punishment, and harm,

including COVID-19 impacts on the lives and experiences of immigration detainees, those on work release, probationers, parolees, and others released from confinement to the outside. In this volume, Bonds, Purser, Stevens, and Zatz, in particular, all amply demonstrate how these groups—and these forms of deprivation and control—must be studied in order to fully understand work and punishment in *all* its facets, iterations, complexities, and forms. That was true before COVID-19 became a pandemic, and it remains true today.

Likewise, while it is palpably a good thing that during early 2020 there was at least some attention paid to the likely effects of COVID-19 on the already-precarious lives of the detained and incarcerated—as well as those paid to punish, control, guard, and rehabilitate them—here too there is a silence that this volume should make us hear. In particular, the vast majority of people enmeshed in penal apparatuses in the American states and territories are also workers. Applying this insight or meta-theme of this volume to the contemporary situation, people are living (and dying) as prisoners, detainees, and people subject to surveillance in the community. But they are also suffering as people pressed or coerced to work under what are likely to be worsening labor conditions. It is too soon to know the details and full scope of COVID-19 on the work lives of the punished, details that will (hopefully) come from careful scholarly research. In the meantime, we should learn from this volume's contributors that this is a topic we must investigate. Just as each chapter of this book makes clear that it is only when we theorize and study work and punishment that we come to fully understand the full role of criminal justice forces in extraction, inequality, predation, vulnerability, and resistance in the United States and beyond, so too is it certainly the case that we will never fully understand the multifaceted impacts of COVID-19 unless we pay attention to the intersections of work and punishment.

In what remains of this conclusion chapter, I offer some thoughts centered around three axes. First, I comment on what I see as a central theme of the volume that speaks precisely to this intersection of work and punishment: complexity and variegation. Next, I try to learn from the chapters and set out some ideas regarding future research in this small but vibrant (and growing!) subfield of work and punishment. Lastly, I close with some prospects and perils of pushing for system reform.

COMPLEXITY AND VARIEGATION

Labor and Punishment: Work in and out of Prison performs an important service in exposing the complexity and variegation that becomes readily apparent when scholars interrogate the intersections of work and punishment. For much of the history of imprisonment in the United States, the practice of making people who are incarcerated work has been cast by elites as a kind of panacea—a way to simultaneously save the state money and reform errant or wayward souls, usually through hard, physical toil (e.g., Meranze 1996; McLennan 2008). We know from research—including Hatton (2018, this volume) that some (perhaps a minority) of the people incarcerated in American jails and prisons speak, at least some of the time, in reasonably positive ways about certain jobs and certain carceral job sites. This can include learning new skills, building self-confidence and self-image, and/or forging new connections with others imprisoned and staff (see also Goodman 2012). There is little cause for celebration in this, however, as emerging research suggests that because prisons are near-universally competitive and difficult places to live and work, even those who manage to find dignity often must do it on the proverbial backs of their compatriots (e.g., Gibson-Light 2020). More generally, that some imprisoned workers speak positively about their jobs ought not to distract us from the simultaneous, overarching reality that coercing prisoners and others to work is in many carceral settings a way of punishing, controlling, and exploiting those who labor; making the institution run smoother and cheaper; and enriching the state and/or private actors.

To help us understand the details of punishment and work vis-à-vis the variegated production of inequality and injustice, each of the chapters herein sheds new light on the intersection of people's *experiences of carceral labor* and the *structures of exploitation and inequality*.

As indicated in the diagram, some of the contributors (in my judgment) more squarely focus on experiences, whereas others are particularly attentive to the meso-level institutions and forces that make and remake inequality and exploitation. Nevertheless, the strength and novelty of this volume is that one side of this Venn diagram is never investigated and analyzed in isolation of the other. As such, the book tacitly recommends a methodological approach that prioritizes this intersection, not by

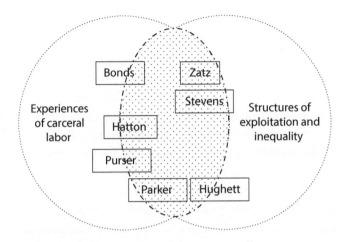

Diagram of *Labor and Punishment's* intersecting themes.

preaching it, but by demonstrating its value through excellent, theoretically grounded, empirical scholarship.

In the zone of overlap, the contributors to this volume theorize and examine work, prisons, and carcerality. It is likely precisely because they pay careful attention to both experience and structure—to the work and who benefits from it—that the chapters of this volume yield rich, nuanced theses that defy simplistic beliefs that carceral labor is a one-dimensional phenomenon.

Two brief examples from this volume will suffice to make the meta-theme of complexity and variegation clear. First, the Milwaukee-based women interviewed by Anne Bonds (chapter 7) discuss the scant vocational and educational training opportunities available to them during imprisonment in Wisconsin. The situation only gets worse after prison; Bonds argues that many feel—and are—virtually abandoned by state actors and institutions post-incarceration (see also De Giorgi 2017; Hallett 2012). From housing to jobs to food, their lives are marked by hardship and precarity, and there is no shortage of forces pushing them into marginal, gendered, low-wage jobs. It is possible that some of those interviewed might benefit from different opportunities and actual supports from criminal justice actors, not (necessarily) the total removal or abolition of work training during and after incarceration. Thus work (and job training) is both exploitative *and* possibly helpful, especially in forms that would lead to meaningful, stable, living-wage jobs.

Second, Caroline Parker's gripping account (chapter 5) of "therapeutic communities" in Puerto Rico shows how these penal institutions—framed to the public as "alternatives" to prison and jail—cannot be reduced to neat or tidy descriptors. The work performed by those confined to these facilities is decidedly menial and degrading, accompanied by a far-fetched claim that those suffering from addiction will, by doing these jobs, somehow magically become "reformed" (whatever that means). Nonetheless, by framing people with addictions as in need of therapy and treatment—even if that treatment is highly problematic and woefully inadequate—these therapeutic communities function as abeyance mechanisms enacting multiple, competing discourses of punishment, deterrence, treatment, and exploitability. We must appreciate all of these discourses if we are to understand the long, peculiar history of these facilities in Puerto Rico; we must recognize multiplicity if we are to think about less harmful practices in Puerto Rico, and beyond.

RESEARCH AGENDAS

Even with the publication of this book, the burgeoning field of study situated at the intersection of work and punishment remains quite small (for now!). Yet whatever it lacks in size it makes up for in richness, interdisciplinarity, and a desire to use questions about work and punishment to breathe new life into old debates. We can now thus take stock of where scholars, students, activists, and others might go next in terms of research. (Related, the challenges and complexities of system reform are taken up briefly in the next subsection.)

First, as Hatton points out (chapter 1), there is an acute need for large-scale, representative data on the many types of work done by people caught up in the US penal system. Although this might include large-sample surveys and quantitative analysis, in so doing we must not lose the voices of the workers themselves. Hatton's own skillful use of interview data in her chapter to map a bricolage of prison work is a demonstration of how this can be done well. Indeed, surveys, interviews, and other methodologies should be combined and intertwined to capture the full-range and complexities of work inside and outside prison walls. What is more, scholars should advocate for the inclusion of criminalized and justice-involved people and immigration detainees in ongoing social science surveys (cf. Pettit 2012).

Additionally, incisive case studies such as the ones found herein are enormously useful for better understanding penal labor, while also making theoretical contributions to wider fields of study. Simply put, we need more. This should include single case studies, as well as examinations of multiple "cases" or "sites" within a particular setting, in order to highlight similarities and differences (e.g., Gibson-Light 2019). One case or several, we benefit from the theorizing and analyzing that comes from this type of research. In the present volume, that includes advancing our theoretical knowledge of penal change (Hughett), kleptocracy (Stevens), carceral labor (Zatz), abeyance (Parker), vulnerability and degradation (Purser), and gendered care work and gendered control (Bonds). Whether based on ethnography, in-depth interviews, historical analysis, legal document analysis, or other methods, textured qualitative studies are essential in shedding light on the nuanced lives of people who are vulnerable, marginalized, and/or exploited.

THE COMPLEXITIES OF PENAL/LABOR SYSTEM REFORM

Readers of this volume know that people subject to criminal justice sanction and immigration control in the states and territories often work in poor conditions; they labor for the primary (and sometimes exclusive) benefit of the forces that imprison and punish them. What can be done? The answers suggested by this volume are—not unlike the empirical stories told herein—complex.

On the one hand, it might well be the case that nothing short of massively downsizing criminal justice apparatuses and immigration control will bring about lasting and significant change. As I write this in June 2020, that no longer seems as infeasible as it did just a few short weeks ago, especially with huge and powerful protests by Black Lives Matter and allies in the wake of ongoing murders by police of Black Americans, including George Floyd. Those protests have already led to many historic gains—including a historic vote by the Minneapolis city council to "defund" and dismantle that city's police force (Willis 2020). Although it remains to be seen what this will look like, and how many other cities follow suit, the impacts on American carceral institutions will be, hopefully, significant.

Coming back to the present volume but continuing the theme of why existing systems might need to be exploded in order to see lasting change, Gretchen Purser (chapter 6) compellingly argues that the stigma of a criminal record functions such that many formerly incarcerated people are forced to take even more precarious and even less desirable ad hoc jobs versus what they might have been able to secure in the absence of a criminal record, parole "conditions," and so on. In this way, the American criminal justice system turns individuals (many already marginalized) into exploited/exploitable people. Likewise, in Jacqueline Stevens's contribution to this volume (chapter 3) on highly coerced work performed by people consigned to immigration facilities (de facto prisons), she shows how private companies can grow rich by exploiting detainees, despite the fact that those incarcerated have committed no crime. Incremental reform is unlikely to significantly alter the power structures and entrenched interests that sustain these practices. Only a deep and abiding commitment to equality, workers' and human rights, and protections against the greed baked into capitalism is likely, under this analysis, to lead to palpably better outcomes for those who are coerced to labor (see also Hatton 2020).

Moving down a layer of granularity, but staying with reasons for skepticism toward incremental reform, consider how easily concepts such as "rehabilitation" can be pressed into service as part of larger mechanisms of exploitation and predation. I have argued elsewhere that in the particular case of California's prison fire camps, imprisoned people can create spaces within discourses of rehabilitation for self-growth and change. It is simultaneously the case that penal officials and politicians can, and do, use rehabilitation, treatment, and so forth as ways to distract public attention from the fact that carceral labor is used to keep an often oppressive system running cheaply and to minimize revolt. Caroline Parker's analyses (chapter 5) of labor "therapy" in residential facilities in Puerto Rico is a stunningly disconcerting case study of these phenomena.

Alongside demanding nothing short of system(atic) reform of the American carceral state, there are some reasons for cautious optimism in these chapters, and, equally important, clues regarding how to move forward in creating a more just and less brutal society. Consider, for instance, Amanda Bell Hughett's analyses (chapter 2) of the elimination and then reinstatement of chain gang–style road work for prisoners in North Carolina during the 1970s. The dominant takeaway is a depressing one: efforts at progressive reform by state correctional leaders were short-lived, swamped by counter pressures to secure cheap labor and beat back growing efforts by incarcerated leaders and their allies to organize and push for better conditions. Yet, this same history suggests another reading coinciding with the first: progressive reform and conservative backlash were inextricably intertwined, sometimes within the very same people. While the net result in this particular case was the reinstatement of the chain gang, there were important and significant actors across a spectrum struggling to establish their vision as dominant. During this dark period of North Carolina's prison history there were real *attempts* to envision and bring about a penal system that included vocational training, wage incentives, and the like, in order to help at least some incarcerated people lead "good" lives post-incarceration. Some real victories were won along the way, including modest (but not-zero) wages for road work and a modicum of legal rights; while these wages may have been at least partially designed to make it more difficult for prisoners to organize, it was wages nonetheless. Regardless of the scorecard one assigns to this period (and it cannot be, overall, a naively positive one), there is the fact that progressive actors and their ideas were overrun and disadvantaged by conservative economic politics, but not eliminated. This means that they were around to fight again, another day (cf. Goodman, Page, and Phelps 2017).

In another iteration of the long struggle, it is worth noting that among the key actors that are well positioned to push for progressive reform in this domain are unions and other forms of organized labor. As Noah Zatz (chapter 4) argues, organized labor has throughout US history mostly fought *against* prison labor, under the theory that goods made by the incarcerated would compete with that of "free labor." This strategy, as Zatz notes, "relies upon casting incarcerated people as dangerous and undeserving" (p. 165). There have been, however, at least a few sporadic efforts to organize the incarcerated by linking to outside groups, including alliances to the Free Alabama Movement and the Industrial Workers of the World. It may be, as Zatz notes, that efforts to organize are more successful with non-incarcerated groups (such as those on work release or probation) precisely because their toil is more likely to be framed as work (versus prisoners, whose labor is seen as something like penance or punishment or rehabilitation). It seems telling that in Canada one of the few successful attempts to organize the labor of incarcerated people occurred during the 1970s at a private (for-profit) abattoir where prisoners worked alongside, and in the same exact jobs, as non-imprisoned workers (House 2018). Focusing also on those outside prison (but formerly incarcerated), Gretchen Purser concludes that "workers' rights advocates need to make a more concerted effort to reach out to and organize this vulnerable segment of the workforce" (p. 231). Indeed, regardless of the details, it is palpably clear that inasmuch as the vast majority of people detained, imprisoned, and subject to penal surveillance and control *work*, we can, and should, fight for the recognition of this essential truth. By extension, we must fight for a panoply of rights and protections that people deserve both *as workers* and *as people*.

Fighting for recognition and rights takes us back to where I opened this conclusion chapter: the COVID-19 pandemic that is currently (as of this writing) dominating public discourse across much of the world. As those held inside prisons, jails, and detention facilities—and their compatriots controlled and surveilled outside physical walls—face new risks and more painful situations due to COVID-19, on top of what is already often a difficult life, now is the time to advocate for massive de-incarceration and the shrinking of the carceral state in the United States and beyond. Thankfully, many of the groups and coalitions currently demanding police reform/abolition in the wake of the ongoing slaughter of Black people by police and other state agents have long recognized that prisons, jails, immigration detention facilities, etcetera form a bloc of penal institutions that oppress and suppress; in this sense, this is not a new call, and those on the frontlines of demanding change are seasoned veterans. As academics, we should join or, at least, very actively support them. It may be that groups such as Black Lives Matter and Critical Resistance, among many others, can gain supporters among people who might not identify as prison or police abolitionists but who are nonetheless ready to declare that no one should be locked up in a place riddled with infections and all the violence, fear, and deprivation that accompanies it. More generally, if the murder of George Floyd was indeed, finally, one too many, may it allow people to see that in the wake of his slaughter nothing short of meaningful and lasting change that reconfigures society, including penality, will do.

REFERENCES

Bain, Beverly, OmiSoore Dryden, and Rinaldo Walcott. 2020. "COVID-19 Discriminates against Black Lives via Surveillance, Policing and Lack of Data: U of T Experts." *University of Toronto News*, April 21, 2020. https://www.utoronto.ca/news/covid-19-discriminates-against-black-lives-surveillance-policing-and-lack-data-u-t-experts.

Carbert, Michelle. 2020. "MP Who Contracted COVID-19 Recovers, Warns Virus Doesn't Discriminate—The Globe and Mail." *Globe and Mail*, April 22, 2020. https://webcache.googleusercontent.com/search?q=cache:9EcYr78Nq2kJ:https://www.theglobeandmail.com/politics/article-mp-who-contracted-covid-19-recovers-warns-virus-doesnt-discriminate/+&cd=4&hl=en&ct=clnk&gl=ca.

De Giorgi, Alessandro. 2017. "Back to Nothing: Prisoner Reentry and Neoliberal Neglect." *Social Justice: A Journal of Crime, Culture and Conflict* 44 (1): 83–120.

Ducharme, Jamie. 2020. "World Health Organization Declares COVID-19 a 'Pandemic.' Here's What That Means." *Time*, March 11, 2020. https://time.com/5791661/who-coronavirus-pandemic-declaration/.

Flagg, Anna. 2020. "Jails Are Coronavirus Hotbeds. How Many People Should Be Released to Slow the Spread?" *FiveThirtyEight*, June 3, 2020. https://fivethirtyeight.com/features/jails-are-coronavirus-hotbeds-how-many-people-should-be-released-to-slow-the-spread/.

Flanagan, Ryan. 2020. "Does COVID-19 Discriminate? This Is How Some Canadians Are Harder-Hit," April 15, 2020. https://www.ctvnews.ca/health/coronavirus/does-covid-19-discriminate-this-is-how-some-canadians-are-harder-hit-1.4897298.

Gibson-Light, Michael. 2019. "The Prison as Market: How Penal Labor Systems Reproduce Inequality." University of Arizona. https://search.proquest.com/docview/2212267563?pq-origsite=gscholar.

———. 2020. "Sandpiles of Dignity: Labor Status and Boundary-Making in the Contemporary American Prison." *RSF: The Russell Sage Foundation*

Journal of the Social Sciences 6 (1): 198–216. https://doi.org/10.7758/rsf.2020 .6.1.09.

Goodman, Philip. 2012. "Hero and Inmate: Work, Prisons, and Punishment in California's Fire Camps." *Working USA: The Journal of Labor and Society.*

Goodman, Philip, Joshua Page, and Michelle Phelps. 2017. *Breaking the Pendulum: The Long Struggle over Criminal Justice.* New York: Oxford University Press.

Hallett, Michael. 2012. "Reentry to What? Theorizing Prisoner Reentry in the Jobless Future." *Critical Criminology* 20 (3): 213–28.

Hatton, Erin. 2018. "'Either You Do It or You're Going to the Box': Coerced Labor in Contemporary America." *Critical Sociology.* https://journals -sagepub-com.myaccess.library.utoronto.ca/doi/10.1177/0896920518763929.

———. 2020. *Coerced: Work under Threat of Punishment.* Oakland: University of California Press.

House, Jordan. 2018. "When Prisoners Had a Union: The Canadian Food and Allied Workers Union Local 240." *Labour: Journal of Canadian Labour Studies / Le Travail: Revue d'Études Ouvrières Canadiennes* 82. https://doi .org/10.1353/llt.2018.0035.

Human Rights Watch. 2020. "Covid-19 Prisoner Releases Too Few, Too Slow," May 27, 2020. https://www.hrw.org/news/2020/05/27/covid-19-prisoner -releases-too-few-too-slow.

Kupers, Terry Allen. 1999. *Prison Madness: The Mental Health Crisis behind Bars and What We Must Do about It.* San Francisco: Jossey-Bass.

Li, Weihua, and Nicole Lewis. 2020. "This Chart Shows Why the Prison Population Is So Vulnerable to COVID-19." The Marshall Project, March 19, 2020. https://www.themarshallproject.org/2020/03/19/this-chart-shows -why-the-prison-population-is-so-vulnerable-to-covid-19.

McLennan, Rebecca. 2008. *The Crisis of Imprisonment: Protest, Politics, and the Making of the American Penal State, 1776–1941.* Cambridge: Cambridge University Press.

Meranze, Michael. 1996. *Laboratories of Virtue: Punishment, Revolution and Authority in Philadelphia, 1760–1835.* Chapel Hill: University of North Carolina Press.

Mills, Alice, and Kathleen Kendall. 2018. *Mental Health in Prisons: Critical Perspectives on Treatment and Confinement.* Cham, Switzerland: Palgrave. https://www.worldcat.org/title/mental-health-in-prisons-critical -perspectives-on-treatment-and-confinement/oclc/1076485903.

Pettit, Becky. 2012. *Invisible Men: Mass Incarceration and the Myth of Black Progress.* New York: Russell Sage Foundation.

Reuters. 2020. "Global Coronavirus Cases Surpass 6 Million," May 30, 2020. https://www.reuters.com/article/us-health-coronavirus-cases/global -coronavirus-cases-surpass-6-million-idUSKBN237001.

Schnittker, Jason, and Andrea John. 2007. "Enduring Stigma: The Long-Term Effects of Incarceration on Health." *Journal of Health and Social Behavior* 48 (2): 115–30. https://doi.org/10.1177/002214650704800202.

Span, Paula. 2020. "How to Improve and Protect Nursing Homes from Outbreaks," *New York Times*, May 22, 2020. https://www.nytimes.com/2020/05/22/health/coronavirus-nursing-homes.html.

Thompson, Dennis. 2020. "America's Prisons Are Breeding Grounds for COVID." WebMD, May 18, 2020. https://www.webmd.com/lung/news/20200518/americas-prisons-are-breeding-grounds-for-covid#1.

Valiante, Giuseppe. 2020. "Criminologists Say Harsh Policing and Big Fines Don't Make People Safer from COVID-19." *CTV News*, April 15, 2020. https://www.ctvnews.ca/health/coronavirus/criminologists-say-harsh-policing-and-big-fines-don-t-make-people-safer-from-covid-19-1.4897820.

Willis, Jay. 2020. "Minneapolis City Council Members Announce Intent to Disband the Police Department, Invest in Proven Community-Led Public Safety." *The Appeal*, 2020. https://theappeal.org/minneapolis-city-council-members-announce-intent-to-disband-the-police-department-invest-in-proven-community-led-public-safety/.

Contributors

EDITOR AND CONTRIBUTING AUTHOR

ERIN HATTON is associate professor of sociology at the University at Buffalo–SUNY. Her research is centered in the sociology of work, while also extending into the fields of inequality, culture, labor, law, and policy. Her recent book, *Coerced: Work under Threat of Punishment* (University of California Press, 2020) examines the work of prisoners, welfare recipients, student athletes, and graduate students; in so doing, it identifies control over status as a form of labor coercion.

CONTRIBUTING AUTHORS

ANNE BONDS is associate professor of geography and urban studies at the University of Wisconsin–Milwaukee, with research interests in urban political economy; feminist geography; and critical theories of race, carceral geographies, and poverty; housing; and criminalization. She has ongoing research on gender, race, and carceral geographies in Milwaukee and on housing policy and urban segregation. Her research has been published in a variety of journals, including *Progress in Human Geography, Urban Geography, The Annals of the Association of American Geographers, Antipode, Geography Compass*, and *Social and Cultural Geography*.

PHILIP GOODMAN is associate professor of sociology at the University of Toronto. His research uses prisons and punishment—and crime and law, more generally—as lenses to understand inequality, penal politics, and the micro-dynamics of everyday life. His research has paid particular attention to race and ethnicity, individual change and behavior over the life course, and penal labor, and has been published in the *American Journal of Sociology, Social Problems, Theoretical Criminology,* and *Law & Society Review.*

AMANDA BELL HUGHETT is assistant professor of legal studies at the University of Illinois at Springfield and an affiliated researcher at SUNY-Buffalo's Baldy Center for Law and Social Policy, where she spent two years as a postdoctoral fellow. She holds a PhD in history from Duke University and has previously served as a law and social sciences doctoral fellow at the American Bar Foundation in Chicago, Illinois.

CAROLINE M. PARKER is a presidential fellow of medical anthropology at the Department of Social Anthropology at the University of Manchester. Her primary research interests are in addiction therapeutics, neoliberalism, and the carceral state. She has published widely in journals of social science and public health, including the *New England Journal of Medicine, Culture, Medicine and Psychiatry,* and *Medical Anthropology Quarterly.*

GRETCHEN PURSER is associate professor in the Department of Sociology at the Maxwell School of Citizenship and Public Affairs at Syracuse University, where she also serves as the codirector for research on activism and advocacy at PARCC. A committed ethnographer, her research centers on labor, housing, and urban poverty governance in the United States. Her research has appeared in a wide range of journals, including *Ethnography, Qualitative Sociology,* and *Critical Sociology.*

JACQUELINE STEVENS is professor of political science and founding director of the Deportation Research Clinic at Northwestern University. Her research focuses on political theories and practices of membership, including deportation law enforcement and the unlawful deportation of US citizens from the United States. Her work has appeared in numerous venues, including *Political Theory, American Political Science Review, The Nation,* and the *New York Times.*

NOAH D. ZATZ is professor of law at the University of California, Los Angeles. He has written widely about legal constructions of work and employment; about work requirements in social welfare, family, and criminal law; and about their interrelation through market/nonmarket distinctions.

Index

addiction, 9, 79, 183–85, 196; and labor
therapy, 9, 179–81, 185–91, 195, 199–200,
203–4; treatment of, 6, 9, 10, 34, 179–
206, 262
Attica, 28, 35, 37, 44, 49, 77

carceral state, 1–11, 20; and addiction treatment, 183–85; and "carceral labor,"
8–9, 10, 39, 133–68, 183, 197, 204, 260;
and capitalism, 10, 98–99, 104, 157, 168,
236; and coercion, 26, 139, 224–27; and
degradation, 9, 133, 145, 166, 218–22,
230; and feminism, 250, 253n4; and
mass incarceration, 1–2, 87–88, 182; and
precarity, 10, 217, 235–52; and welfare
state, 4–5, 151, 164, 168, 169n2, 215,
253n3. *See also* incarceration; prison
labor
Corcraft, 27, 35, 36, 37, 49. *See also* prison
labor
community service, 24, 134, 153, 156, 158–62,
164, 166, 167. *See also* carceral state;
parole; prison labor; probation

diversion programs, 134, 135, 160–62. *See
also* addiction

exploitation: and carceral labor, 217, 227,
228–31, 261, 263, 264; and immigrant
detention, 86, 90, 99, 103–9, 264; and
Jim Crow, 137, 157; and labor therapy,
180, 181, 190, 203; and non-carceral
labor, 38, 135; and prison labor, 18–19,
24, 25–27, 75, 88, 136. *See also* prison
labor; work and employment

ICE: and carceral state, 8, 94–98; and
for-profit detention centers, 8, 92–94,
98–110; and immigrant detention,
89–113; and labor, 86, 90–98, 106–10. *See
also* immigrant detention
immigrant detention, 6, 8, 10, 86–113; labor
within 86, 90–98; lawsuits against, 105–
10. *See also* ICE
incarcerated people: "prison life," 236, 238,
240, 242, 250, 252; resistance and activism of, 7–8, 19, 33, 60–61, 64, 65, 67–68,
71–76, 252; work experiences of, 25–38.
See also incarceration; prison labor
incarceration: and economic precarity, 1, 2–4,
6–7, 11, 39, 228, 236, 239–52; and gender, 10, 235–40, 242, 244–52; and Jim
Crow, 18–19, 89, 137–40; and labor

Founded in 1893,
UNIVERSITY OF CALIFORNIA PRESS
publishes bold, progressive books and journals
on topics in the arts, humanities, social sciences,
and natural sciences—with a focus on social
justice issues—that inspire thought and action
among readers worldwide.

The UC PRESS FOUNDATION
raises funds to uphold the press's vital role
as an independent, nonprofit publisher, and
receives philanthropic support from a wide
range of individuals and institutions—and from
committed readers like you. To learn more, visit
ucpress.edu/supportus.

Milton Keynes UK
Ingram Content Group UK Ltd.
UKHW042058290923
429652UK00006B/371